What Everyone Is Saying
About *Start Up Financing*

"Bill Stolze has an outstanding track record as an entrepreneur and a business school teacher, and *Start Up Financing* contains just the kind of useful, down-to-earth advice any entrepreneur needs to get the capital to start an exciting new business. It's full of useful tips."

—Peter S. Prichard, author of *The Making of McPaper: The Inside Story of USA Today*, and president of The Freedom Forum

"Bill Stolze has done it again—this time by demystifying that labyrinth of sources, terms and tricks of the trade regarding the ultracritical small business subject of obtaining capital. As he did with his legendary book *Start Up, An Entrepreneur's Guide to Launching and Managing a New Business,* he has cut through the mystery, complexity and baloney of an important small business issue and brought clear thinking, clear writing and personal experience to it. Entrepreneurial readers of *Start Up Financing* will not only significantly enhance their chances of raising the money that they seek, but they'll go into the process with a lot less ignorance and fear."

—Fred Beste, managing partner of Mid-Atlantic Venture Funds

"Once again, Bill Stolze offers a book with creative, but practical and sound advice for entrepreneurs. What he is saying is true, in the absence of bank or venture capital financing, today's entrepreneurs must consider financing their growing businesses in imaginative ways, as did the very successful businesses profiled in the last chapter of the book. These success stories, alone, make *Start Up Financing* well worth its cover price. Entrepreneurs take heed of Bill Stolze's astute and succinct financial advice, 'But when no other road is available, take the one you can find.'"

—Mary L. Woita, assistant state director, Nebraska Business Development Center

"A great many options are currently available to entrepreneurs who need financing for early stage companies. In his new book, *Start Up Financing*, Bill Stolze explores a wide range of these options in his own effective, clear-cut and user-friendly style."

—Paul Brentlinger, general partner, Morgenthaler Ventures

"Bill Stolze has a unique capacity to present valuable information in actionable terms. *Start Up Financing* is worth more than the money."

—Louise Woerner, founder and CEO, HCR, Rochester, New York

"In my opinion this book contains important, fundamental reading for any person considering entering the world of entrepreneurism. Bill Stolze has 'been there' and he knows how to help others achieve."

—Tom Golisano, founder and president, Paychex, Inc.

"One of the first questions I am asked by budding entrepreneurs is: 'Where do I find the money to launch my business?' Bill Stolze provides an answer in his book *Start Up Financing*. It is a practical approach to solving the mystery about funding a new venture. Its strength is an in-depth evaluation of 'what to do' and 'how to do it' that makes *Start Up Financing* a must read book for those who want to start a business and acquire the capital. Also, lecturers in entrepreneurship will find it an excellent textbook to use in the classroom because it is a combination of theory and practical experience. It is a winner!"

—James N. Doyle, lecturer in entrepreneurship, Simon Graduate School of Business, University of Rochester and former president of Sarah Coventry, Itnl.

"I found *Start Up Financing* to be a well organized, easy to read volume that should be put on all entrepreneurs' must read list. It addresses many of the normally left out aspects of business decisions in addition to being full of critical information. I found it to be both an excellent reference guide and a quality read."

—Joanne Bauman, regional director of the Small Business Development Center, Binghamton University

"Bill Stolze has done it again. Another tour de force! His first book *Start Up* is a best seller and one of the most widely read books in the world on how to launch and manage a new venture. Now he has written a book on how to finance a new venture that tells it like it really is. It is packed with invaluable advice, experience and insights on how to raise the money you need to launch a new venture. If you are looking for financing for your business, this book is a must read."

—Dr. Warren J. Keegan, director of the Institute for Global Business Planning, Pace University, NY, and author of *Global Marketing Management*

"Bill Stolze's new book, *Start Up Financing*, is another sure winner. Written in the same pithy, no-nonsense style as his first book, this one fills a definite need in one of the most important, yet misunderstood areas of entrepreneurship. Filled with the practical, down-to-earth wisdom that has become Bill's trademark, it is sure to be a most welcome handbook on the shelf of anyone trying to start or grow a business. I highly recommend it for giving students a dose of the real world."

—Lanny Herron, professor, Department of Management, University of Baltimore

"In the early 1990s William J. Stolze, founder and president of RF Communications, distilled the years of experience which he had gained as a practicing entrepreneur in a fresh and unique text called, *Start Up, An Entrepreneur's Guide To Launching And Managing A New Business. Start Up* was unique for several reasons. First, *Start Up* provided a more comprehensive coverage of the various issues associated with starting a business than any other text in the field. At the same time, *Start Up* was significantly briefer than most other texts because Stolze spoke directly to the core issues and concerns in each area of start up activity. And perhaps most importantly, *Start Up* accurately reflected the realities of the world because of Stolze's tremendous knowledge base. As a result, *Start Up* became one of the leading entrepreneurship texts of the 1990s, and was adopted by many of the leading graduate schools of business in the United States.

Now Stolze has prepared a new text, *Start Up Financing,* which is again based on his personal and professional experience in the field of entrepreneurship. And once again, Stolze's insights and ability to cut to the core of the issues promise to redefine the area of new venture financing.

I am, therefore, happy to strongly recommend Stolze's *Start Up Financing* to all of those interested in starting their own business. It is a source of wisdom and advice that will make your own start up far easier, and wisdom that would take you years to accumulate on your own."

—Charles W. Hofer, regents professor of Strategy & Entrepreneurship, University of Georgia

"This is a splendid practical book on how to finance your business from one who has been there and done it. It should be read by every entrepreneur. Particularly valuable is the survey of different sources of financing and how to tap them. Bill Stolze tells you how to get money from your relatives without destroying family relations and how to get money from venture capitalists without giving away your business.

Bill Stolze tells you what lenders and equity investors are looking for and how you can use them and other sources of funds to make your business grow."

—Peter Faber, partner, the law firm of McDermott, Will & Emory, New York

START UP FINANCING

An
Entrepreneur's
Guide to
Financing
a New or
Growing Business

By
William J. Stolze

START UP FINANCING

An Entrepreneur's Guide to Financing a New or Growing Business

By
William J. Stolze

CAREER PRESS
3 Tice Road
P.O. Box 687
Franklin Lakes, NJ 07417
1-800-CAREER-1
201-848-0310 (NJ and outside U.S.)
FAX: 201-848-1727

START UP FINANCING
ISBN 1-56414-271-X, $16.99
Cover design by L & B Desktop Publishing & Printing
Printed in the U.S.A. by Book-mart Press

To order this title by mail, please include price as noted above, $2.50 handling per order, and $1.50 for each book ordered. Send to: Career Press, Inc., 3 Tice Road, P.O. Box 687, Franklin Lakes, NJ 07417.

Or call toll-free 1-800-CAREER-1 (NJ and Canada: 201-848-0310) to order using VISA or MasterCard, or for further information on books from Career Press.

Library of Congress Cataloging-in-Publication Data

Stolze, William J.
    Start up financing : An entrepreneur's guide to financing a new or growing business / by William J. Stolze
        p.   cm.
    "This book is a follow-up to my first book, 'Start up, an entrepreneurs guide to launching and managing a new business' ... now in its fourth edition" --   Introd.
    Includes index.
    ISBN 1-56414-271-X
    1. Small business -- Finance. 2. New business enterprises -- Finance. 3. Commercial loans. 4. Venture capital.   I. Title.
HG4027.7.S85   1997
658.15'224--dc21
                                                                97-17795
                                                                    CIP

Contents

Introduction

Most books on the subject of the financing of start up or growing companies are written by bankers, venture investors or others, whose backgrounds are as providers of capital. The problem here is that the bankers' chief responsibility is to make loans only under circumstances when the loan is almost certain to be paid back, and many people in the venture capital industry seem almost proud of the fact that only about one out of 100 companies trying to get an investment succeed.

This book is different in that my background is primarily as an entrepreneur. I started a very successful company, RF Communications, Inc., in the long range radio communications business and helped a number of other companies get started and raise their initial capital. In addition I taught entrepreneurship in MBA programs at the University of Rochester and Rochester Institute of Technology for about 10 years, which brought me in contact with many students, both young and experienced, seriously considering starting businesses. Also, through the years I counseled and advised several hundred people who were either planning to become entrepreneurs or who had recently started their own businesses.

By no means do I consider myself to be a financial expert. My viewpoint is the viewpoint of an entrepreneur, struggling to get a business going, who has the problem of trying to raise the needed capital for the business they would like to start.

Many of the things I say are likely to be in conflict with what you read about in other books on the subject or are issues that some writers do not consider important enough to mention. Whether you agree with everything I say is less important than that you consider these issues to see if they apply in your situation. If they do, my comments may help answer some questions you may have. I do not suggest that you do not read other books about financing a new business. Learning about the problems from every possible viewpoint can only be good.

Starting a business is hard. The outstanding successes you read about in the more popular national business media represent only a minuscule fraction of the new businesses started by entrepreneurs each year. Do not let the fact that a company like Netscape Communications Corp., which incorporated in early 1994, shipped its first product later in that year, raised several million dollars of capital from private investors during its first year or so in business and then raised more than $100 million in an initial public offering (IPO) within the next few years, make you think that the problem of raising early stage capital is an easy one. Do not think that this is apt to happen to you. It is very, very unlikely.

Be prepared to struggle and be prepared to be at considerable personal risk, both financial and emotional. As you work to get your new business going do not be surprised when you conclude, as I did, that to most problems an entrepreneur faces there are no right or wrong answers. There are no equations or formulas to guide you. The best you can hope for is an answer that works. You will never know whether doing something differently would have been better or worse. Making the problem even more difficult is that the answer to almost every question you ask anyone begins with the words, "It depends."

Of all the problems I have sought professional help on through the years the ones in which there was the least agreement from the "experts" were those involving finance. I sought guidance from bankers, from people in the investment community, from venture capitalists, from heads of finance in both large and small companies and from other entrepreneurs. Eventually I reached the point where I kept asking the "experts" until I found one who agreed with me and then I did what I probably would have done in the first place.

One part of this book that I strongly urge you to read is Chapter 29. I tried to include brief descriptions of how a number of entrepreneurs financed the formation of their businesses. Included are a variety of different types of businesses, each of which seemed to have some kind of unique problem. Several of the examples are companies that now have sales of several hundred million dollars while some are much, much smaller.

Each of the entrepreneurs overcame many problems in raising capital and most used money from a number of different sources. To me this says that persistence, imagination, and selling skills are important qualities to have in order to succeed in raising capital for a new business.

This book is a follow-up to my first book, *Start Up, An Entrepreneur's Guide to Launching and Managing a New Business,* now in its fourth edition. It is used either as a text or in small business programs at more than 50 colleges and universities. I encourage you to read my other book since it covers many nonfinancial issues that are crucial to achieving success when you start a business. It is available from most major book store chains or can be ordered directly from the publisher, Career Press.

I welcome comments or questions from readers on any of the issues I discuss. You can contact me through the publisher. Good luck to you in your effort to become an entrepreneur. I wish you success.

Chapter 1

What's the First Step?

....

When an entrepreneur begins planning how to finance his or her new business one thing that is important to keep in mind is that money isn't everything. For a new business to succeed it must do many things right, not just raise capital. The strategy of the business must be sound. It is important that you have created an offering, either product or service, that addresses a market with a need for that offering. It is important that you have assembled a management team with the skills and experience to run the business. Finally, it is important to remember that raising money, by whatever route you choose, requires selling skills as well as entrepreneurial skills.

You must identify the things that will be attractive to potential investors or lenders and present them in a way that convinces them that your chances of succeeding are good.

Also, it is important to remember that many companies have succeeded in raising millions and often hundreds of millions of dollars only to find a few years later that somehow things did not work out as they expected and the business either filed for bankruptcy or simply ceased operations.

As an example, 10 or 12 years ago I personally made a $100,000-plus equity investment in a new business that had what appeared to be a great idea for a new, high-tech product. The founder had great skills at raising capital. He successfully raised more than $70 million during the 10-year existence of the company but never managed to develop a market for the new product. They got a few orders for miscellaneous research and development programs along the way but never enough to come anywhere near supporting the business. After 10 years the company ceased operations.

Obviously I lost all of my investment as did the people and organizations who invested the large amount of money the company raised from others. In my judgment this company did not fail because it ran out of money, it ran out of money because it failed.

Hardly a week goes by that you do not read in *The Wall Street Journal* or other business publications of companies that raised huge amounts of capital and, for various reasons, filed for bankruptcy. So I repeat again, money isn't everything.

The remainder of this short chapter will discuss a number of the key issues that, in my opinion, are the things you can do and the strategies you can follow that will improve the chances of your business succeeding. You may already be aware of many of these and be going down a road that you feel will lead to success. In any event, reading what I consider to be crucial issues in determining whether a company will be successful will either confirm the steps you have already taken or suggest some other things you might consider. These are the type of things potential investors will examine very carefully in deciding whether or not to become financially involved with your business.

Here are some of the questions you should ask:

1. Should I start the business alone or with a team? Many people starting a business have never run a business before and are unlikely to have all of the necessary skills. Starting a company with a team, a small group of others with skills that complement yours, in my opinion, greatly improves your chances of success. Bringing together what I call a Mr./Ms. Inside and Mr./Ms. Outside can combine people who have product or service skills with people who have marketing, management and financing skills. These skills are not usually found in the same person. While teaming has both advantages and disadvantages, I believe the pros far outweigh the cons.

I read of a recent survey of 200 fast-growth companies that showed that 54 percent were started by two people, 40 percent by three or more and only 6 percent by one person. While there are some drawbacks, this is pretty powerful evidence that teaming has a lot of merit. I also think that raising early stage capital from any source is usually easier for companies started by a team of entrepreneurs than for those started by a single individual.

2. What is my distinctive competence? The next thing you should do is to try very hard to identify some distinctive competence that you or the members of your team have that can serve as the basis of the business. This is often the idea for the product or service upon which the business will be based, but it can also be other things such as marketing skills, financing skills, etc. The issue here is that you do not have to be good at everything but you must be very good at something. Another way of putting this is that you should not try to learn a new business at the same time you are trying to start a new business. Build on a strength.

Obviously, most potential investors will look at this issue very carefully.

3. What advantages do small businesses have? Another good thing to do is to analyze the large companies with which you will undoubtedly be competing and try to identify areas in which they have a natural advantage over small companies. Large company advantages usually are the result of access to large amounts of capital. The benefits from this include things such as having full product lines, large direct marketing organizations, being able to manufacture in large quantities which usually results in lower costs (economies of scale), etc.

Then try to identify the things the small companies can do that give them a natural advantage over large companies. These may be harder to identify. Small company advantages could include a willingness and ability to accommodate the unique requirements of small groups of customers, the flexibility to move fast on almost every problem a business faces and a willingness on the part of senior management to spend time with customers. The start up business should obviously emphasize those things where they have a natural advantage and avoid those things where the large companies have a natural advantage.

4. How can I differentiate, concentrate and innovate? These three things are of great importance to a new business. Try to lead—not follow. If your offering is the same as your larger competitor your only approach to getting more business is to drop your price, and that is the road to Hell.

Try to find a niche, either in a product niche or a market niche, at which you can excel. Niche strategy is almost always the best basic strategy for a business, regardless of its size. The small company's best approach is to select a niche that is "the right size," neither too large nor too small. The niche should be large enough to provide a reasonable opportunity to succeed but not so large as to attract too many large company competitors.

It is also very important to find ways to innovate in all aspects of the business. Innovation in product and service are obvious but it is also possible to innovate in pricing, marketing, customer service and many other aspects of the enterprise. These three words, "Differentiate, Concentrate, and Innovate," are of crucial importance in any new business.

5. How do I offer my customers "better value"? Next, I suggest that you very carefully examine your pricing strategy. Some people consider the pricing decision to be part of the marketing process. I do not. I consider the pricing to be one of the fundamental strategic decisions of a new business. The reason for this is that people do not make their purchase decisions based upon price alone—they make them based upon value, and value equals benefits divided by price. If you surround your offering, whatever it may be, with benefits that your customers value you will be able to sell at a higher price.

This means that the likelihood of your business being profitable will increase dramatically. If you make a list of a half dozen or so of the best companies you can think of, regardless of the industry, I think you will find that they all follow this approach to pricing. Clearly, potential investors will be highly impressed by your strategy decisions on this issue.

6. How do I finance the business? Finally, when you have gone through the above process you reach the point where you can intelligently estimate the financial needs of the business. Then you should try to identify sources of capital that might be appropriate and what steps you should take to raise that amount of money.

Interestingly, there are two questions that should be kept very much in mind when thinking about the problems of financing a new or growing business.

They are, "What can you do to raise more capital?" and "What can you do to need less capital?" This idea might be better described as raise more and spend less; either or both of these will help you solve the financing problem of getting a business going.

Notice that securing financing is only one of a number of things entrepreneurs should do to improve their chances of success. Making the decision process even more complex is that some of these decisions are highly inter-related. So starting a business, becoming a successful entrepreneur, is a complex process requiring that you do many things right, or almost right. Many potential entrepreneurs have discovered to their immense embarrassment and perhaps financial ruin that money is not enough. In the words of Mary Kay Ash, the founder of Mary Kay Cosmetics, "Money isn't everything. You also have to know what you are doing."

Chapter 2

Basic Questions About Financing

....

I have assumed in writing this focused book that you, as an entrepreneur, have developed a business strategy that you are satisfied with and are now trying to raise the money needed to get your business underway. What do you do next? I believe the process of financing a new business requires that the entrepreneur start by answering the following four questions:

1. How much money do I need? This is done best by making a detailed cash flow projection. To do this you must first project how your company will develop a revenue stream from the sale of whatever it is you are trying to sell. This is followed by a projection of expenditures, the cash outlays that will be required. Subtracting expenditures from revenues tells you the amount of money you will need. This is called cash flow. A crucial point in the life of every new business is when the direction of cash flow goes from negative to positive. This

must happen before the firm runs out of money. In its simplest terms the furthest negative point on the cash flow projection represents the amount of capital the firm needs. This is discussed in detail in Chapter 5.

2. How much money can I put into the business myself? You must determine if you have the resources and/or personal borrowing power to supply the amount of money that will be needed to reach the point where cash flow goes from negative to positive or if you must raise money from others.

3. How much of the ownership in the business am I prepared to give up? and **What risks am I prepared to take in return for the money I need?** If the answer to question two is that you need money from outside sources, you must then decide the amount you think you can raise from others, either through borrowing or through the sale of a part of the ownership of your business—equity financing. If you sell equity in the business you must also decide what percentage of the ownership you are prepared to give up in return for the additional capital you think you need. This is also a very tough decision because the business does not have enough financial history to accurately estimate a value.

4. Where do I look? Finally, you have to decide what the best way is to close the gap between what you can invest personally and what you need. There are many places you can look for additional capital, each with advantages and disadvantages. This is a complex decision, one that this book will try to help

you make. When thinking about this question, remember that most companies during their early years are likely to need to raise money from more than one source.

Sounds complex, doesn't it? In a way it is very complex. If you cannot raise all of the capital you think you need you may have to go back and re-examine your strategy, perhaps changing it to match the amount of capital you can raise. On the other hand, if you have a very good concept for the business, describe it clearly and effectively in your business plan and accept the fact that raising capital is a selling problem, not a problem related to the business you hope to start. It may not be as difficult as you expect.

Chapter 3

Fundamentals of Financial Statements

I was very fortunate when I decided to become an entrepreneur because shortly before I took the step I had the good fortune to go to MIT under a Sloan Fellowship and receive a Master of Science (SM) in Industrial Management. This program included two courses in accounting which, for me, were the most difficult courses I had taken since thermodynamics in undergraduate engineering school. Learning accounting seemed at least as difficult as learning a foreign language.

Many, if not most, entrepreneurs start their businesses without the benefit of an accounting background. This is unfortunate because an understanding of the various financial statements they will have to deal with would make the business easier to run and much more likely to succeed. It would also make obtaining financing much easier. This chapter is intended to review some accounting principles that I believe can

contribute meaningfully to the success of a new business.

In general there are four financial statements that an entrepreneur should understand. They are: Balance Sheet, Operating Statement (profit and loss), Backlog, and Cash Flow Projections. The following few pages review these in sufficient detail so that, hopefully, they will no longer be a mystery.

Balance sheet

Shown in Fig. 3A is a simplified balance sheet for a typical small business. It includes two categories of information. Assets are shown on the top and liabilities on the bottom. Assets are all of the tangible things of value that the company owns. Liabilities list the people or organizations who have a claim on these assets. Assets must always equal liabilities.

There are two types of assets. Current assets are those things that can usually be converted to cash without

Fig. 3A

The XYZ Corporation
Annual Balance Sheet
For the Periods Ending December 31, 1995 and 1996
(All figures in dollars)

ASSETS	1995	1996
Current Assets		
Cash	$40,000	$69,684
Accounts Receivable	80,000	90,000
Inventory	40,000	60,000
Total Current Assets	$160,000	$219,684
Fixed Assets		
Land & Buildings	$90,000	$93,000
Equipment	30,000	35,000
Less Accumulated Depreciation	(15,000)	(20,000)
Total Fixed Assets	$105,000	$108,000
TOTAL ASSETS	$265,000	$327,684
	=======	=======
LIABILITIES & EQUITY		
Current Liabilities		
Notes Payable	$25,000	$30,000
Accounts Payable	30,000	35,000
Accrued Expenses	8,000	8,000
Total Current Liabilities	$63,000	$73,000
Long Term Liabilities		
Term Loans	$50,000	$45,000
Total Long Term Liabilities	$50,000	$45,000
TOTAL LIABILITIES	$113,000	$118,000
	=======	=======
OWNER'S EQUITY		
Capital Stock at Par Value	$10,000	$10,000
Stock in Excess of Par Value	50,000	50,000
Retained Earnings	92,000	149,684
NET WORTH	$152,000	$205,684
TOTAL LIABILITIES	$265,000	$327,684
	=======	=======

much difficulty. Fixed assets are the things that cannot readily be converted to cash but still represent value, such as a building or manufacturing equipment.

The first asset item is usually cash and cash equivalents. This one is simple— it is either money in the bank or money invested in short term, very safe securities to which the company has immediate access. Be careful when you invest excess funds that they are put in something that is almost certain to retain its value.

One entrepreneur I know, after his company went public, had several hundred thousand dollars to invest. Rather than a certificate of deposit or other short term security, he put the money in IBM stock at a time when its price was more than $150 per share. This was obviously an unwise thing to do for a number of reasons, the most important being that investors do not buy stock in a company so that the entrepreneur can play the market. The other was that even though IBM stock is readily converted to cash, in this situation the price of the stock soon dropped well below the purchase price and stayed there for a long time. I do not know how long the entrepreneur held the stock, but clearly this was an unwise way to manage the resources of the company.

Accounts receivable is usually the second asset item. This is the money owed the company by customers to whom its products have been shipped. Sometimes these receivables are almost as good as cash, and sometimes a few customers will never pay. Hopefully, the "no pays" are very small in number.

The final item in current assets is inventory. Inventory also has several categories that are usually shown as parts, work in process and finished goods. These are often not shown on the balance sheet. Determining the value of inventory is somewhat complex in that there are several acceptable approaches that can be used. They are: "first in/first out" or "last in/first out." The reason for the difference is that the cost to replace materials in inventory usually changes over time because of inflation and other factors. Therefore, the value of more recently purchased inventory may be different than that of inventory purchased earlier. The main effect that this has on the business is the way it affects the cost of the products you sell, which in turn affects the profits shown on the operating statement and the taxes the company may be required to pay.

I personally prefer "first in/first out," the more conservative approach, because the remaining inventory number will be closer to reality, i.e., the cost to replace the items shipped. Add up all of the above and you have the total of current assets.

Fixed assets usually include tangible items such as land and buildings, manufacturing equipment, expensive office equipment, etc. These are things that a company needs in order to operate the business that normally cannot be converted to cash rapidly to pay other obligations. Since these assets, except for real estate, have a finite life, and in theory must be replaced sooner or later, their value is decreased each year by a factor called depreciation. For example, if a piece of production equipment has an expected useful life of five years, each year its value as an asset should be decreased.

Here again, though, this number is sometimes confusing in that there are several ways to handle depreciation. One is to depreciate at a constant rate over the expected life of the asset, called straight line depreciation. The other is to assume that the asset's value decreases faster early in its life and to depreciate it faster in early years and at a lower rate in later years. This approach also has an effect on profit. I do not have a strong feeling about which method of depreciation is best for the new company to use. I guess the answer is, "It depends."

Add up all of the above and you have a fairly accurate summary of the tangible things of value that the business owns.

Not listed on the balance sheet as assets, however, are a number of intangible items that might be of immense value to the company. They may, in fact, be the most valuable things it owns. This includes things such as patents, trade marks, the cost of developing the products upon which the business is based, market penetration, etc. This issue is fairly complex and extremely important and is discussed in more detail in Chapter 4.

Liabilities have three components: current liabilities, long term liabilities and owner's equity. In some balance sheets these titles may vary, but the meaning is pretty clear. Liabilities are obligations that the company has to others.

The first liabilities are usually notes payable and current portion of long term debt. These are the money borrowed from others (banks, etc.) which must be repaid during the current accounting period. This is sort of the opposite of cash and cash equivalents.

Following this is accounts payable, which includes money you owe the suppliers of material you purchased from them such as inventory, machinery, office supplies, etc. The final item in current liabilities is accrued expenses which are wages owed employees and taxes owed taxing authorities that had not been paid at the end of the accounting period when the balance sheet was prepared.

Long term liabilities include things such as long term loans and mortgages on buildings or property, i.e., indebtedness that is not due until a later accounting period.

Finally there is owner's equity which is the difference between total assets and the sum of short term and long term liabilities. In effect, it is the value of the business to the owners.

Owner's equity also usually has three categories. The first is the par value of any stock owned by either inside or outside investors. Next is investment in excess of par value which is the amount paid by investors over and above the par value in order to purchase the stock they own.

The reason there is a difference between the par value of the stock and the price the investors paid for the stock is that companies usually set par value as low as possible because it often determines the incorporation fees that must be paid to the state in which they are incorporated in the event the company operates at a loss and pays no income taxes. In many states it is unwise to issue stock with "no par value" because in this situation the states may assume that the par value is one dollar, which may be higher than you want.

The next item is retained earnings, which is the total earnings of the company, either positive or negative, that have been accumulated since the company began. In a new business, retained earnings are likely to be negative, which reflects operating the business at a loss. Hopefully, retained earnings will become a positive number as soon as possible, which says that the value of the shareholders' investment has increased.

The total of par value of the stock, investment in excess of par value and retained earnings is the net worth of the business.

And that is all there is to the balance sheet. It is very important that an entrepreneur understand this because it is usually a fairly accurate representation of the financial condition of the business. There is some latitude on how several items are handled, but these are usually explained in the notes to the financial statement, which should be read as carefully as the numbers.

Operating statement

The operating statement (sometimes referred to as a profit and loss statement) describes the financial performance of the company over a specified period of time. This period may be monthly, quarterly or, at the longest, annually. Fig. 3B shows an operating statement for a typical small business.

A common way to present this is to show the performance in the prior period as well as the performance in the present period. This will give the reader a chance to compare the two periods and draw a conclusion about how the company is doing and if any progress is being made.

The first line of almost every operating statement is net sales. This is the value of all products that have been shipped or services that have been provided to the company's customers less any discounts that may be available to the buyer at the time they pay their bill. Net sales would include both sales where payment is due immediately as well as sales where payment may be due over a longer period of time.

Here again there are a number of questions that might be asked. Does a sale require that the customer be billed? Does a sale require that the customer accept whatever it is that was supplied? Does a sale require that the product actually be put on a truck, or is being on the loading dock or in the shipping room sufficient? These are games that some companies play that are very hard for the reader to figure out other than to depend on the ethical standards of whomever it was that prepared the statement.

The definition of a sale that I like is that the product must have in fact been shipped and the customer invoiced.

The next line is usually cost of goods sold. This should include all of the expenses of creating the thing or service that has been sold that can be identified as being directly used in the creation of the product or the providing of the service. Cost of goods sold should not include expenses that are of a general nature that are spread across the entire business.

The difference between net sales and cost of goods sold is the gross profit. Hopefully gross profit will be a big percentage of net sales.

The next group of items on the operating statement is operating expenses.

Fig. 3B

The XYC Corporation
Annual Operating Statement
For the Period Ending December 31,1995 and 1996
(All figures in dollars)

	1995		1996	
	Dollars	% of Sales	Dollars	% of Sales
Net Sales	$500,000	100.0	$600,000	100.0
Cost of Sales	300,000	60.0	350,000	58.0
Gross Profit	$200,000	40.0	$250,000	41.6
Operating Expenses				
Salaries & Wages	$ 60,000	12.0	$ 70,000	11.6
Payroll Taxes	9,000	1.8	11,000	1.8
Rent & Utilities	10,000	2.0	11,000	1.8
Insurance	7,000	1.4	8,000	1.3
Marketing	40,000	8.0	45,000	7.5
Supplies & Misc. Expense	3,500	0.7	3,700	0.6
Accounting & Legal	3,500	0.7	3,700	0.6
Depreciation	5,000	1.0	5,200	0.9
Total Operating Expenses	$138,000	27.6	$157,600	26.2
Net Operating Income	$ 62,000	12.4	$ 92,400	15.4
Less Interest Expense	(5,000)	(1.0)	(5,000)	(0.8)
Taxable Income	$57,000	11.4	$87,400	14.6
Less Income Tax	(19,380)	(3.9)	(29,716)	(5.0)
Net Income	$37,620	7.5	$57,684	9.6

This is usually a long list of things that cannot be identified as reasonably attributable to a specific product or service. Included here are things such as accounting and legal expenses, the president's and his or her secretary's salaries, insurance, building maintenance and repair, the company plane (God forbid), and everything else of a general nature.

Subtracting operating expenses from gross profit gives you net operating income. From this number subtract interest expense to reach net pre-tax income. This, hopefully, is also a positive number.

Finally, subtract taxes, if any, to get net income. This is the so-called "bottom line" of the business. While net income is not nearly as important a tool for the management of a business as the balance sheet it is the number that seems to be of greatest interest to potential lenders and potential investors in evaluating the performance and long term potential of the company.

If the company pays dividends to its shareholders these are deducted from both cash and retained earnings. This means that the net worth of the company will decrease but the assets will still equal liabilities.

Cash flow projections

These are critical to any new business, because if cash flow does not go from negative to positive before you run out of cash and other sources of capital, the company will in all likelihood become insolvent. Remember that even companies that are profitable can be forced into bankruptcy while still showing a net profit. One reason for this apparent inconsistency is that if the company makes a major capital purchase (manufacturing machinery, for example) all that affects profit is the depreciation during the period while the total out of pocket cost affects the cash balance. Cash flow is discussed in detail in Chapter 5.

Backlog

Here again you will find some disagreement as to the importance of this number. Backlog includes orders that a business has received for its products or services scheduled to be shipped at a later date. The first reaction that most people have is that the bigger the backlog the better.

I do not agree entirely with this position because companies are not in business to have backlog, they are in business to have sales. High backlog can be the legitimate result of good marketing and lots of unexpected orders that are challenging the manufacturing department, or it can be the result of poor scheduling, product deficiencies, poor planning that slows down deliveries, etc.

High backlog usually provides a lot of comfort to management and investors. However, an ideal backlog to me would be the amount necessary to run your factory at a planned pace that does not result in either a large finished goods inventory or your falling behind in deliveries to the point where you lose orders.

Another way to think about what represents ideal backlog is the amount of orders to cover one production cycle of whatever it is you are doing. This is a very hard balance to achieve, but it is a better goal than simply saying you want a very large backlog.

Ratios

As your company grows you may want to use ratios to help you decide how you are doing. Some managers depend on ratios more than on the numbers. My inclination is to use ratios occasionally but to depend more on the numbers.

Some of the more common financial ratios used are:

1. Net profit as a percentage of sales.

2. Earnings per share.

3. Inventory turnover.

4. Debt as a percentage of total capital.

5. Return on equity.

6. Average collection cycle.

You should use these ratios and any others that you find helpful in the management of your business. My feeling is that they are most helpful when comparing performance during one period to performance during a prior period. In effect they help you decide whether you are on an uphill or a downhill slope.

Summary

That is all there is to the accounting information that will be most helpful to you in running your new business. It is also the financial information that will be required by any person or organization providing capital to your company. There is really nothing very complex about these numbers once you understand that the vocabulary accountants frequently use is much different than the vocabulary used by ordinary people such as entrepreneurs. The same problem of differences in vocabulary often exists when conversing with lawyers, bankers and doctors. To be a successful entrepreneur you should track cash flow with a vengeance, watch your balance sheet like a hawk and try to keep backlog at a level consistent with the capacity of the company to perform. To be a wealthy entrepreneur you need to watch your profit and loss statements as well because that is what many potential investors use as their guide to your performance as the head of a company.

Chapter 4

Assets Not on the Balance Sheet

There is another category of assets that does not show up on the balance sheet. These assets are things to which it is difficult to assign a tangible value. Cash is easy—all you have to do is look in your checkbook or call your bank. But how can an accountant determine the value of the skills of the management team, a patent, the design work needed to develop a product, market penetration, store location, etc.?

This type of asset does not appear on a balance sheet and does not show as something of value to the company. However, any one or group of these may be the most valuable assets that the company owns. When trying to raise capital for your business, it is crucial that these items, and any others of a similar nature, be listed separately from the balance sheet and described in detail because they may be the most important things a potential investor or lender uses to make the decision as to whether to become involved with your company.

Unfortunately, it will also be difficult for you to determine the value of this group of assets. However, because of their importance to the lender or investor, you must tell a good enough story that the person reading your business plan or investment proposal can determine to their own satisfaction the "real" value these items have in influencing the future of your business.

The following is a list of some of the more important "non-balance-sheet-assets" and how you might handle these in presenting your story.

Management. To most equity investors, surely, and probably most lenders as well, the quality, skills and experience of the management of a company may be the most important factor in determining whether they have any interest in providing money. If you ask many venture investors what the three most important factors are in determining success in a new business they will frequently answer, "Management, management and management." So this is a very important factor.

My suggestion on how to get this message across most effectively is to have a short section in the Executive Summary of your business plan describing the most important managers with a brief summary of their background and experience in running a successful business. Describe their key skills and how they complement each other. Then in the body of the plan include an organizational chart showing their specific role, their relationship to each other and a little more detail about their background. And as an appendix include a one or two page resume listing all relevant experience.

This may sound like overkill but believe me it is not because the management group is a very important part of the decision by any investor or lender as to whether they are interested in working with you.

Product. The money you invested in the design and development of the products or services that form the basis of your business normally does not show as an asset on the balance sheet. Usually it is expensed during the period in which the design and development occurred. Here again these products or services may be of immense value and represent a key strength in the minds of investors or lenders. In this case you must describe the product or service in some detail along with an indication of its most important features compared to competitive products other companies are selling to the same customers. What benefits do you offer that will make your product more attractive than alternatives? What sales have you generated to date? Is the product profitable?

Market penetration. This, in my opinion, is one of the most important assets a company might have. The fact that you are already selling something to a focused group of customers is an immense strength. In the case of my company, RF Communications, we sold long range radio equipment to customers all over the world. Our selling organization included a small marketing group located at the home office in Rochester, N.Y. But the main selling was done by independent agents and distributors with whom we had relationships and who were located in each country in which we did business.

This meant that for someone to compete with us in these overseas markets they would also have to find marketing representatives in each country who were as good as ours. In many countries there were just one or two people or organizations available with the skills needed to sell such complex products. The combination of a product line with many innovative and unique features together with a long standing relationship with a strong group of agents and distributors was an extremely valuable asset—hard for other companies to duplicate. Interestingly, for most equipment in our line we had no patents, and market penetration was a far more important strength.

Depending on the nature of your business, it is of great importance that you identify and describe in detail the assets your company has that are not included on the balance sheet. These must be described in detail in a way that an investor or potential lender, not familiar with your business, will be able to understand. It is extremely important that you be careful not to use too much technical jargon and complex descriptions in order to get your point across.

Chapter 5

Homemaker's Theory of Cash Flow: Forecasting Capital Needs

A number of years ago I began teaching a course titled "Entrepreneurship and New Venture Management" to second-year MBA students at a prominent graduate business school. To my amazement, I discovered that the students had virtually no understanding of cash flow, particularly as it applies to a start up venture. Since then I have read informational booklets written for entrepreneurs by several national public accounting firms. To my further amazement, I found that the discussion of cash flow in some of these booklets was almost useless to an entrepreneur.

Cash flow is, by far, the most important financial control in a start up venture and almost every small business, and every entrepreneur must fully understand its significance.

The accounting definition of cash flow is sometimes quite complex but usually comes down to net profit plus depreciation, both being noncash items in the operating statement. This number is sometimes adjusted by several other things such as increases or decreases in receivables, payables, investing activities, etc. While this approach should give a pretty accurate indication of cash flow, I personally consider it too complex for the average non-accountant entrepreneur to understand.

A far better way to define cash flow, at least for a start up, is that it is the difference between cash receipts and cash expenditures—the difference between the money you take in and the money you spend.

It is imperative in planning a new business, or in managing a growing business, to do a cash flow projection on a regular basis. A cash flow projection must be a key part of your business plan. It is the only way for you to have any assurance that you will be able to meet the financial obligations of your business. It is the only way to be sure that you will not come to the office some day and suddenly discover that the business is insolvent. As one entrepreneur said, "You cannot meet a payroll with depreciation." Some people describe managing a start up venture as "a race against insolvency," and they are right.

A cash flow projection is also extremely important to both equity investors and lenders. It is an indication to them that you know what you are doing and the money you are trying to raise will do the job you expect it to do.

Sample Cash Flow Projection

	Jan	Feb	Mar	Apr	May	June	July	Aug	Sept	Oct	Nov	Dec
Receipts												
Product A												
Units Ordered	5	5	7	7	9	9	9	9	9	9	9	9
Units Shipped	0	3	6	7	8	10	10	9	9	9	9	9
Cash Receipts	0	0	0	24	48	56	64	80	80	72	72	72
Product B												
Units Ordered	0	0	2	5	5	5	3	3	4	4	4	4
Units Shipped	0	0	2	3	4	4	4	4	4	4	4	4
Cash Receipts	0	0	0	0	10	15	20	20	20	20	20	20
Product C												
Units Ordered	1	1	3	3	3	3	3	3	5	5	10	10
Units Shipped	0	0	0	1	2	2	2	4	6	8	8	8
Cash Receipts	0	0	0	0	0	10	20	20	20	40	60	80
Total Cash Receipts	0	0	0	24	58	81	104	120	120	132	152	172
Expenditures (All cash)												
Rent	5	5	5	5	5	5	5	5	5	5	5	5
Salaries	10	15	20	30	40	40	40	40	45	45	45	45
Benefits	2	3	4	6	8	8	8	8	8	8	8	8
Telephone	2	2	3	3	3	3	3	3	3	3	3	3
Materials	2	2	8	10	12	20	50	50	50	50	50	50
Capital Equip		15					8				10	
Misc.	1	2	2	4	1	1	2	2	2	2	2	2
Total Cash Expenditures	22	44	42	58	69	85	108	108	113	113	123	113
Net Cash Flow	-22	-44	-42	-34	-11	-4	-4	12	7	19	29	59
Cumulative Cash Flow	-22	-66	-108	-142	-153	-157	-161	-149	-142	-123	-94	-35

In my opinion, the most useful way to forecast cash flow in a meaningful way is to first project cash receipts from all sources. When I say cash receipts, incidentally, I mean cash in the bank. Orders are not cash receipts and invoices that you send out are not cash receipts. A deposited check is close. Cash receipts are cleared checks. And even here you run some risk that you will have returns. Subtract from these the projected cash expenditures. A purchase order placed with a supplier, a bill, or even a check that you mail is not a cash expenditure. A check that clears your bank account is a cash expenditure. This is a very simple concept. By keeping all of the above in mind you can forecast cash flow in a reasonably intelligent manner. Keep track of the cash input to the firm and subtract the money that you spend. I call this the Homemaker's Theory of Cash Flow.

The average homemaker is a master at managing money. This includes the housewife, professional woman or man—whoever is managing the finances of the family. They worry not at all about profit and may not even know what depreciation means. What they do know is that if they continually spend more than they take in they will soon be in pretty big trouble. It is the same with a new company. Almost every new company begins its life with limited capital and it is necessary to project and manage cash flow carefully to run the business intelligently.

As an example, the illustration shows a cash flow projection for a typical start up company.

When projecting cash flow, you must consider when orders will be received, manufacturing cycle, shipping schedules and collection delays. In this example, I assume the company has three products that go into production within a few months of each other. I also assume a collection cycle of 60 days. Expenses, of course, start almost immediately. A personal computer and simple spreadsheet program will be of immense help in projecting cash flow. Even though the example I use is for a product business, cash flow is equally as important for a service business.

These projections are very difficult to make with any degree of confidence. About the only thing you can be sure of in a forecast of cash receipts is that it will be wrong. Should that stop you from making the forecast? Absolutely not. What it does tell you is that projections of cash receipts must be constantly reviewed and updated.

Projecting cash expenditures, on the other hand, is easy. These include rent, salaries, telephone expenses, purchased materials, etc. Most expenditures are both known and controllable and can be projected with a fair degree of accuracy. However, here again, they should be constantly reviewed—not so much for accuracy but to be certain that your spending rate is consistent with the most current projection of cash receipts.

Anyone can forecast expenses, but it takes someone with real business sense to project orders, shipments and cash receipts. Students doing a business plan for the first time invariably get bogged down when they try to project cash receipts. They simply cannot deal with the uncertainty.

I suggest that you do these projections on at least a monthly basis, and under certain circumstances they might even be done weekly. For a new company, a quarterly or annual cash flow projection is of no use. The bottom line in the projection is cash flow on a cumulative basis.

I find cash flow most understandable when plotted as a graph shown here.

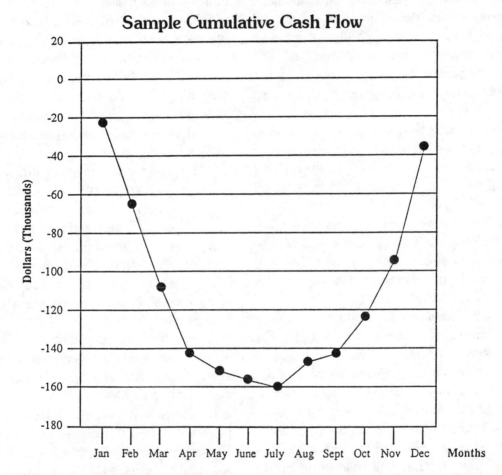

Sample Cumulative Cash Flow

A critical point for all small businesses is when cumulative cash flow reverses direction from negative to positive and starts to head north. This is a milestone that every company must reach sooner or later, the sooner the better.

Every business has financial obligations that must be met. They cannot be deferred if the company is to survive. Payrolls must be paid on time; they cannot be deferred, except perhaps for the owners of the business. Withholding items such as income tax, social security, etc., must be paid or the company can incur large penalties. And the obligations of debt must be paid, both interest and principal, or the company risks being forced into bankruptcy by its creditors.

So it is easy to see the importance of keeping very close track of cash flow—it may mean survival.

Also, the cash flow projection is the best way for a business to forecast its capital needs. As a practical matter, the lowest negative point in the graph indicates in simplest form how much capital will be needed to finance the operation of the business. The point where the cash flow projection reverses direction is the absolute minimum amount of cash that you must have to survive.

When deciding how much credit you will need from lenders or equity from investors, you should obviously include a safety factor when using this system to allow for contingencies. I already suggested that the only thing you can be sure of is that these projections will be wrong. This means that when you begin arranging bank credit or raising equity capital you should aim at raising 25 percent or 50 percent more than your projections indicate will be needed. In this example, where the projection shows that about $350,000 will be needed, you should probably try to raise between $400,000 and $500,000.

You may have noticed that the cash flow example I used is for a product business where the order flow is not seasonal in nature. Certain types of businesses are very seasonal, which makes the cash flow problem even more difficult. For example many retail businesses have a big concentration of sales just before Christmas. This means that for a

month or two the inflow of cash is likely to be very high. However, for sales to be high the store must have in inventory by Thanksgiving just about everything it expects to sell between then and Christmas.

If your business is selling to retailers you will probably begin receiving orders in mid-summer for delivery in October and November. Here, the likelihood of the retailer paying its bills before the end of the year is fairly low. In this situation you are apt to have a big surge of accounts receivable in October, November and December, hopefully to be reduced at about year end. Situations like this make cash flow projections very difficult and the need for dependable sources of financing very important. This approach to forecasting cash needs is a simple yet effective way to project the capital needs of a business that will be of great value to the entrepreneur.

Finally, you might ask who in the new company should make these projections. The only one qualified is the head of the company. Do not let your accountant do the job. He or she may be able to handle the expense projections, which are easy to project because they are identifiable and controllable. But your accountant is likely to panic when he or she tries to project orders, shipping schedules, revenues, and cash receipts. I cannot emphasize enough the importance of continually tracking cash flow as the major financial control available to an entrepreneur.

As I finish this chapter I am reminded of a personal experience I had several years ago on the subject of cash flow. A young man I knew owned a retail fish store that had serious cash flow problems. It was located in a relatively affluent suburb of a medium-sized city. He contacted me to ask if he could come in for some counsel and possible suggestions on how he might improve his cash problem. Of course I said that he could and a few days later he and his bookkeeper came to my office.

They explained how their business seemed to be prospering but they were always running out of money. The first question I asked was had they done a cash flow projection. They did not answer directly but I could see from the look on their faces that the question they had was, "What's that?"

I proceeded to give them a brief lecture on "Cash Flow 101," essentially covering the things I described earlier in this chapter. They said they would do one immediately.

Then I decided to question them on some of the aspects of managing a business that I thought might apply in their situation, even though I know virtually nothing about the fish business. My first question was, "Suppose you raised the price on every item you sell by 5 or 10 percent. How much do you think this would affect your business?" Their answer was, "Probably very little." Then I said, "Try raising your prices a bit at a time to be sure."

My next question was, "Do you sell retail only or do you also sell wholesale to restaurants or other fish distributors?" The answer was that they sold to

both. However the over-the-counter sales were always for cash so there was never a collection problem. But the wholesale part of the business, in addition to requiring a discount from normal retail prices, was usually very slow paying. My suggestion was that perhaps it would be wise to either completely forget that part of the business or only sell to people who paid their bills promptly.

My next question was, "Do you have a kitchen in your store?" The answer was yes because some of the items they sold were pre-cooked. I asked whether they used the kitchen on weekends and the answer was, "Only occasionally, when someone wanted to use it who was catering a wedding or Bar Mitzvah." I asked why he didn't make this a regular practice so that the kitchen was always used on weekends without incurring additional cost. He said he would give it a try.

Then I asked, "Do you use all of the space that you have and do you sell other things that might be of interest to someone purchasing fish, such as utensils, condiments, etc.?" He said he did not but someone had recently approached him to rent a corner of the store to put in a rack that offered these other items. I asked what was taking him so long to do that because in addition to providing a small amount of rental revenue it may also increase their fish sales. He said he would try to make some kind of deal as soon as possible.

When we were finished, I could tell his and his bookkeepers' heads were spinning because the handful of simple actions I suggested might very well solve their cash flow problems. I like this example because it shows how a little imagination on improving cash flow can be of immense help in managing a business and substantially reducing capital needs.

That is all there is to cash flow. Do not let anyone tell you that it is complex. It is not. It is extremely simple in concept, yet crucial to the new firm, both in running the business and in raising outside capital from any source.

Chapter 6

How Much Money is Enough?

The previous section suggested a way of estimating the capital requirements of a new business by using detailed cash flow projections. This gives you an idea of the capital you can expect to need, based on the type of business you are trying to start and the scale of operations suggested in your business plan. It is the amount of capital that you would like to have to get the business underway. Ideally, you would like to approach a banker or venture investor and ask for the amount you desire and walk away with a check. It's not that simple. The capital projection is only a first step.

The next step is to try to determine how much capital you can reasonably expect to raise, and what you should do if you cannot raise the amount you think you need. Further questions are: Should you try to raise all of the capital you need at one time or should you do it in stages? And, is it desirable to raise more capital than you require?

As a practical matter, there are eight sources of financing that should be considered, each of which is discussed in detail in a later chapter. They are:

1. Personal savings and borrowing.

2. Borrowing from relatives, friends and business associates.

3. Borrowing from banks and other professional lenders.

4. Individual venture investors.

5. Professional (Institutional) venture funds.

6. Corporate venture investors.

7. Going public.

8. Federal, state and local governments.

Under what circumstances you should try to use any or several of these sources is a complex question. If you are fortunate enough that your business grows faster than you expect you will probably find it necessary to use two or more of these sources either for short term or long term financing.

However, the main question I want to cover here is what you can do if you cannot reach your financing goals from any combination of the above sources.

Suppose, for example, you think you need $350,000 to get your business going as planned, and find you can only raise $200,000. What next? You have two choices. One is to take the $200,000, get the business going as best you can in accordance with your plan, and attempt to raise additional capital at a later date. Another alternative is to go back to the drawing board. Go over your business plan and try to devise a different strategy that requires only $200,000. How can this be done? First, you should carefully examine both the projected cash receipts and projected cash expenditures and try to figure out what you can do to speed up the receipts and delay the expenditures. But this will probably not close the entire gap.

An important strategic decision a new business must make that greatly affects cash flow and is covered in more detail in my other book is whether to be a product company, a service company, an advice company or some combination of these. An example of a product company would be the manufacturer of personal computers, lawn mowers or printed circuit boards. A service company might be an accounting firm, law firm or retail store and an advice company would be a consultant of some sort.

Many start up businesses follow two or even all three of these options.

We faced this decision at RF Communications in developing our initial strategy. If we were to be a product company—that is, to try to have a line of proprietary radio communication equipment—we had to design the product, build prototypes, set up a manufacturing facility, get orders and make shipments before we could expect our first cash receipts. This process takes at least 12 to 18 months and requires a lot of capital. As an alternative, we could have become a service company, that is, go to the Army, Navy and Air Force and try to get development contracts and studies. Government contract business is the high-tech equivalent of a service business. In effect, we would be selling man-hours of staff time to design military products to government specifications. The advantage of this strategy is that you perform the work, send an invoice once a month, and in a relatively short time pick up a check. Not much up front cash is needed.

As a consultant, of course, you provide whatever service it is you are providing and also send an invoice once a month and get paid fairly promptly. In fact, some consultants even require an advance payment of some sort, which makes the cash flow problem even easier.

To RF Communications, the major difference between a product business, a service business and an advice business was timing of cash flow. The product business is capital intensive, it needs a lot of initial investment before cash receipts can be expected. With a service or advice business, positive cash flow can be expected fairly early, frequently within weeks or just a few months.

Our goal at RF Communications was to have a line of proprietary products. This was very important to us because we believed it would result in a more profitable and stable business. We thought we could raise enough capital to do this but were not certain. As a hedge, we also aggressively pursued contract work and consulting work at the same time and within a few months had several large contracts. In effect, our game plan emphasized the product business and used contract work to provide cash flow to keep the company running until our products came on stream. From time to time we also did consulting for other firms as a way to generate both cash and sales leads for our products.

Even if you have a product business, there are strategies that can reduce the capital needed. A new company should buy as many components and sub-assemblies as possible from outside sources rather than setting up its own manufacturing facility. More and more companies are doing this, both as a way to conserve capital and as a way to avoid adding certain very expensive, specialized skills within their own organizations. Today this is usually called "out-sourcing."

I suggest you do a careful job of estimating the amount of capital you need for the kind of business you want to have. If you don't like the answer, shift the strategy as much as you must to match the capital you can raise. Forecasting the capital needs of a start up is an empirical process. You may have to do it many times before you are satisfied with the result.

Now let's suppose you encounter the opposite situation where you are able to raise more capital than you need. Suppose, for example, that you can raise $500,000 when you think you need only $350,000. What then? You will be surprised when I say too much capital also has some drawbacks.

If you are borrowing, it will probably require higher interest rates and make it much harder to get the loan. If you are taking the equity route and raise more capital than you need you may be selling your stock too cheaply. It may be better to take $350,000 and perhaps a modest amount more, the amount you think you need. One or two years later, if you are meeting your plan, you should be able to borrow more readily or sell stock for a higher price. This means lower borrowing risk and less dilution will be required to raise the additional capital.

A second reason is that having more money than needed takes the pressure off the management of a new business. Offices will be larger, facilities will be more elaborate, salaries will be higher, more support services will suddenly appear, etc. All of these consume cash and none contribute in meaningful ways to the success of the business. This is a very important issue.

A third more subtle reason why a start up should not raise more capital than it needs relates to the skills of the entrepreneurs. One of the major risks in a new venture is the uncertainty as to whether the team of entrepreneurs have the skills that it takes to run a business. If they do have the skills, more money should not be difficult to obtain. If they do not, the sooner they learn it and stop trying, the better.

I believe there is such a thing as a right amount of start up capital for a new venture, not too much and not too little. You want enough to give you and your team a fighting chance to achieve the goals you set out but not so much that you either borrow too much or sell your stock too cheaply, spend money in an imprudent manner, or try to continue the business beyond the point where it becomes obvious that you will not succeed.

Paul Hawken, in his book *Growing a Business*, said that he and his partner started the very successful Smith & Hawken garden equipment mail order business with $100,000, even though they had access to much more at the time. This was the amount they were comfortable with and the amount they thought necessary to do the job they had in mind.

Few financial experts are likely to agree with these comments. Almost no business failures occur because of lack of money. It is almost always the excuse but seldom the reason. The real reason businesses fail is because of poor product selection, poor market selection, poor marketing or just plain poor management. For more on why companies fail, please see Chapter 28.

Chapter 7

Where and How to Look for Financing

Many if not most entrepreneurs need outside financial support of some sort to start or grow a business. This support is usually either a loan of some sort or an equity investment resulting from the sale of stock in the new business. The level of difficulty in getting financial support depends upon many factors, but I think it is safe to say that raising money is never easy.

Some experts suggest that raising money has a seasonal quality. For example, it is probably a waste of time to approach a wealthy individual for an equity investment either in the middle of the summer or the middle of the winter. People with large amounts of money to invest are likely to be away on vacation during the summer months or in a warmer location during the winter months. The right time to approach them is likely to be in the spring or fall.

Other experts say that raising money is more cyclical than seasonal, and they are also probably right. A number of years ago I did some research and found that in the upstate New York area during the 1960s, about 100 companies raised their initial outside capital by going public. Some used an underwriter; most did it themselves. My company, RF Communications, was one of the first.

A more recent study I conducted, which I will describe in more detail near the end of this chapter, showed that during the 1980s, in the same region, a larger number of companies raised more initial capital from private investors than from any other source.

During the first half of the 1990s, initial public offerings (IPOs) have become very, very popular again, being done mostly through established brokerage firms, both large and small. Many companies in the past few years have raised millions of dollars to finance businesses that were barely underway and, at the time, still not profitable. In some cases the companies had not even shipped their first product to a customer. Articles in the business press now suggest that this surge in IPOs may have come to an end or will before long.

The best place to look for outside capital during the rest of 1990s is not yet entirely clear.

First, a course on selling

Before listing and commenting on various sources of financing, I would like to describe an experience I had that substantially altered my view of this important issue.

In late 1991, I spoke at an outplacement seminar at a state university in New York. Schools in the state system faced substantial reductions in financial aid and were in the process of making staff cuts to balance their budgets. This seminar, which lasted two days, was organized to help those facing termination find a job. My role was to describe starting a business as an alternative.

One of the other speakers was discussing making contacts, writing a resume and being interviewed. A man in the audience, very upset by his situation, raised his hand and said, "I know nothing about finding a job. I have not done it in many years. Every time I apply anywhere there are 20 or 30 other applicants for the same job. What am I to do?"

Even though this was not my assigned subject I could not restrain myself. I interrupted him and said that whether he liked it or not he had just changed professions. Last week he may have been an assistant registrar or a data processing specialist but this week he had suddenly become a salesman. And, he had only one product to sell—himself. He may not like being a salesman and may not want to be a salesman, but if he wanted to find a job during difficult times, he had better get used to the fact that he was now a salesman.

His next question was, "What is the state going to do to help me?" I answered, "Probably nothing." Then he asked, "What would you do if you were me?" I suggested he do the same things I did early in my career when I made the transition from design engineer to salesman.

I would immediately find a course in selling that I could take. Go to the library where they undoubtedly have several shelves full of books about selling. Read them all. Soon you will understand that selling is a process that has well established techniques and procedures that are followed by almost every successful sales person and these techniques work. Learn them and apply them. This will be an immense help in finding a job because your competitors, the other 20 or 30 applicants, almost surely have done nothing to improve their selling skills.

Why am I telling you this story as part of a chapter on where to look for financing for your new business? The reason should be obvious.

When you, as an entrepreneur, decide to try to raise outside financial support for your business you, also, have just changed professions. You are no longer an entrepreneur, or design engineer or the distinguished founder of a hot new start up company. You are now a salesperson, whether you like it or not.

And, what is it you are trying to sell? You are selling your concept for a business. You are selling your management team, your idea for a product or service, your assessment of a market opportunity. In short, you are selling your plan for a business. To raise money today you had better learn how to sell because if you don't, your chances of success are virtually nil.

What do I mean by selling? Well, first you develop leads, then you separate the prospects from the leads. A prospect is someone who needs what you are selling and who can afford what you are selling. This is a little tricky to comprehend when your goal is raising capital, but it must be done.

Next, you analyze your competition and plan your approach and your sales pitch. Then you figure out how to answer the objections and negotiate and close the deal. All of these things are standard selling techniques. They are skills you seldom learn in business or engineering schools, but you had better learn them now if you expect to get financing, whatever its source.

Where do you look?

At last we get to the main subject of this chapter. This discussion assumes that the entrepreneur has determined how much capital is needed to launch the new business. The question to be resolved is how to find that much money. This is another complex question for which there is no right or wrong answer. Possible sources of early capital for the entrepreneur include the following, each of which is discussed in greater detail in a later chapter:

1. Personal savings and borrowing. Whether this is a reasonable source depends on the nature of the business you are trying to start and the amount of personal resources you have over and above what you need to live on. It further depends on how big a personal risk you are willing to take.

Most entrepreneurs finance the early start up stage of their business with personal savings. If the company is formed by a team, it is their combined personal contributions. This amount of money, though often quite small, can sometimes pay the cost of building prototypes of products, limited market research, filing a patent application, getting a service business off the ground, incorporating, and the preliminary steps of more formal financing.

Service businesses, particularly, do not require much capital, and I have seen a number of such ventures use only the personal savings of the founder and spouse as well as retained earnings of the business. If you have ample personal resources available, whether to use them rather than seeking outside investors is a decision only you can make. On one hand you keep complete control; on the other you reduce the financial risk and increase the potential.

2. Borrowing from relatives, friends and business associates. Another source is loans from family, friends or business associates. This approach has its pros and cons as well. Borrowing money from this group probably does not require lengthy negotiation or your committing all of your personal resources to guarantee the loan. But it does represent a very large personal obligation and could seriously affect your relationship with whomever it is you borrowed from.

For example, at this point you will probably want to think about some kind of formal agreement with your lenders. Chances are you will need an attorney to set up the arrangement in acceptable legal form. As you bring in more and more outside individual lenders you may decide to either incorporate, form a Limited Liability Company (LLC) or set up some kind of legal partnership.

However, keep in mind that some people say that the best way to turn a good friend into an enemy is to borrow money from him, so this approach also has its disadvantages.

3. Banks and other professional lenders. Banks and other professional lenders are other sources of financing and may be used alone or in combination with yet other sources. However, this type of borrowing is a complex and difficult problem for a new business. The bank's reward for making a loan is usually limited to interest and it rarely has the opportunity to increase this reward if the company that borrows is exceptionally successful. Its main goal, therefore, when making a loan is to be sure that the interest and principal will be paid back. If the borrower's business runs into unexpected trouble the lender wants to be as sure as possible that the loan is protected by enough guarantees that it will have a good chance of getting its money back, even in the case of bankruptcy.

Any loans you are able to get from these sources will probably have to be secured with a personal guarantee, which puts all of your personal assets at risk, including your home, savings accounts and investments, and anything else of value you may have. Because of this, many entrepreneurs are reluctant to borrow from a bank to get their business underway.

4. Individual venture investors. Individual investors have become a common source of capital in recent years. They are sometimes called "angels." These are usually people who are interested in investing in new businesses, understand and are willing to take the risk and are willing to wait a number of years for a return.

5. Formal (institutional) venture capital funds and small business investment companies. These are other possible sources of capital. They can be either private groups or groups backed by the Small Business Administration. They usually have large amounts of money available to invest in new businesses. However, it may be very difficult for an early start up business to get money from this source.

6. Corporate venture investor. Another source of capital that may also be an alternative is another company. Many large firms in recent years have established internal venture investing groups, sometimes formal and sometimes informal, that are willing to invest in new businesses. The goal is either to expand their business in a direction that they are already in or as a form of diversification.

7. Going public. Selling stock to the public is usually not considered a reasonable approach to raise capital for a start up business. Almost every financial expert you are likely to ask will advise you against even thinking about this alternative. However, I suggest you do think about it as many companies have gone public very early in their corporate lives, either through the use of an underwriter or on their own. Recently, the Securities Exchange Commission, which regulates the public sale of securities, has eased some of the restrictions on small businesses going public, which may make this route more attractive again.

8. Federal, state and local governments. The federal government, most state governments and many local governments have financial programs intended to encourage people to start businesses. They also provide financial support to help existing businesses grow. The purpose of most of these programs is to create jobs. Creating jobs may not be your highest priority as an entrepreneur. But that in no way conflicts with the government's goal, because if you succeed in your business, the probability is you are also creating jobs. Both sides win.

A study of venture capital sources in Rochester

In 1988, I conducted a study of venture capital sources in the Rochester, N.Y. area and surrounding counties. A list was compiled of all firms I could identify that raised their first outside capital between Jan. 1, 1980 and Mar. 31, 1988. A second list was compiled of the companies from this original group that raised capital a second or third time during the same period. I included five sources of venture capital—individual investors, going public, formal venture capital funds, corporate investors, and minority small business investment companies. I did not include borrowing as one of the sources even though I am quite sure many of these companies also used borrowing of some sort as they got going.

Table I on page 54 summarizes how 65 companies raised their first outside capital. Table II lists how 29 of these 65 companies raised capital a second or third time during the same period. Many of the companies on this list continue to operate. I have no information as to whether the situation in other sections of the country is similar to Rochester, but I see no reason for much difference.

While this survey is not entirely up to date, it does gives an entrepreneur some guidance as to how a large number of new businesses raised early capital. I do not have good data on how many of these companies are still in existence nine years and more after the survey, but I do know that quite a few are doing very well.

Table I: Sources of First Outside Capital

	#	%	Dollars
Individual Investors	42	64.6%	$22.5 Mil
Going Public	16	24.6%	30.3 Mil
Venture Capital Funds	5	7.7%	6.8 Mil
Corp. Venture Funds	0	0%	
Minority SBICs	2	3.1%	0.2 Mil
Total	65		$59.8 Mil

Table II: Sources of Later Capital

	#	%	Dollars
Individual Investors	8	27.6%	$11.3 Mil
Going Public	8	27.6%	37.3 Mil
Venture Capital Funds	8	27.6%	14.4 Mil
Corp. Venture Funds	5	17.2%	31.0 Mil
Minority SBICs	0	0%	
Total	29		$94.0 Mil

Scams

In recent years, with so many new companies trying to raise equity capital, some of these firms have become the target of unscrupulous scam artists. These vary from people who agree to raise the capital you need but require large advance payments to others who in fact do sell the company's stock but then proceed to manipulate the stock price in ways that can seriously endanger the company for which the money was raised.

Some states have begun holding seminars to advise entrepreneurs on the process of raising money. In at least one case the manager of the seminar estimated that about 20 percent of the attendees were unscrupulous promoters "looking for their next pigeon."

The Feb. 12, 1996 issue of *Business Week* included an article that suggested a number of things a small business can do to avoid being ripped off. They are:

- Beware if someone wants to sell shares or reincorporate your company out of state, or do a large stock split. These hallmarks of the penny stock scam are now being applied to small cap stocks.

- Beware promoters promising easy venture capital or business loans, particularly if they for ask up-front fees.

- Check references by getting written evaluations of the firm's service from former clients. Phone references may be accomplices.

- Check credentials with state securities or banking regulators. Be especially careful if promoters are in another state.

- Have a lawyer read the fine print of any agreement. Some contain fees that must be paid in cash, whether or not your company receives capital; others require turning over up to 10 percent of equity.

This same issue of *Business Week* describes a number of specific examples where several small companies in desperate need of capital have been badly hurt and even driven out of business.

So be careful.

There is no right answer

Which of these approaches is best? It's hard to say. There is seldom a right or wrong answer, and the best you can hope for is an answer that works. The following chapters will discuss each of these alternatives in some detail, giving the pros and cons of each, how you approach each source, and the problems of negotiating a deal.

Chapter 8

Personal Savings and Borrowing

Many people who start businesses do so using only their own personal resources. This is usually done under one of two circumstances. One is where you are very rich and can afford to invest your own money to meet all of the financial needs of the new business; the other is where the business you start simply does not need much money and what you have or can borrow, even though it may be a fairly small amount, is enough to get the business going.

The first example does not need much discussion. For instance, if Bill Gates, one of the founders of Microsoft, were to someday decide to leave that company and start another business I doubt whether he would be under much pressure to either borrow or raise equity capital from outsiders to get the new business underway. The Oct. 14, 1996 edition of *Forbes* magazine estimates Gates's net worth to be in the range of $18 billion, which should be enough to start any kind of business known to man. Interestingly, though, if Gates were to start another business, people would probably be lined up halfway across the United States trying to buy a piece of it. This is commonly known as, "He who has, gets."

I also suspect Gates would not be likely to be reading this book for suggestions on how to find lenders or investors.

The other example is different and much more likely to happen. It is where the business is not capital intensive, you are anxious to own it all and it simply does not need more money than you are able to provide. What kind of businesses might these be? They are mostly service or knowledge businesses of some sort that just do not take much money to get underway.

One of my daughters is a certified public accountant with an MBA who specializes in taxes, either for small businesses or individuals. About 10 years ago she set up her own practice working from her home in a town near Bridgeport, Conn. After getting her first few clients she rented a small office to give the business the appearance of being "more professional."

After a year or two, her annual billing rose to about $50,000, which provided her a decent income while remaining free of debt. Shortly after that, she moved from Connecticut to Columbia, Md. Being a pretty bright young woman, she did some research on whether an accounting practice can be sold rather than simply abandoned. She learned that the standard in the industry was that an accounting practice was worth about one year's billings, payable over five years.

She did a little better than that and after moving started another similar business from her new home and cashed a check for a little more than $10,000 for the next five years. In this example, my daughter started two businesses, both quite successful, with her own resources, without either borrowing or selling part of the business.

I know of many other small business owners who have done the same thing in areas such as consulting, training, computer programming, public relations, etc., where their skills as entrepreneurs and their ability to get orders and/or clients fast made it possible for them to get the business going on a profitable basis completely on their own resources. Incidentally, whether the entrepreneur is a man or a woman, having a working spouse can make this approach much more realistic.

A variation on this is for the individual to start the business entirely on his or her own resources, knowing full well that before long they will need additional financing for the business to either survive or grow. This approach has both advantages and disadvantages. The major advantage, in my opinion, is that the further a business is down the road the easier it will be to raise additional money, either from lenders or investors.

The major risk is that even further down the road you may still not be able to raise more money. In this situation, as we already discussed, you will have the choice of reducing the scope of the business to match the money you can raise or simply abandoning the business and starting over from scratch.

Except for the few examples mentioned above, I think it is usually a better idea to start a business using, to the greatest degree possible, other people's money. I say this for two reasons. The first is that the personal risk is greatly reduced, especially if the money you raise is from the sale of equity; the second is that the access to greater amounts of capital may greatly increase the growth potential of the business compared to what it would be using your own resources alone.

Chapter 9

Family, Friends and Business Associates

If your financial needs exceed your personal ability to invest your own money or borrow on your own credit worthiness, the next place many entrepreneurs look for help is loans from family members, personal friends or business associates. These would be people who, almost without exception, know you well and are acquainted with your skills and ability. As I mentioned earlier, borrowing from this group also has its pros and cons.

When I started RF Communications, I had to raise $5,000, which was my share of our start up money and which I did not have. This may not sound like much money now, but in 1961 it was about one third of a year's salary. One person who gave me help, in the form of several thousand dollars, was my father. He was by no means wealthy but all of his children were grown and through school and he had a decent, fairly well-paying management job in the printing industry. He had always been ready to help me out with any problems I faced during my life and all it took was a brief telephone call to get a check. There were no loan agreements, due diligence investigations or the need to prove my credit worthiness. I was his son and he was ready to help me along any path I was embarking on. We did not discuss it at the time but in my mind this was a loan that I was obligated to pay back at some point regardless of the difficulty or hardship it may have caused me.

What are the negatives of this? It is hard to say. Perhaps there aren't any. The amount of money involved, if lost, would have had little effect on my father's standard of living or retirement income, and I know it gave him great pleasure to help me out.

Of course it would have been far better if my father had been Ross Perot or Sam Walton, but that was beyond my control. When it comes to picking a father you normally have no opportunity to influence who you end up with. But, within his limited means, the money my father let me have at the time I was starting a business was extremely helpful, almost crucial.

I never borrowed from any other members of my family, friends outside my family or business associates. However, if I had done so I think I would have wanted some kind of formal agreement. For one thing, I would have insisted on paying interest and on some kind of regular repayment schedule.

It may be that we could have established a limited partnership of some sort in which there would have been an opportunity for greater rewards if the company succeeded, but would not have any personal liability if it did not. Another way to give them the opportunity for gain beyond the value of the loan should the company prosper would have been to agree to give or sell them some of my personal stock at a later date, at a predetermined price based upon the value of the stock at the time of the loan, either in repayment of the loan or as a reward for their support.

Whether such an agreement is in writing or not will be determined by the nature of the relationship, but in general, in situations such as this I usually think a formal document is desirable. It does not have to be a 20-page agreement loaded with "boilerplate" but perhaps just a page or so outlining what you both understand to be things to which you agreed. Good judgment suggests that it should at least be reviewed

by a knowledgeable tax lawyer to avoid future surprises.

I am an active sailboat racer and have owned sailboats for many years. From time to time, two friends purchase a boat together as equal partners in order to have the use of half of a better boat than they could have afforded on their own. In these situations I always suggest they put in writing how either of the two owners can get out of the deal should their personal circumstances change, such as a job change, a move to another city, etc. I have found that it is always easier to agree on how a situation such as this will be handled at the start, when the relationship is a happy one, than later on, when one party or the other has a problem and needs to get out.

Incidentally, what I usually suggest, should they ask my advice, is that the partner who wants out should name a price at which he will either buy or sell his or her half of the boat and the other person has the choice of whether to buy or sell. Another approach, of course, would be to simply sell the boat and divide the money they get.

A final way to handle a loan from family or business friends is to form your corporation or limited liability company before the loan is consummated and have a loan be to the business rather than to you personally. Obviously, you should also be willing to give them your personal guarantee in addition to the company's obligation. This makes the personal loan more like a bank loan and could be a way of avoiding future animosity should you encounter difficulty paying the lender back. On the plus side it also gives you a way to provide the lender with additional rewards in the form of warrants or conversion privileges should the company prosper.

One important negative of borrowing from either relatives or friends is that any of the loan arrangements I have discussed can put a serious strain on the relationship which, in the long term, could ruin the friendship. Here again, this is a situation where there is no fail safe advice I can give other than that you try to anticipate as many possible problems as you can before they happen, when it will be much easier to reach an agreement satisfactory to both parties.

Another thing to consider in these types of arrangements is the tax implication of whatever you do. In a formal loan between a parent and a child, for example, if it exceeds $10,000 it probably should include interest, at the prevailing rate. If you, as the lender, receive interest it must be declared as income. If you, as the borrower pay interest, under certain circumstances it may be declared as an expense.

Two of my children went through divorces and needed loans from their father in order to purchase a house. These loans were both in the high five figure range. They paid me regular interest, which I declared on my tax return as income. When they finally reached the point that they could pay back the entire loan, I told them both that I did not

want their money and I would forgive the principle of the loan. This ended the whole situation except for the fact that I had the obligation to deduct the amount from the $600,000 estate tax exemption which would come into effect at the time of my demise.

There is another possible way to do this if the amount is not too high that may avoid all tax issues. As you probably know, the IRS permits annual gifts of up to $10,000 from one person to another without any tax implications. They do not even need to be reported on your tax return. If you are married your spouse can also make a $10,000 gift at the same time—a total of up to $20,000. And if you make the gift in December you can make another in January of the following year which means you can get a total of as much as $40,000 from your family or friends with no tax liability on either side. I have done this with each of my children to help them establish a personal retirement program and to all of my grandchildren to set up a college fund for use by them when they reach that age.

The amounts of money that can be gifted without tax implications may be sufficient to finance a new business. Whether this money is ever paid back is your choice, but be very careful of the tax impact.

Another thing you must keep in mind is that all of the above comments about tax issues refer to the federal tax agency, the IRS. However, most states and some local governments may have tax regulations that are different than those of the IRS. I know New York state does and probably many other states do as well.

I do not pretend to be a tax expert and the rules regarding these actions are almost always complex and change from time to time. So I strongly advise you to consult your tax accountant and/or tax lawyer for expert advice at the time any transaction of this type takes place.

Chapter 10

Banks and Other Professional Lenders

....

Sooner or later almost every new business reaches the point where it must borrow money from a bank or other professional lender. If your company has equity investors and is operating in the black this becomes almost a routine process where the banks may be pursuing you more than you are pursuing the banks.

On the other hand, for many small businesses where raising money through other sources is not possible, for whatever reason, borrowing from a bank can be a harrowing and very difficult experience. However, there are things that you can do to make the process easier, and these may mean the difference between success and failure.

In 1951, when I was a young engineer raising three infant children and earning a salary that just about permitted the family to exist with a reasonable degree of respectability, I eventually reached the point where I decided to purchase a new car. We were living in New York City, at the time and I had accepted a position with a company in Rochester, N.Y. Both my wife's family and mine thought we were nuts to leave New York City but I had decided that commuting a total of about three hours a day to and from Manhattan from the outskirts of Queens was just not an acceptable way to spend my life.

This move meant we had to have a new car in place of the 15-year-old jalopy we were then using. My dear father had given us a $1,000 war bond as a wedding gift six years earlier, therefore we needed about $800 more to buy a new Ford—money we did not have. You may have noticed that new cars were far less expensive then.

This meant going to a bank for the first time in my life to get a loan. I was scared stiff because I had the false impression that the bank was doing me a great favor in lending me $800 secured by a $1,800 new car plus all of my personal assets. I did not have much savings but I had a good job with a lot of earning potential.

Soon I became much wiser and realized that banks are in business to make loans, they are not doing the borrower a favor. Unless they can find good borrowers who will pay interest and principle in a timely, dependable manner they will not survive as banks. Banking happens to be a very competitive industry.

This says that borrowing is not totally a financial problem, it is also a marketing problem. And, there are many things an entrepreneur can do to help secure a loan.

The personality of the bank

Companies and organizations have personalities just as people do. The personality of the firm is generally determined by the personal style and personal values of the senior management. I do not suggest that this is either good or bad. It simply is a condition that prevails and should be recognized.

What does this have to do with bankers? Well, banks also have personalities. Some are aggressive, others are conservative and cautious. Some are people-oriented, others are stuffy and formal. Some are willing to work with small, new companies, others consider them a nuisance. Since you will undoubtedly want a close working relationship with your banker, it's important that you're comfortable with the personality of the organization you select.

Determining the personality of a bank is not easy. One way to start is to

talk to present and former customers. Another way is to interview some senior officers at a number of banks, being very candid in the process. By doing this you are more likely to be satisfied with your choice.

In addition, you must recognize that even though banks have unique personalities, the day-to-day relationship in all cases is based on working with one person or a small group of individuals within the larger unit. These tend to be person-to-person relationships.

You must decide whether you are comfortable with the person assigned to your account. If you are not, talk to the head of the organization and ask that someone else be assigned. If for some reason your request is refused, change banks.

The cost of banking

The cost of services from a bank is another complex issue. They are expensive in the form of interest and/or fees. In your effort to keep your expenses down, I suggest you deal with the question of the cost of whatever banking services you use in an open and aggressive manner. Ask for a list of hours spent, rates charged, services provided and fees charged other clients.

Do not hesitate to challenge any items you consider unreasonable. Very few people do this. The minimum benefit is that they will be more careful in the future and the likelihood is that they will simply reduce the charge. In all cases, removing the irritant will lead to a better relationship.

How banks look at their customers

You deal with banks in a number of ways. First, you will surely need many of the services they provide. For example, a payroll account, a regular checking account, a safety deposit box or as registrar and transfer agent for your stock if you are publicly owned. These are services for which, in some form or other, you pay a fee. Then, sooner or later, you are likely to need to borrow from your bank either short term for working capital or inventory, or long term for a mortgage on a building or an expensive piece of capital equipment. The service part of the relationship is simple. It becomes more complex when you start to borrow.

Also, remember the underlying philosophy most banks have when lending. They do not make loans when they think there may be any significant risk. Some people think that banks adjust the interest rates up and down to compensate for risk. That is not the case. If they think there is significant risk—no loan. I discussed this question recently with two bank presidents. One said I was entirely right, the other said it was not true. Test it yourself.

The next thing banks worry about is how they will be paid back. They want to see their interest covered by earnings and the principal covered by liquidation of whatever the money was used for. For example, if the loan is to finance a capital purchase, it must be paid back from depreciation. If the loan was to finance receivables it must be paid back when the receivables are collected.

As a practical matter, you will have no trouble borrowing from most banks provided you do not need the money very badly. In this way the bank can be pretty sure the loan is safe and will be paid promptly. Establish your line of credit and perhaps even borrow when you do not need a loan, and repay promptly. Sounds silly, doesn't it? But believe me, this is good advice. There is nothing like a history of good credit to make you attractive to a banker.

During the late 1980s and early 1990s, many banks experienced serious financial difficulties. The number of bank failures was on the verge of becoming a national disaster. The federal agency that insured bank deposit was forever running out of money. Many of the foreign loans made by the large commercial banks were turning bad as were many of the more borderline domestic real estate loans. These were very hard times for the banking industry.

Recently banks have made a comeback. However, another factor has made it difficult for small businesses to get loans. With interest rates at almost all-time lows, banks can get nearly as good a return putting their money into U.S. government securities, where there is no risk, as they can from loans to private firms.

How does this affect the small company trying to get a loan from a bank? The bottom line is that it is still very hard. What could have been an acceptable loan situation five years ago may not even be considered today. I don't have any clever answers to this dilemma other than to suggest, as is suggested in other sections of the book, that you better have a pretty good business plan and better be a pretty good salesperson if you want to be successful in obtaining a loan.

Other factors affecting the relationship

Most banks, when lending to small companies, demand the personal guarantees of the owners and possibly other officers of the firms. This means that you must pledge as security all your savings, the equity in your home and everything else of value that you own. The banks' logic is that if the officers do not have enough confidence in the company to personally guarantee the loans, it is too risky a deal. I feel very uncomfortable guaranteeing loans and have always refused to do so. Nonetheless, my guess is that until your company has substantial sales and earnings, personal guarantees might be necessary in order to get a loan.

It seems that new bank customers almost always get better deals than present customers, so shopping around is often a good practice. Obviously, it is not acceptable to change banks every six months. However, you can change once in a while. You can let your current bank know that it is a possibility, and you might even do business routinely with more than one bank.

Finally, I have found it very difficult to determine with any degree of certainty what banks charge for their services. For instance, you borrow money at an agreed-upon interest rate and then learn that you are expected to keep a sizable balance in your account at zero interest. We all know about mortgage loans where, in addition to interest, you must pay several points of closing costs, plus the cost for the bank's attorney to protect the bank against you.

Pledging receivables

One thing that many companies do is to borrow money while they are waiting for their receivables to be paid by their customers. This is situation for which a bank will frequently lend you money. However, it is unlikely that they will lend the whole amount and they will almost surely require you to pledge the receivables to guarantee the loan.

If you have a good relationship with the bank they will continue to allow the checks from your customers to be sent directly to you and you have the obligation in turn to reduce the loan. In other situations the bank may require you to notify your customers to send their checks directly to the bank or to a post office box over which the bank has control. This assures the bank that they will receive the money for which the loan was to be used.

Most companies do not like this arrangement because it alerts your customers to the fact that your financial position is weak and may affect the customers' willingness to do business with you in the future.

I do not have any clever solution to this problem other than to have a sufficiently good banking relationship that they do not decide it is necessary to notify your customers of the loan arrangement.

Leasing

Another way to obtain long term financial support for your business is to lease equipment whenever you can rather than making an outright purchase. A lease is in many ways similar to a loan where the equipment being leased is the security. This is sort of the equivalent of renting the equipment rather than buying it. In some leasing situations, the lessee (you) may have the option to purchase the item at a greatly reduced price after an agreed upon period of time.

Depending on the specific situation leasing may be a more expensive approach than outright purchasing, based on what the firm leasing the equipment considers a reasonable return. The best type of leasing arrangement is when you can lease directly from whomever it is that is selling the item to you rather than through an intermediary. In this case the value of getting the order and prospects for future business may encourage a lower lease rate.

Leasing has several other advantages over a long term loan to purchase the same asset. Among these are the following:

1. A lease may cover the entire cost of the item being leased which long term loans normally will not do.

2. Leases are usually simpler documents than loan agreements and contain fewer restrictive covenants. Also, in some situations a lease may be tax deductible in situations where an outright purchase is not. Consult your tax accountant or tax attorney for advise on this issue.

3. Finally, a company that is unable to get a long term loan may have much less trouble getting a lease.

So companies that are borderline borrowers may find leasing an attractive alternative.

Interest rate calculations

When you borrow from a bank or any other lender there are several ways to compute interest that affect the cost of the loan. Three ways that I know of are simple interest rate, discounted interest rate and floating interest rate. There may be others.

In the simple interest rate approach the payments on a loan are constant over the life of the loan and the interest rate is fixed at the start. Regular payments are required at the end of a specified period, usually monthly. But the amount credited as interest and the amount that the principle is reduced are different each period. The interest the borrower pays is the interest due on the remaining principle, which changes as the amount of principle decreases. Most mortgage loans use this system.

In the discounted interest rate system the interest for the loan is discounted in advance so the borrower does not receive the face value of the loan but that amount less interest. This means that the effective rate is higher than using simple interest.

The last commonly used system is the floating rate method. In this approach the interest rate is not fixed but would be a variable such as prime rate plus 3 or 4 percent. In this system interest is calculated similar to the fixed rate system but the amount of interest that must be paid is calculated each day based upon prime rate. This means that the amount the principle of the loan decreases each period will vary depending on fluctuations in the prime rate and you will not know in advance what that rate will be. I understand that the most common system used today is the floating rate system.

As may be obvious, I am far from an expert on this issue and you should consult your accountant, not your banker, for further counsel.

Other issues

An additional factor that may have an effect on your short term borrowing is that banks normally require that the borrower be out of debt for 30 or 60 days each year. This assures them that the company is not using a series of short term loans for long term commitments.

And be sure to read the loan agreement used by the bank very carefully. These vary between lenders but many contain restrictions that you might consider unacceptable. This could include things such as maintaining minimum levels of working capital, restrictions on salaries and dividend payments, additional borrowing, and use of assets.

Each of these types of things restrict you, at least to a degree, in how you manage the business. Sometimes the onerous conditions can be negotiated out of the agreement and in other circumstances they may cause you to consider changing banks.

A final piece of advice that will help you maintain a good banking relationship is to be certain that you keep the bank well-informed about how your business is doing. This is done in detail at the time you get a loan but the borrower should make it an important personal obligation to keep the bank up to date on how your business is progressing since that time—either good or bad. If things are going well they will consider the information as a pat on the back for making a smart loan. If things are not going well they will learn about it sooner or later, so probably learning it from you sooner is better. Also they may be able to give you advice and suggestions that will help you overcome the problems causing your difficulties. And, of course, you must always be truthful and candid in bringing problems to the bank's attention.

So, you can see from the above that financing a business with money borrowed from a bank or other lender is a fairly complex transaction about which the average entrepreneur is likely to have little knowledge. And mistakes can have costly consequences. So I usually advise people beginning to utilize bank borrowing to read other comprehensive books on the subject and to get advice from people more expert in the subject than I, such as an experienced account-ant or business lawyer.

Included in the appendices of this book are samples of short term and long term loan agreements used by a major bank in making loans. The bank has asked not to be identified, but I think the things in these agreements are pretty standard. Please understand that these are intended to be read as examples, not as documents that must be accepted; they are subject to negotiation and change. The exact terms you will be re-quired to accept may vary depending on many things, such as how long you have been in business, how much money the principles have put into the business, whether you operate at a profit, your cash flow projections and many other things. But these sample agreements give you an idea of what your negotiat-ing starting point is apt to be.

The following chapter was written by a women who has 10 years' experience in commercial lending and who is on the loan committee of two New York state agencies that make loans to small busi-nesses. She said that many small busi-nesspeople are extremely naive when applying for a loan and do not present a very attractive deal to the lender. Her comments will give you a good idea of the things commercial lenders find im-portant and may improve the odds of your getting a loan.

In summary, borrowing money for the purpose of either starting or grow-ing a new business is a perfectly accept-able, though often difficult way to fi-nance a business. But as I said at the beginning of this book and over and over again in the various chapters, your selling skills may be more important in obtaining a loan than your business skills. Do not forget this very important piece of advice.

Chapter 11

How to Obtain a Loan

This chapter was written by Victoria Posner, a Trainer and Consultant based in Rochester, N.Y. (716-461-3531; fax 716-473-7764). Victoria has 10 years' experience in commercial lending, and teaches banking and finance to bankers, investment managers, and other financial professionals. She also teaches a number of workshops on financial planning for small business. Victoria sits on two nonprofit micro-loan committees: the New York State Rural Venture Fund, sponsored by Rural Opportunities, Inc., and the Minority and Women's Revolving Loan Fund, sponsored by the Urban League of Rochester. She writes a monthly column for the newsletter "Small Business Success." She holds a BA from Connecticut College and an MBA from Wharton School.

Getting a loan is a hard road

Borrowing to start a business is not easy. However, the problem is often not that there is no money available but rather that many people do not want to put in the time and effort necessary to submit a good package to potential lenders. Lenders ask for an awful lot of information. It takes a great deal of work to put it all together and you may well wonder why so much information is requested. Well, lenders need to know as much as possible to make good decisions.

No lender should take inordinate risks. When banks do that we all end up paying—remember the savings and loan crisis? For a lender there is a great deal of "downside risk" and virtually no "up side" potential. If the business fails, the loan goes down the tubes; if it succeed, the lender gets the money back with a little interest but does not share in the profits.

So it is important that the lender be prudent, since there are no windfall profits to offset losses.

At the same time, it does not benefit you to take on debt that cannot be repaid. The likely result is a failed business and, often, personal bankruptcy. Of course, everyone thinks that his or her idea is a sure winner. But the failure rate of start up businesses tells us otherwise. As unpleasant and as disappointing as it may be, getting turned down for a loan may be the best thing that can happen to you. It should make you stop and rethink your whole idea through again. That doesn't mean that you should give up, just that you need to do more work.

The need for personal information and guarantees

Since your business is a start up, lenders rely on your ability and integrity. Therefore, they need to know as much about you as possible. Most lenders will ask you for a lot of personal information in addition to information about your proposed business. Typically you will be asked for a complete resume, several years of income tax returns with all supporting schedules, a personal financial statement listing all your assets and liabilities and a recent report from a credit bureau (unless the lender can access the credit bureau directly). Many people balk at these requests but it is standard procedure.

You can also expect the lender to ask for personal guarantees from you and your spouse and a lien on any major assets such as a home. Don't be surprised, this is also fairly standard. If you want a loan you will have to supply the requested items.

There will usually be some sort of application you must fill out. It may range from a simple one or two pages to a long, detailed document. Many of the questions will already be answered in your business plan. You will be tempted to write "See Business Plan" over and over. Don't do it! As boring and as tedious as it is, answer each question fully and completely. While you may not understand the need for this redundancy, there usually is a good reason. For example, banks must compile information on loan applications into statistical reports for regulators. Searching through your entire package would be very time consuming so they ask for the needed information on the application document.

The business plan is critical

The heart of your package is your business plan. It is a constant source of amazement to me to see what people put together and call a business plan. Having a good business idea but only some vague notion of how to accomplish it just won't cut the mustard with lenders. Time and time again I see applicants come to the loan committees on which I sit with what can only be described as half-baked business plans. They follow the right format but there is no meat. Just having the right chapter and section headings does not constitute a good business plan. This may seem obvious but it isn't.

People make the most amazing mistakes when putting together their business plan. So I would like to give you some do's and don'ts that can make a big difference between success and failure.

1. Make sure it is very clear to the reader just what the business is. I have read plans that talk around it but never say exactly what the writer intends to do. Sometimes the individuals use a lot of industry jargon thinking that they are being precise. But you can't expect everyone to understand. Make it very clear, in simple language, what you are doing or making and exactly who the customer is. Lenders are not inclined to approve a loan if they can't even tell what the business is. Pretend you're explaining it to a group of 10-year-olds who know nothing about the business world. That ought to do the trick.

2. Do not make broad, unsubstantiated statements like "It is a known fact that..." If you can't support statements with good, solid data, don't make them. Whenever I read something like that I know it should read, "In my opinion..." However, there is little room for opinions in a business plan. Lenders want real facts. Document, document, document. Spend time in the library doing research. Be able to support everything you say, every number in your projections. Vague ideas and shot-in-the-dark guesses just won't do. And don't rely on, "I've worked in this industry (for someone else) for 20 years so I know what I wrote is true." If you really do know what you are talking about, you should be able to back up your assertions with facts from reliable sources.

3. Similarly, watch the adjectives— "There is a dire need..." A dire need? Are people dying, is the world heading for nuclear holocaust because your product or service isn't available? Negative adjectives are particularly dangerous. I had a client who made a number of negative statements about his largest competitor. That competitor had been in business for many years so it must have been doing something right. Indeed, I had personal experience with the competitor and knew it to be a well-run operation. Knocking the competition does not build your case, so don't do it.

4. Make sure your numbers make sense. Many people who start businesses are product people (engineers, for example) or marketing people. Almost everyone hates numbers. But the bottom line is that it is the bottom line that determines whether the lender gets the money back. So you have to spend time with your numbers and make sure they make sense. Here are a few classic errors:

   a. The numbers do not jibe with other sections of the business plan: In one business plan I reviewed, the marketing section called for local television advertising. The financial plan showed $200 per month for advertising expense. This ought to buy about five seconds at 3 a.m. once or twice a month on the bowling channel.

b. Not anticipating price increases: I reviewed a set of projections where utility bills remained at the same dollar figure for three years. Even if you don't use more power over the years it is unlikely that the rates will stay constant.

c. Presenting only annual projections: Preparing projections month by month for the first year is tedious, hard work but very necessary. Some people finesse this by making an annualized projection and then dividing the figures by 12 to fill in the blanks for each month. That defeats the purpose of monthly projections. Virtually every business has peaks and troughs. The lender wants to know if you can get through the slow months. If not, you're out of business and the loan goes down the tubes.

d. Not including a list of assumptions to explain how you got your numbers: The lender wants to know how you arrived at your figures. This should be provided line by line starting with a detailed discussion of your sales. You can't just pick a number. You must have good, solid reasons.

e. Numbers that don't make sense: I saw a set of projections where the gross profit margin went from 35 percent in the first year to 60 percent in the third with no explanation provided. (Gross margin in percent is defined as [sales-cost of goods sold]/sales multiplied by 100.) It's possible, I suppose, but you'd better tell me how you plan to achieve that.

f. Not telling the lender how the money will be used: It is important to let the lender know how you are going to use the money, dollar by dollar. You can't just say, "inventory, equipment and working capital." You need an itemized list of exactly where the money will go, supported by price quotations, price lists, etc., where possible.

5. Discuss the risk. It's great to have a positive attitude but you've got to be realistic, too. There is no business without risk. None. Risk is everywhere. If you don't discuss risk then lenders are going to assume you haven't thought about risk. That scares them to death. They know you can't possibly plan for every single contingency, but they want to know that you've thought about the major risks and of some way to manage them.

Of course, risk is not always negative. There is the risk of succeeding beyond your expectations. I reviewed a business plan once of someone who was going to manufacture a sophisticated craft item. The product was beautiful and I could see where orders could well be way in excess of projections. Since it took some artistic skill to make the product, I wondered what the owner would do if that happened. Failure to meet orders on a timely basis usually means you don't get repeat orders. In the owner's plan he/she had identified several skilled people who could be hired if the need arose. I was very impressed. The loan was granted. The business has done well.

6. Be prepared to answer questions about your plan. The applicant whose profit margins went from 35 percent to 60 percent in two years said he or she was "not a numbers person," that the accountant had prepared the projections, and so he/she couldn't really explain them. The loan was not approved. If you are going to own a business you have to have some understanding of numbers. How else will you know how you are doing, where the problems are, etc.? When you tell a lender that numbers aren't "your thing" what you are really saying is that you don't want to own a business. You are better off working for someone else. You must be able to answer virtually any question about any aspect of your business plan.

7. Do not be excessively wordy. Whoever is reading your business plan is a busy person. Don't waste his or her time with long, florid passages when a few well written sentences will do. I've read business plans that went on for 40, 50, 60 pages or more that could easily have been reduced to just 10 or 15 if only the writer had eliminated all excess language. Don't repeat yourself ad nauseum. People like to go on

about things such as how they are going to beat the competition with better service and a more customer-centered approach, for example. That's a pretty vague statement and repeating it on every page does not improve it. Stick to the facts, state them clearly, and don't repeat them unnecessarily. The point isn't to write a long business plan but a good business plan.

Reviewing the plan

Have your business plan read by as many people as you can. You want them to read for two purposes: mechanics and content. You would be amazed how many plans I see with gross spelling, grammar, and arithmetic errors. I firmly believe that if you don't care enough about your business to do a great business plan, why should I care enough to put money on the line. Don't leave the important proofreading task to yourself alone. We all tend to see what we think we wrote so we miss the errors. Get a couple of people to read your plan for the mechanics, even if they know nothing about business. Tell your kids you'll pay them 50 cents for each error found; it will be money well spent.

You also want at least one person whose business judgment you trust and who you know will give you truly honest feedback to read your plan. The best person for this job is a good outside consultant—someone who has seen a number of different business plans, who has experience lending money, and who won't worry about losing a friend by being truly honest. That will cost you more than a few dollars but will be well worth it in the long run. It is important to find out where your business plan falls short before you hand it to a lender.

And now the good news

Finally, here are a few words of encouragement. There are lenders out there who want to help small businesses. There are banks that will lend to you, though you may have to search around. Generally small, local banks are your best bet, although some larger banks might have funds available under their Community Reinvestment Act programs.

You may be able to get a Small Business Administration (SBA) guarantee to support a loan with a bank. Here the SBA guarantees part of the loan reducing the risk for the bank. In most cases you have to go through the bank; the SBA rarely deals directly with borrowers. Unfortunately, if you are truly a start up business, the odds of getting an SBA guarantee are slim. However, if you have been around for a while, even just a year, you may qualify. If you are interested in this type of loan it is advisable to check with the bank you are dealing with to be sure you have the latest information.

Another SBA option is the 504 Certified Development Company program (CDC) If your company is exporting to foreign countries, there is the SBA Export Revolving Line of Credit Program (ERLC).

Recently, the SBA has streamlined the application process and has been approving/denying applications within a few days; it used to take anywhere from a few weeks to a few months. For the latest information on SBA programs you should contact your nearest SBA office or call the SBA's free bulletin board service at 800-697-4636 using any general communication software for your modem (set your speed at 9600 baud; parity:none; data bits:8; stop bits:1). This bulletin board contains all sorts of information for small businesses including a lot of downloadable software. (You can reach the bulletin board on the Internet at: http://www.sbaonline.sba.gov.)

There are finance companies that specialize in small businesses. You must be sure to check these out carefully since there are bogus operators in the field. If a firm asks for a significant, up front "application fee"—run, don't walk, as fast as you can in the opposite direction. Before dealing with any of these ask your bank or SBA office for references.

Interest rates charged by legitimate finance companies are usually higher than those charged by banks. But remember, your problem is access to credit—loans at prime don't do you any good if you don't qualify for them.

Many state, county, and local governments have funds to assist small businesses located within their regions. A few telephone calls may lead you to one of these sources. Look in the government section of your telephone book for offices of economic development. It may take more than one or two calls to locate these but persistency may well pay off.

Finally, there are a lot of nonprofit organizations with micro-loan funds. These are usually loans of less than $250,000 and can be as small as several hundred dollars, to buy sewing machines for a small alteration business, for example. The SBA sponsors some of these, so a call to your nearest SBA office will lead you to the ones in which they are involved. Another way to find some is through the Association for Enterprise Opportunities in Chicago (312-357- 0177).

As you can see, the picture is far from bleak. If you do your homework carefully you should be able to find some money.

Chapter 12

The Importance of Control: Who Needs It?

Many entrepreneurs, when trying to finance a new business, seem to be obsessed with the subject of control. The 51 percent number is magic. Admittedly, it is desirable to own as much of the company as possible; however, control is not nearly as important as most people believe.

This issue often determines whether the entrepreneur will be willing to have outside investors, thereby giving up some of the ownership of the business. The alternative is usually to try to raise all of the outside financing it might need through borrowing, thereby usually giving up no ownership. My advice to entrepreneurs planning the financing is not to let the issue of control have too great an influence on their decision.

The more important issues are the questions of risk and potential. How much personal risk are they willing to take and how will the inability to raise sufficient capital limit their growth are the key issues?

Digital Equipment Corp. (DEC) is a classic example. When Ken Olsen raised his first $70,000 of venture capital, he gave up about 77 percent of the company, keeping only 13 percent for himself and distributing the rest to other founders.

Today, Olsen owns less than 2 percent of DEC stock, but it is worth millions of dollars. Even though DEC has had its ups and downs through the years, its introduction of the mini-computer revolutionized the computer business at the time.

My advice in negotiating with a venture investor or an underwriter selling stock to the public is to give up as little of your company as possible in return for the money you are trying to raise. But don't panic if your share of the ownership drops below 50 percent.

The bottom line here is that if you are doing a good job running the company, if your sales are increasing and you are realizing a good profit and if you consistently meet the goals of your business plan, you have nothing to worry about regardless of whether or not you control a majority of the stock. On the other hand, if none of the above is happening and the company is floundering, you have plenty to worry about, even if you own all of the stock. My point is that even the founder must earn the position of head of the firm. And you only earn it with good performance.

Assume, for example, you have to give up 70 percent of the stock to outside investors in order to raise the capital you require to start the firm. So what? When venture investors put money into your business they are investing in you and the team you put together. A major factor in the investment decision is their evaluation of your ability to build and manage a business. As I mentioned earlier, many venture investors, when asked what the three most important factors were in their decision to invest in a start up, answer, "Management, management, and management." The last thing in the world they want is to run your business. If they thought that was likely to happen they would not invest. A bank considering making a loan to a new company will in all likelihood give you the same answer.

Suppose the company is not doing too well. You should be the first to suggest that someone else might be better than you at running the business. Perhaps you should play a different role, director of engineering or sales manager for example, rather than president. Let someone else run the show.

The management skills needed to run a successful business are different for a start up than for a $10 million company, and they are different for a $10 million company than for a $100 million company. Some entrepreneurs can make this transition—many cannot. More important in the long run for you, your employees and your investors is that the company survive and thrive rather than your remaining in control.

Do the best that you can when structuring a financial deal, be it a loan or an equity issue. Try to keep as much of the control of the business as possible. But don't forget: It's more important that you have the opportunity to start the company than that you own 51 percent of the stock and remain the boss forever.

Several months ago a man came to visit me to get my reaction to an idea he had for a business. It involved developing and marketing a relatively complex technical product. I do not remember exactly what the product was but I do recall that it was a complex device and seemed like a good idea. When I asked him how much money he thought he needed he said, "About $2 million." Then I asked him what percentage of the company he was prepared to give to an investor for that amount of money. He said, "Forty-nine percent."

I then asked if he realized that attempting to sell 49 percent of the business for $2 million implied that the company was worth $4 million. I explained to him that he had not developed the product on which the business would be based, he was not certain that the product would produce all of the good things he forecasted and that he had never built even a preliminary model. Obviously he had no orders and made no shipments. In my opinion the company was surely not worth $4 million and was probably not worth anywhere near $2 million.

He next asked what I suggest he do. I said he had to decide what was most important to him. Was it to have the opportunity to prove whether or not his idea could be the basis for a successful business even though he might not have majority ownership? Or was his goal to own a majority interest in a company that might never get started? He left shaking his head in disbelief. I lost contact with him and do not know whether he was ever able to raise the capital he wanted, but my guess is that if he stood his ground on the 49 percent issue he would be trying to raise capital forever.

In addition, there is another more practical consideration that you should keep in mind especially when issuing equity as your source of capital. If you have any significant number of shareholders, say 10 or more, the likelihood of their joining forces against you is low unless you really screw up in your job. If your stock is publicly owned, the chances

of a stockholder revolution are almost nil. We all know about publicly owned, multimillion dollar corporations in which the management holds only a tiny fraction of outstanding shares. Since they usually load their board of directors with friends and/or employees, they must be guilty of gross mismanagement for their job to be in jeopardy.

This situation has been somewhat challenged lately at IBM, Eastman Kodak, Apple Computer and several other companies where the board of directors replaced the CEO with an outsider, but it is still generally true.

As I described in detail in another chapter, at RF Communications the four founders first formed a legal partnership in which we were all equal. Then we incorporated and divided the stock in proportion to our expected role in the company. My reward for being founder and president was to have a little more stock than the other three, or about 33 percent. Then we sold stock to the public to raise our initial capital and my percentage dropped to about 20 percent. Over the next eight years we raised equity capital on four other occasions, each time further diluting my share of the ownership. We also used both short term and long term bank borrowing to help us out between stock issues.

When we finally merged, I only owned a little more than 10 percent of the stock. But this was 10 percent of a very big pie. Had I insisted on maintaining a controlling interest in RF Communications we could not possibly have achieved the results that we did. My personal rewards would surely have been much, much less. I can honestly say that I never worried about having control.

In the long run, if the company succeeds, there will be more than enough to go around and your rewards will be great. If the company fails it does not matter how big a part of it you own. Set your ownership goals high, but don't be greedy.

Chapter 13

What Investors Look For

To many entrepreneurs starting a company, the idea of raising capital from outside investors is very appealing. However, it is important that the entrepreneur fully understand the serious implications of such a move.

The benefits are fairly obvious. By using other people's money instead of your own, the financial risks are reduced considerably, often to zero. And, by having more capital available than you can invest yourself, borrow or generate from earnings, you can adopt a more aggressive strategy, and hopefully, grow faster.

Two disadvantages of having outside investors are the issues of dilution of ownership and control, which most entrepreneurs are far too concerned about. These questions were discussed earlier.

Another more important disadvantage, though, is that by having outside investors you, as the head of the company, assume a very substantial obligation to do all you can to provide these investors with a return on their investment consistent with the risk, and to provide them with liquidity, that is, a way to sell their stock for cash.

Think of your relationship with an investor as being similar to the relationship between a borrower and a bank. An equity investment from a shareholder is a liability, and liabilities must be paid back. The main difference between outside investors and a bank is that investors have different expectations and are usually more patient. Venture investors typically expect a minimum of a five to 10 times return on their investment over a period of about five years. You should not even think about selling stock to outsiders unless your venture has reasonable potential for this kind of appreciation.

In addition, you have a very strong obligation to find some way for your investors to achieve liquidity, to convert their stock into cash, within a reasonable length of time. As a practical matter, the two most common ways to accomplish this are for the company to either go public or merge with another firm.

Telling your investors that they will achieve liquidity from the dividends your company will pay, or that you will buy the stock back according to a formula, is a good way to make it very difficult to raise capital. Venture investors do not make high risk investments for the purpose of getting dividends. If that were their intention they would buy stock in a public utility. They probably will not believe you or will find the formula unacceptable when you suggest the company is prepared to buy back its stock at some future date.

What I suggest is that when an entrepreneur accepts money from an outside investor, he or she assumes a very strong obligation to provide a return to that investor consistent with the risk, and a very strong obligation to provide eventual liquidity. It probably requires that the company either go public or merge. If you cannot accept this, do not take on outside investors.

Chapter 14

Individual Venture Investors

I am an individual venture investor, having been heavily involved in a number of start up businesses. As you might expect, I am more familiar with this source of venture capital than with the other sources. My experience with other types of institutional venture capital funds is limited, but I have augmented my personal experience with the comments of two friends who manage a very large and a medium-sized formal (institutional) venture fund, respectively. I have personal experience with one corporate venture investor, have been closely associated as a consultant to a large company's internal venture activity and again have augmented my own knowledge with comments from others who have been involved with this type of investing.

There are several other sources of venture capital that I have not mentioned, such as R&D Limited Partnerships and Small Business Investment Companies (SBIC). The R&D Limited Partnership seems to be out of favor because of changes in the tax laws. The SBIC, for all practical purposes, is quite similar to an institutional venture fund except that its source of money is usually from loans guaranteed by the Small Business Administration rather than institutional and private investors.

With this as background, let's look at the pros and cons of individual investors and informal venture groups as sources of start up capital. This includes individuals or small informal groups who invest their personal money in new ventures. They are often entrepreneurs who have started their own companies and have money they are willing to put at risk. Individual venture investors are either willing to or insist on being closely involved with the business as directors, informal advisors, or mentors. This type of investor is often called an "angel." I read an article recently about venture investing and it said that "angels" currently invest about $10 billion a year in more than 30,000 companies nationwide.

The major advantage of dealing with individuals or small groups of venture investors is that if the entrepreneur can catch their interest, deals can be consummated fairly rapidly and the deals are likely to be simple and straight forward. Also, this type of investor may be more willing than other sources of venture capital to finance an early start up.

In general, individual investors have goals similar to the entrepreneur, i.e., to make a lot of money through high risk, long term investments. However, many, having been entrepreneurs themselves, have an understanding of the problems of starting a business, and their involvement can be valuable.

Finally, even though individual investors and informal groups are likely to be fairly sophisticated, they often make their investment decisions intuitively, without too much lengthy and involved due diligence investigation. The deals they cut will be less onerous than the deals you are apt to get from an institutional venture capital fund or corporate investor.

On the negative side, even though the total amount of money invested each year by individuals is very high, the amount they will invest in each particular deal may be limited. In addition, once having made an initial investment, individuals or informal groups often have little interest in providing a second or third round of financing. And the contacts these investors have with the investment banking and brokerage communities may be somewhat limited.

Individual venture investors may be hard to find. There are few formal channels available to establish contact, and the entrepreneur may have difficulty in locating people with the kind of money required.

One possible way of meeting possible individual venture investors is through what is known as venture capital groups or venture capital clubs. I organized such a group in Rochester about 12 years ago called the Rochester Venture Capital Group. Initially it had about a dozen members who met for breakfast every month or so. At each meeting one or two entrepreneurs presented a description of their business with the intention of raising some equity capital. Quite often they were successful.

Soon the group grew to about 50 members or so but many of the new members were service providers rather than successful entrepreneurs. This included a number of bankers, lawyers and CPAs. These groups justify becoming members on the basis that some of their clients are potential investors and are too busy to attend regular meetings. This may be true in some cases, but I think their main reason for joining the group was either to find an occasional new client or simply to keep abreast of new business activities in the upstate New York area.

The program has varied over time. Initially we had three speakers at each meeting, each of whom had 10 or 15 minutes to describe their business idea and then follow-up with interested potential investors privately after the meeting. Presently the group has only one speaker at each meeting with more time to present a case. The speaker also gets some detailed reaction from the group on the strengths and weaknesses of the proposal.

If you are trying to raise capital from these types of people you should check out whether such a group exists in your area. Your local chamber of commerce, SBA office or Small Business Development Center should be able to help you. There are many of them across the country and as a minimum it will give you a chance to network among people with investment interest. Even if you are unable to raise the capital you want it will be a good source of contacts.

Until recently, private placement offerings (the sale of stock to individuals or small informal groups) could only be made to a limited number of potential investors and the company had to establish investor criteria—the minimum each investor must contribute and what income or net worth an individual must have to qualify. In effect, the Securities and Exchange Commission (SEC) permitted the sale of this type of high risk security only to investors who were capable of fully understanding the risk, having their money tied up for an extended period and who had sufficient personal resources to afford a loss in the event the company went under. Stock sold in private placements was also restricted in that it could only be resold under very limited circumstances.

In 1992, the SEC amended its Rule 504, which controls this type of stock sale, substantially reducing or eliminating many of the restrictions previously in place. The purpose of the amendment was to make it easier for small companies to raise capital using this route. Among other things it permits a company to promote the offering more broadly, to sell stock to a greater number of buyers, made it easier for the buyers to sell the stock they purchased, and eliminated the need for the Private Placement Memorandum (a detailed description of the offering and the risks involved). It does not, however, reduce the companies' obligations under the anti-fraud rules of the federal securities laws to be completely open and honest in their dealing with the investors.

My suggestion is that your first step in trying to raise capital from individual venture investors should be to prepare a document, similar to a Private Placement Memorandum, describing the business in detail even though it may no longer be a legal requirement. These only need to be 20 or 30 pages in length but they should clearly describe both the risk and opportunity of the investment. The information must be absolutely true and complete, and should accurately describe both the positive and negative aspects of the business. Much of the information can be drawn from the business plan. An important part of this document is a description of the number of shares you want to sell, the price, and what you intend to do with the money. It would also be a good idea to include a list of present shareholders and what they invested in order to get the stock that they own.

Even with the changes in Rule 504, I strongly recommend that under no circumstances should you conduct a private placement without the advice of a knowledgeable lawyer completely familiar with security regulations. These can be complex transactions subject to both federal and state regulations.

You may conclude from what I have said that the private placement is just too complex to bother with. That is not the case. As mentioned in Chapter 7, in the Rochester area, between January 1980 and March 1988, 42 companies raised approximately $32 million from individual investors. I know many people who are interested in making this kind of investment. They understand and are comfortable with the risks. Their hope is that they may find a situation where their investment may appreciate 30 or 40 times.

Raising money through a private placement usually requires a large amount of time from the senior people in the firm. Many potential investors are likely to visit the company personally to meet the principals, see the facilities and ask questions about the business. If you happen to include among your personal acquaintances a half dozen or so millionaires, this will be of immeasurable help. Failing this, I suggest you try to find one or two highly visible, successful entrepreneurs who, if persuaded to come in on the deal, may attract others.

An example of a Rochester company that successfully used individual investors for its initial financing is Ormec

Systems Corp., a manufacturer of high-tech precision motion control systems used in automated manufacturing. Its customers include Eastman Kodak, for its film manufacturing operation; Johnson & Johnson, for the manufacture of pharmaceuticals; the Harrison Division of General Motors, for the manufacture of automobile radiators; and many others.

I met two of the four founders of Ormec in an entrepreneurship class I spoke to. At the time, the two key people were engineers working for Eastman Kodak. After getting to know them and their business I decided to invest personally and brought together a group of four other successful entrepreneurs. Together we provided $300,000 of start up money in return for a 40 percent interest in the company. The two key founders quit their jobs and the company was off and running. Four of the outside investors became board members.

Ormec has since raised about $1 million of additional capital in two subsequent private placements and now has about 130 shareholders. Recently they made major investments in building a large national network of distributors and representatives and in developing a new, very advanced product line. This investment in building the business paid off at the time. Sales went over $10 million and they were well in the black.

In 1994, Ormec spent about $1.3 million in a stock buy-back at a price of $12 a share proportioned to investors, according to the number of shares each offered back to the company. Some shareholders offered all of the stock they owned, others offered none, and many offered some but not all. In every case that I know of the sellers realized a gain. It varied from about 20 to 1 for the very early investors to about 2½ to 1 for later investors.

In the last two years, Ormec's performance fell off somewhat and in fiscal 1996 it experienced a loss. This was caused by a number of factors including a major investment in another new product. They are now well into the black again, and hopefully will soon reach the point where either a public offering or merger with a larger company will be considered.

For Ormec, money from individual investors made it possible for the founders to leave their jobs at a large company for which both worked, get the business underway and establish the company as an important supplier in its industry. As many entrepreneurs have learned, individual venture investors can be a good source of capital for a new business.

Chapter 15

Formal (Institutional) Venture Capital Funds

The venture capital industry has been one of the major growth industries of the 1980s and early 1990s. At the end of 1996, about $28 billion of equity capital was managed by venture capital funds.

Venture funds are usually limited partnerships where the bulk of the money is supplied by passive limited partner investors, such as insurance companies, college endowment funds or corporate retirement funds. The investment portfolio is then managed by a general partner or group of general partners. They seek out and evaluate investment opportunities, negotiate deals, manage the follow-up activity and participate in various ways in the companies in their portfolio, often as members of their board of directors.

The formal venture capital industry has structure, and there are a number of directories available that list the various funds, amounts of capital available,

industry focus, and addresses and telephone numbers of the managing general partners.

One such source of information is *Galante's Complete Venture Capital & Private Equity Directory*, which contains an extensive list of venture funds and their areas of interest, and is available from Asset Alternatives, 180 Linden St., Suite 3, Wellesley, MA 02181 (617-431-7353). Its cost is $395 on either disk or hard copy or $495 for both. The disk version of this directory is compatible with many popular personal computer programs which make rapid searches possible based upon about a dozen different criteria.

Another source is *Pratt's Guide to Venture Capital Sources*, from Venture Economics, a Division of Securities Data Publishers, 40 W. 57 St., #1100, New York, NY 10102-0968 (800-455-5844 or 212-765-5311). The price of the 1997 edition is $325. It includes an introductory section about the venture capital industry and lists just about every venture capital fund in the United States and Canada and its area of specialization.

Even though these directories are fairly expensive, they both contain much cross referenced information that can save you hours and hours of effort trying to find a venture fund that may be interested in your type of situation.

A *Directory of Small Business Investment Companies* can be obtained from the Associate Administrator for Investment at the U.S. Small Business Administration, Washington, DC 20419 (202-205-6510, fax 202-205-6959).

Another way for a company to reach venture investors is by attending Venture Capital Forums that are held on a regular basis in many sections of the country. They are intended to give entrepreneurs the opportunity to present their deals to groups of venture fund managers. Contact your chamber of commerce to learn if there are any of these forums held in your area.

One of the more important advantages of dealing with an institutional venture capital fund is that it has access to large amounts of money. For example, I have read that in 1995 venture funds raised about $4.4 billion of new money, an all time record. Except for the small funds, their minimum investment is frequently in the $500,000 to $1 million range and they can often put together deals requiring $5 million or more. In addition, it is quite typical for this kind of venture investor to make

second and third infusions of capital as the company grows.

Another important benefit that venture funds offer is an excellent window on the investment banking industry. At such time that the company goes public, the managers of the fund can be a valuable source of help. In general, the goals of this type of venture investor are similar to the goals of the new enterprise, that is, to grow the business and make a lot of money. However, the venture fund may be more impatient to cash out on a deal, which could force the company into a merger or public offering sooner than it wants.

Finally, the general partners are usually diligent in their participation on the board of directors of the companies in their portfolio. Because they are frequently involved with other similar companies, they can be an important source of experience and expertise.

However, in spite of the above list of advantages, I urge new companies seeking capital from venture funds to proceed with caution. Entrepreneurs recognize the risks associated with starting a business. They may not be familiar with the risks of dealing with venture investors.

Among the disadvantages of trying to raise capital from a venture fund is that the process can be very slow. Venture funds are typically deluged by proposals and business plans from companies seeking money, and most funds operate with a limited staff of people who are all extremely busy. Their response time can be slow. Some people familiar with the venture industry suggest that a business plan submitted without a personal introduction has almost no chance of receiving attention.

Because they have a fiduciary responsibility to their limited partners, venture funds go through an extensive due diligence process. Commonly, they retain consultants, expert in the specific industry, to investigate the products, markets and competition of the new venture. This process can take weeks and months to complete and can be very demanding on the time of the entrepreneur.

Another disadvantage is that venture capital funds impose some very tough conditions that many entrepreneurs consider entirely unacceptable. For instance, it is not unusual for them to demand some form of convertible preferred stock, one purpose of which is to give them preference over other shareholders in the event of liquidation. Also, they frequently require anti-dilution protection if stock is ever sold at a lower price, strong representation on the board of directors, control over salary levels of managers, and the latitude to take over the company if certain financial criteria are not met. These conditions are outlined in what is known as a Term Sheet.

The advice I give to people beginning negotiations with a venture fund is to ask for a copy of the fund's standard term sheet at the start rather than at the end, as this may avoid unexpected surprises and a lot of wasted time. You will likely be told they do not have such a thing because terms vary so much

with the deal. Then ask for a copy of the term sheets of several recent deals, or the term sheet of an investment they made in a company similar to yours. Sample term sheets of large and medium sized venture funds are shown in an appendix in the back of this book. These samples are intended to give you an idea of where the venture fund will begin negotiations. Where the negotiations end depends on the exact situation in the company seeking funds.

Most onerous, though, in dealing with venture funds is the valuation they set on the company, which determines the price they are willing to pay for the stock. My experience with venture funds is that they drive tough financial deals.

It is extremely desirable for entrepreneurs to negotiate with a venture fund at a time when they do not need the money too badly, and to have at least several sources of venture capital competing for the deal. It is not unknown for an unethical venture fund to deliberately protract negotiations so long that the company is desperate for money, then nail them to the cross in setting a price. The expression "vulture capitalist" has some basis. This term suggests that you should try to check out the references of a fund before you get into serious discussion.

Entrepreneurs should be very careful in approaching venture funds to avoid the appearance that they have unsuccessfully approached a large number of other potential investors. Communication between funds is fairly efficient and the fact that you have shopped the deal and been turned down by a number may make your situation untouchable to others.

From my contact with venture funds I have concluded that when you get past the public relations hype, many of them are really not very venturesome. Part of this results from the fact that they must report regularly to the limited partner investors, who, in turn, are managed by financial types whose performance is continually under review. Either consciously or unconsciously they want investments that will make them look good in the short term. An entrepreneur trying to raise money from a venture fund to finance a raw start up faces a very hard road.

Entrepreneurs dealing with venture funds had better not be thin skinned. A few years ago a friend of mine was invited by the manager of a large, well known fund to come from Rochester to Boston to meet with the partners at 3 p.m. the following afternoon. After being kept waiting for two hours, he was told he had 15 minutes to present his story.

If you do approach a venture fund, remember that the managers control large amounts of money and the world seems to beat a path to their doors. Financial power, like political power, can distort one's sense of values. Also, the general partners of venture funds are almost always incredibly busy. Typically, they travel three, four and five days a week. They are overwhelmed with potential deals, some of their past deals may be in serious trouble and they are deluged by telephone calls from impatient entrepreneurs. This frenetic existence can cause impatience and unintended slights.

In approaching an institutional venture capital fund, the entrepreneur should remember that the main goal of the fund is to make a profit for themselves and their sources of money. This is probably your main goal, but if other goals are of equal or greater importance, such as providing a place for your children to work or providing some benefits to society in general, the chances of getting an investment from an institutional investor goes down dramatically.

Another thing to keep in mind is the various stages a company may go through during its corporate existence and that some of these stages are of much more interest to a venture fund than others. The stages are:

1. Start up. This is the formative period of the existence of a new business. Some specialized venture funds will invest in the start up stage of a company's existence, but most will not.

2. Development stage. Here a company has probably raised some capital from private sources, completed the development of its main product, perhaps secured a patent, built some units and possibly even sold some. This stage is of more interest to a venture fund, and if the heads of the company have a successful record starting other businesses, the chances of getting an investment may be pretty good.

3. Growth stage. In this stage the company is up and running and perhaps even operating in the black. It has gone through the initial period of getting some market acceptance and needs additional funds to achieve growth. This is a situation that many venture funds are looking for. It is not overly risky and the opportunity of participating in the fastest growth phase of the company can still be quite high.

4. Running well. Here the company is doing quite well and needs additional funds for such things as a new factory, an acquisition, etc. Venture funds may be interested in investing at this stage even though they may have missed the period of rapid growth and their chances of in-vesting at a very low price are not too good.

5. Other stages. This would include helping an entrepreneur buy an existing unit of another company that it is trying to sell off, take over a turn around situation where the company has been doing very poorly but a new management thinks it knows how to get the ball rolling again, etc. Here the likelihood of getting an investment from a venture fund varies considerably depending on the exact situation. Some funds may be interested in these, others may not. Again, a very important factor is the background of the people who will be running the business after an investment is made.

Another thing an entrepreneur should remember is that a crucial part of the decision process in getting the interest of a venture fund is the business plan of the company. Chapter 20 of this book is devoted to the business plan but its

importance cannot be over emphasized. The plan tells the potential investor a number of things, including details of the business and the market the new company plans to address, the background of the management, financial projections and possible exit strategies, but mostly it tells them the general business sense of the people trying to raise money.

The plan should describe the new business in a way so that the opportunities are clearly presented but should not be so optimistic that the intuitive judgment of the management is brought into question. This is a hard balance to achieve. Personally I do not like business plans that use the words, "Our conservative projections are ...."

So my advice to entrepreneurs seeking investment from venture capital funds is to be very cautious. Talk to other entrepreneurs who have been down the same road, and most importantly, try to do all of your money raising when you do not need the money too badly and while you still have options.

To give you the other side of the story about working with institutional venture capital funds, I asked a friend of mine who manages a large institutional fund to write the next chapter of this book about how to improve the odds of attracting this type of investment. I urge you to read that chapter because it balances out some of my views which may be biased toward the entrepreneur.

Finally, the subject of venture capital funds is covered here in only a few chapters. This is a subject that could be and is the subject of entire books. Go to your local book store chain which will surely have at least a few on its shelves devoted entirely to the subject. I own one named *Venture Capital Handbook, An Entrepreneur's Guide To Obtaining Capital To Start A Business, Buy A Business Or Expand An Existing Business,* written by David Gladstone and published by Prentice Hall. The copy I have came out in 1988 but later editions may be available. Gladstone takes you through the entire process of working with a venture capital fund from start to finish in far more detail than I have and his is a very good book.

Chapter 16

How to Get a Venture Investment

This chapter was written by Paul S. Brentlinger, general partner in Morgenthaler Ventures, a venture capital firm based in Cleveland, Ohio. The Morgenthaler firm manages approximately 300 million in venture capital assets representing a wide variety of industries and types of investment. Earlier, Paul was senior vice president of Finance and vice president of Corporate Development at Harris Corporation. Paul has an MBA from the University of Michigan and is a member of Phi Beta Kappa. He is a director of a number of companies in which Morgenthaler invested and the chairman of the board of trustees of the Cleveland Institute of Art.

There is a lot money out there

If you believe the company you started can grow to a large size, and if you are willing to work in partnership with investors who own a significant share of your company's equity, you probably owe it to yourself to consider seeking capital from an institutional venture investor. Institutional venture capital comes from 600 or so professionally managed venture capital firms in the United States plus a small amount from abroad. They manage venture type equity investments on behalf of pension funds, foundations, university endowment funds and other institutional sources of money.

At the end of 1996, institutional venture capital firms in the United States were managing about $28 billion of equity capital. During 1996, these firms invested $10 billion in 1,500 different companies. More than 80 percent of this investment went into two industries—information technology and life sciences.

By comparison, it has been estimated that some 250,000 individual "angel" investors invest $10 billion to $12 billion annually in some 30,000 companies. These "angels" are usually relatives, friends or neighbors of the entrepreneur. "Angels" have investment approaches and objectives that are different from those of institutional venture capital firms. This chapter focuses entirely on the investment process used by institutional venture capital firms, not individual investors.

Analyze your goals

The primary objective of some entrepreneurs is to build a comfortable, medium-sized company that is always subject to their personal control, that is designed to finance the family's yacht or Florida condominium, and which will provide jobs for children and relatives. These are legitimate objectives, but they are incompatible with the objectives of institutional venture capital firms.

To obtain money from institutional venture capitalists, it is important that you understand their goals. Pension funds, endowment funds, foundations and others that entrust the investment of their money to venture capitalists expect a rate of return significantly higher than the return on investment attainable from buying publicly traded common stocks.

To illustrate, if the Standard & Poor's stock average has produced an annual rate of return of 10 to 12 percent over the past five to 10 years, venture capital should produce a return in the 15- to 18-percent range.

Because some venture capital investments are total failures, and a number of others will produce minimal returns (these are called the living dead),

the venture capitalist must see an opportunity for a very high rate of return, in the 30- to 40-percent range on any individual investment opportunity.

With this in mind, the venture capitalists are strictly equity oriented investors. A share of the ownership of a company is what creates an opportunity for substantial capital gains. Venture capitalists do not lend money at six points over prime rate.

Entrepreneurs seeking institutional venture capital funding must therefore be willing to share equity ownership and give up a significant degree of control of their enterprise.

Are you a candidate for a venture investment?

In general, venture capitalists prefer to invest in companies that are candidates for selling stock to the public within five years or so. In today's world that probably means the company should have the potential to generate annual sales revenue in the $50 million range within that time frame. It is also essential that the company's products or services address markets which investors believe to be large and rapidly growing—the kinds of markets which attract attention from professional securities analysts.

To work toward public ownership requires a totally professional approach to management. This probably means a willingness on the part of the entrepreneur to work with a board of directors comprised of a majority of outsiders, including venture capitalists. Also, the company must have the ability to generate financial statements prepared in accordance with generally accepted accounting practices and audited by Big Six accounting firms, and the ability to develop an effective multilayer management team. This list is illustrative—it is by no means all inclusive.

How to approach a venture capital firm

With all this in mind and if you believe your objectives are consistent with those of institutional venture capitalists, how is the best way to approach a venture capital firm?

It is highly desirable to arrange an introduction through a mutual acquaintance. Lawyers, accountants, consultants, private investors or friends who have a personal relationship with the venture capital firm represent ideal points of entry. Rightly or wrongly, institutional venture capitalists rarely invest in companies that make a cold "over-the-transom" approach.

The business plan is crucial

Once the introduction has been made, the submission of a well-thought-out business plan is a key part of the process. Chapter 20 illustrates this point.

In reviewing a business plan the venture capitalist probably will concentrate on the following issues:

The business concept. What market is being addressed? Is a large and growing economic need being addressed?

Product or service. Does the product or service offer a genuine competitive advantage? Why will people buy this rather than buying alternative products or services? Will customers pay a premium price? Is there patent protection? Are there barriers to entry? Are there powerful competitors? Can the company be the low-cost producer?

Management team. Are members of management experienced in the market being addressed? Do they have a track record of success? Have the managers previously been winners? Is the management team totally committed to the success of the enterprise? Is the team motivated and hungry? Is the team capable of growth as managers as the company grows?

Financial aspects. How much capital is needed? Is the business capital intensive? Will additional rounds of private venture capital investment be required before the company is cash-flow positive? Are the financial projections realistic?

Valuation. Will the venture capital investment buy enough shares in the company to produce the opportunity for at least the 30 to 40 percent return on investment described earlier? What is the probable exit strategy? Is the company a candidate for a public offering, and if so, when and at what multiple of earnings? Is the company a candidate for acquisition at a high price by a larger company?

Why does the process take so long?

In a somewhat different vein, most venture capitalists like to co-invest in early stage companies with other strong venture capital firms. By doing so they share the work load and financial burden. You must ask if your company is one that is likely to attract an investment from other well-financed venture capital firms capable of offering constructive collaboration. The individual venture capitalist will think about whether he or she would like to put his or her reputation on the line by introducing the deal to a friend in another venture capital firm.

Once an investment opportunity gets beyond the initial screening step, a series of meetings will take place between the venture capitalist and the company's management team. These meetings represent a critically important step. Venture capital investing involves a long-term partnership relationship with the management team. Before an investment is made, there must be sufficient personal interaction to ensure a mutual belief that the venture capitalist and the management have the same objectives. It is important that the people concerned will be comfortable working together over a period of several years to accomplish their mutual objectives.

If there appears to be a strong mutual interest regarding the investment, the venture capitalist can be expected to do a lot of reference checking regarding the management team. In many cases, the venture capitalist will also use outside consultants to advise on the technology and the market prospects. As an entrepreneur seeking venture capital funding, you have to be willing to share detailed information about your products and technology, and about yourself and your colleagues, as part of this due diligence process.

You are, of course, entitled to receive assurances from the venture capitalist that proprietary information will be held in confidence.

Upon completion of the due diligence, the venture capitalist must make a go/no go decision. Most venture capital firms require that one of its partners recommend any specific investment—a partner must act as a sponsor or champion. Your personal relationship with the venture capital partner looking at your company is of vital importance—the partner is unlikely to champion an investment in your company unless he or she believes an effective relationship can be developed.

Reviewing the steps

To summarize, in order to attract an investment from an institutional venture capital firm, the following conditions must exist:

1. Your personal objectives must be consistent with those of the venture capital firm.

2. You must be willing to share equity ownership and a degree of control with the venture capitalist.

3. You must submit a business plan that presents a compelling case for your business concept, products, management team and probable financial results.

4. You must be prepared to have a lot of personal interaction with the venture capitalist in the course of an intense due diligence process. This will often require the sharing of your trade secrets.

5. You must be prepared to value your company at a level that satisfies the risk/reward criteria applied by the venture capitalist.

You get a lot of help beyond money

If your company receives funding from a group of strong venture investors, the ultimate benefits can be very rewarding. Good venture capitalists do not stop work after the investment is made—they contribute more than money.

They can be helpful in such areas as arranging customer contacts, in executive recruiting, in shaping financial strategy and in attracting strong underwriter support when the time comes for an initial public offering.

While the venture capital process may appear to be long and arduous, enormous wealth has been created for entrepreneurs who have successfully traveled the path. Examples include companies such as Genentech, Sun Microsystems, VeriFone, Cisco Systems and Cardio Thoracic Systems.

Your challenge will be to add your company to this list of venture capital backed winners—you may have a chance for personal immortality by being able to put your name on the newest building of your favorite university, or the latest addition to the Metropolitan Museum of Art. There is not much to lose if you try.

Chapter 17

Corporate Venture Funds

A third source of venture capital is the corporate venture investor. In recent years a number of large corporations have established venture funds, sometimes formal and sometimes informal, for the purpose of investing in new ventures. In most of the cases that I know of, these investments are made in situations that are generally related to the main business of the investing organization, even though this is not always the case. In some, the goal is to diversify the business, not expand it in areas in which they are already active.

Among the advantages of raising capital from corporate investors is the potential source of both technical and management expertise as well as money. They often have access to fairly large amounts of capital, they can be quite venturesome and, because they have goals other than pure financial gain, they may not drive as hard a deal as a venture fund.

The major drawback of using corporate investors as sources of venture capital is that they often want some way to eventually gain control of the company in which they invested. This will sometimes be in the form of a buy out provision with price based on a predetermined formula. Obviously, this constraint can put a serious limit on upward potential for the entrepreneur.

In thinking about obtaining financing from a large company, the entrepreneur should keep in mind that large firms use at least two primary approaches to venturing. The first and most common is called intrapreneurship. This is the process that many large firms use to encourage people already employed by the firm to identify and bring into existence new businesses or new products that will benefit the company. The companies assist and encourage people with entrepreneurial qualities to evolve new ideas that can be financed and supported by the firm as a way to expand its business.

The second approach is to provide financing, similar to the way used by venture capital funds, to become involved in ventures outside of their present organization. These new ventures will usually not be 100 percent owned by the sponsoring company and may or may not be based upon ideas for products or services that originated within the company. Also, with this approach the entrepreneur may be able to own a reasonably large percentage of the equity in the new venture thereby greatly increasing the potential for financial reward if the venture succeeds.

Intrapreneurship. The purpose of this book is mainly to assist an entrepreneur in starting a business independent of a parent company, not as part of a company for which the entrepreneur is already employed. However, in some cases intrapreneurship may be a good way for an entrepreneur to proceed and the following describes two programs I am familiar with that give you an idea about how these programs work. A few of the large U.S. companies very heavily involved in intrapreneurial activities are 3M, Hewlett Packard, DuPont and Motorola. There are many, many others.

One of the most successful intrapreneurial programs that I am familiar with is the PostIt™ program at 3M. It is an incredibly successful and profitable new product area that evolved entirely from within the company. It led 3M into a new business area that a few years ago did not exist.

Another case of intrapreneurship that I am familiar with that was not as successful as 3M's is a very large company that had an internal department whose function it was to locate potential entrepreneurs, mostly from within the company. They were seeking ideas unrelated to the company's current product offering. This was intended to give the company the opportunity of diversifying into other types of businesses.

Here when the internal venture coordinating group either located or was approached by someone with what appeared to be a good idea, they would assist them in doing market research and in the preparation of a business plan. This would then be presented to an internal review board, consisting of a group of senior executives of the sponsoring company, whose function it was to decide whether or not to fund the new activity. Even though these ventures were fully owned by the sponsoring company, they were physically located in an outside facility away from the company's other plants.

They undertook about 16 of these new ventures in a period of about two years and provided them with considerable capital. Several years later, the company decided that this system was not working well and they terminated the program. They either sold off the new businesses, re-absorbed them into some department of the parent company or simply abandoned them. They spent millions of dollars trying to get into these new, unrelated businesses with this approach and it turned out to be almost completely unsuccessful.

For potential entrepreneurs within the company, though, it gave them a chance to start a business with considerably less risk than going out on their own. However, it also had considerably less potential. As best I know, only one of the ventures had a modest financial reward for the founders over and above their salaries and none of the people involved came anywhere near becoming rich in the process. Many of the people in these new ventures ended up working for the parent company again so they were really not at risk.

External ventures. The following describes several situations I am familiar with where the sponsoring company takes a substantial equity position, but not necessarily control, of a start up business.

One interesting example of a new business whose initial financing was from a major corporate investor is Microlytics, which was founded by a former employee of Xerox Corp. My familiarity with this situation is a result of knowing the entrepreneur who was seeking the investment and providing some counseling to him during negotiations. I also own a small number of shares of stock in Microlytics that the founder gave me in appreciation for my help.

This one seemed to have turned out badly for everyone involved since Microlytics recently filed for bankruptcy. However, from the entrepreneur's viewpoint, even though the company was not a success, it gave him a chance and the financing necessary to start a new business. If it had been a success he would have fared very well financially. It did not succeed, and I assume, he did not come out so well. I will tell you a little about the background of Microlytics because it is a very interesting situation.

The founder had a long background of running a number of his own businesses and seemed to have many important entrepreneurial qualities. When Microlytics came into existence its intention was to enter the personal computer software business. Its initial product was a program named *Wordfinder*, a spelling checker and thesaurus. This was at the time before every word processing program included these as built in features. One of Microlytics's goals was to license its spelling checker and thesaurus software to companies offering word processing programs.

Initial financing was a $400,000 investment from the venture capital arm of Xerox. In making this investment, Xerox required that Microlytics raise a matching amount from private investors, which the company did without too much difficulty. In addition to capital, Xerox gave Microlytics access to several other products.

At the start, everything seemed to go well. Several years later, Microlytics merged with Minneapolis-based Selectronics, which had a line of handheld spelling checker/thesaurus products. Because Selectronics was a publicly owned company at the time, they kept that corporate identity. More than two million of these handheld spelling checkers were sold, but unfortunately severe competition kept profit margins very low and the company ran into serious financial difficulties. The combined company name was then changed back to Microlytics and they abandoned the hardware business.

During several years of severe ups and downs, the company worked hard to expand its product offering and get the operation back into the black. Xerox helped them during these very hard times. A recent newspaper article about Microlytics said they requested that their stock be unlisted because of the expense of filing the regularly required SEC reports. An unlisted stock can still be traded but its appeal to potential investors is apparently less than if it were listed.

Shortly after that, the company filed for bankruptcy. For the founder of Microlytics, the corporate venture capital route was a good approach to its initial financing since it gave him the opportunity to see whether he had the skills and ideas needed to create a profitable business with a minimum of personal risk. He worked very hard for a number of years before leaving Microlytics. For Xerox and the other outside investors it did not turn out so well.

My personal experience with these corporate investing programs is that they vary considerably from company to company. In the Xerox situation I just described, the company had a formal venture fund that operated somewhat independently of the parent company.

Another approach I am familiar with is used by a company that is in the military electronics business. The company became associated with an existing institutional venture capital fund which moved one employee to the city in which the company was headquartered. His job is to actively seek out possible venture opportunities from within the company. The difference between this and the prior example is that the people in the venture capital fund were required to raise about half of the needed capital from other outside venture fund investors. From the sponsoring company's viewpoint this gave them at least some assurance that the specific deal had been reviewed by several independent and experienced venture investors, with each performing some due diligence. This, hopefully, will increase the possible success of the spin-off company.

This program has only been underway for a short period of time and I do not know what the results have been. I do believe that several new businesses have been started. My general feeling is that having the deals reviewed and approved by professional venture investors unrelated to the sponsoring company greatly improves the chances of their succeeding.

Notice that in the two examples where large companies provided financing to new businesses outside the company, one is unsuccessful and one "too early to tell." But both summaries are from the viewpoint of the investor, not the entrepreneurs. In both cases the entrepreneurs successfully raised the capital needed to try to start businesses. One of them did not succeed, but at least he had the chance. So even with all of the shortcomings these examples are a way for the potential entrepreneur to give it a try.

Two other questions that might be asked are, "What is the best way to locate a company that might be a source of early financing?" and "What would be the best way to approach them?" These are questions to which I do not have a good answer. I suggest regularly reading business publications such as *The Wall Street Journal, Business Week, Fortune, Inc., Forbes*, etc. Occasionally there are articles describing various companies financing new businesses. There are also several books devoted to large company venturing which describe the programs in a number of organizations. Then I would contact someone within those companies, at a very high level with a personal introduction if possible, and send them a brief summary or a copy of my entire business plan. The business plan should be "customized" to match the interests of the company to which it is being sent and carefully written to generate interest.

Finally, I would put on my salesman's hat and go to work.

Chapter 18

Staying Private/Going Public

Most financial experts advise new companies not to go public too soon. I'm not sure I agree with this conclusion and will describe some of the benefits of a company going public for its initial financing, which can be considerable. This may be done using an underwriter or by the company itself. The earlier you go public the more likely you will have to do so on your own.

But first, a word about the disadvantages. One of the major drawbacks of going public with a new venture is that you will bring in small investors. Even though your offering circular or prospectus will describe the risks in great detail and with great emphasis, the typical small investor may not fully understand them. The head of a start up company has enough problems without having to worry about the "widows and orphans" among the shareholders who cannot afford to lose their investment.

A second frequently cited drawback is that it puts unreasonable pressure on management to achieve short term profitability in its desire to keep the price of the stock up. I see nothing wrong with management being under pressure to achieve profitable operations early. My experience is that most entrepreneurs have no trouble figuring out reasons to defer profits, and pressure in the other direction is likely to be good rather than bad.

A third disadvantage is the cost of going public. Legal fees and printing costs for a public stock offering may be considerable, and if you use an underwriter to sell the stock, commissions may also be considerable. This does not worry me too much either because it's an accepted fact that the cost of raising capital can be high and there are things a company can do to keep these costs down.

A fourth disadvantage is the time required. In most cases you will need approval from the Securities and Exchange Commission (SEC), which can be a long and complicated process.

Finally, there is the possibility that the price of your stock will fall below the offering price, which may make it both difficult and costly to raise more capital at a later date. This should be a real concern, but it is somewhat offset by the possibility that the price of your stock may increase, making it easier and less costly to raise more capital at a later date.

The importance of this list may be serious or not serious at all. It obviously depends upon the specific situation. How about the advantages?

For one thing, going public is a way to avoid using venture investors. It usually results in at least several hundred small shareholders rather than a handful of very large ones. The public is likely to be easier to deal with.

A second advantage is that you are almost sure to get a higher price for your stock. As discussed previously, venture investors drive very hard financial deals with many other restrictions. The public is likely to be less demanding.

Another benefit is liquidity. Stock purchased in a public issue can be traded freely by outside investors. The people who help you get started are not forced to leave their money tied up for five years or more. The founders will also have greater liquidity, at least to a degree. There still remain substantial restrictions on when and under what circumstances the founders, officers, directors, and/or major shareholders can sell stock. Restrictions notwithstanding, stock in a publicly owned company is somewhat easier to sell.

Still another benefit of public ownership is that the company becomes more visible. Among other things, this means that hiring new employees will be easier, and doing business with other companies will be easier. One example of this is that small, publicly owned companies are more likely to use stock options as a way of attracting new employees to a much greater extent than big companies. In a 1990 survey of about 100 companies that had recently gone public, more than 50 percent of the respondents listed enhanced credibility with customers, suppliers, banks, etc., as the most important benefit.

Also, for senior people in the venture, increased public visibility can result in the job being more fun. Communicating with shareholders, having contact with them, and conducting annual meetings are all things that can make the job more interesting, especially when the company is doing well. These may not be so much fun when the company is doing badly.

A final benefit of being publicly owned will only be realized when the new venture decides to sell out or merge with a larger company. It is my experience, both as a seller and a buyer of companies, that the price paid for a publicly owned company is almost always higher than the price paid for a privately owned company. In the case of a publicly owned company, the price is normally the quoted price plus a premium. If the company has done well and can catch the fancy of the investing community, the price may indeed be high. I have seen fairly large transactions where the acquiring firm paid 40 or 50 times the earnings and more. In negotiated deals for privately held companies, the price earnings ratio used is likely to be much lower. The message here is that if you are positioning your company to be acquired, going public first can have considerable merit.

Let me tell you about my experience going public as a way to raise start up capital. Rochester, N.Y., during the 1960s, was a hotbed of new venture activity. I researched those years in some detail and learned that during the decade about 100 companies in the upstate area had initial public stock offerings. The company I started, RF Communications, was one of the first.

RF Communications came into existence during the summer of 1960. Our experience raising our initial capital by going public is described in detail in a Chapter 29 and will not be covered here. It was probably the only alternative available to us to get our business underway, and in both the short and the long term, had many benefits.

During the late 1980s the government made available a faster and far less complex way for small companies to raise capital by going public. It is known as SCOR, Small Company Offering Registration. By early 1997, I believe about 40 states had adopted the SCOR registration process.

The purpose of SCOR is to establish a standard disclosure process in a Questions and Answers format that is acceptable to both the Securities Exchange Commission and the various state regulatory bodies. It is not a way to avoid registration but it simplifies the disclosure process.

Among the restrictions in SCOR are that the maximum amount of money that can be raised is $1 million and the stock must be priced at $5 per share or higher. I cannot tell you which states have approved the use of SCOR, but I suggest you check with your attorney whether your state is among these if you are seriously considering going public.

Recently I learned about a very good Internet web site devoted entirely to small companies considering going public. Its address is http://www.scor-net.com. I recommend that readers try this site as it has much information that could be of great value.

More recently, the SEC introduced a new registration process known as Regulation SB. It is a system of simplifying the disclosure process, but it can also be used by larger companies. Among other things, to be eligible to use Regulation SB the company must have revenues of less than $25 million. Forms and instructions for using Regulation SB are available from the SEC. This and other changes in the securities regulations are intended to simplify and accelerate the registration process for going public and cut the cost of raising capital for small firms.

I am by no means an expert in registering a company's stock for a public issue. I strongly urge anyone planning to do so to seek counsel from a lawyer completely familiar with the process. The SEC regulations are complex, as are the regulations of various states, and it is necessary to register in each state in which you intend to sell stock. The problem with registering in states is that their regulations vary widely and the costs of registration can grow fast.

Be sure to check references of the lawyer you choose. Several months ago, I was approached by an entrepreneur for suggestions about raising capital and I soon discovered that the advice he was getting from his lawyer was, in my opinion, completely out of date. I suggested he go back to him to be certain they were on the right track.

In 1995, companies in the United States are estimated to have raised about $29 billion of new equity by going public for the first time. Many of these, of course, were fairly well established companies with attractive performance records, but never the less this is a huge amount of capital when compared to the $3 billion to $10 billion raised each year by several thousand companies from venture capital funds and the billions raised each year by about 30,000 companies from individual investors. Even though 1995 may not have been a typical year for public offerings, the numbers are still mind boggling.

Finally, a word of caution. From recent articles I have read in business publications it seems that many companies going public during the past few years have been successfully sued for large sums by groups of their initial investors. The reason for these lawsuits is that the stock price dropped substantially a short time after the offering because of a downturn in business. The lawsuits claimed that the companies should have known trouble was brewing and failed to disclose the possibility in their prospectuses or offering circulars at the time the stock was first sold. These are often class action suits and they are very expensive to defend. An article I read in *The Wall Street Journal*, written by the head of a California company subject to such a lawsuit, said that the estimated cost of defense would be so high that they decided to settle even though they were quite sure they had done nothing illegal and would probably have won the case had it gone to trial.

The way to avoid this problem seems pretty clear to me. First, you must be absolutely and completely honest when you describe the business and financial situation of the company. You should probably only go public when you are virtually certain that the business is on an upward path that will last for a while. Try to be as sure as you possibly can that sales and earnings will continue to increase for a fairly extended time following the offering.

Congress recently passed a law making it harder to sue companies for faulty projections. However, even with this new law in effect, my advice is for a publicly owned company to be extremely cautious when making public projections of future sales and earnings.

For a new company raising capital for the first time by going public, estimating future sales and earnings is very difficult to do with any degree of confidence. If you estimate too conservatively it will be more difficult to sell the stock. If you estimate too optimistically it will be easier to sell the stock, but you may be in for trouble if you miss your goals and the stock price drops sharply soon after the offering.

Shareholder lawsuits sometimes involve financial judgments against the officers and directors as well as the company. It is obviously desirable to have officers' and directors' liability insurance as a way to give you some degree of protection, but this type of insurance is apt to be expensive and possibly not even available.

So be careful.

Chapter 19

What Is Your Business Worth?

In the early stages of a business, most entrepreneurs have a very difficult time trying to determine what their company is worth. A venture investor calls this the "valuation" of the deal. In effect, what you must decide is what percentage of your company you are willing to sell for how much money. Because start up companies have little or no operating history, the valuation is usually set mostly by estimates. The following describes the process a venture investor is likely to go through.

The first thing a venture investor will do is to look at the sales and net (after tax) profit you project in your business plan five years or so in the future. Assume for this discussion you expect annual sales to be $15 million and net profit to be 5 percent or $750,000. Based upon the venture investor's knowledge of the market, your competitors, your product and your management as well as advice from consultants, he might

decide that this is too optimistic. Let's say he cuts it back to $10 million in sales and $500,000 net profit.

Having determined to his satisfaction what your company's sales and net profits might be five years in the future, he then tries to estimate what the value of your company will be at that time. He estimates what a reasonable price earnings (P/E) ratio for your stock is likely to be. He will probably assume something in the range of 10 to 1 or less, not 40 to 1 or 50 to 1. Therefore, in the minds of the venture investor the value of your company five years from now, if you meet your plan, is your net earnings times the P/E ratio, $500,000 times 10, or $5 million.

Next, he will ask what is $5 million five years from now worth today, or what is its present value. To do this calculation you must assume a rate of return. Venture investors want a rate of return in the range of 25 percent to 50 percent, which is high because of the risk involved. For this example let us use 36 percent. The present value of $5 million five years from now at a 36 percent rate of return is a little over $1 million.

This means that in the mind of the venture investor your company is presently worth about $1 million. Therefore, if you are planning to raise $600,000 of capital, the venture investor will want to own 60 percent of your stock. Going through this process always shocks the entrepreneur by how low the valuation comes out to be.

Another factor that can affect the valuation is that many entrepreneurs in the early stages of their business make personal loans to their companies. Also, when they work for less pay than they could ordinarily expect, they often show the differential on their balance sheet as deferred salaries. Their hope is that they will be reimbursed later from the capital they raise. I always advise against this practice. When an entrepreneur puts money into the company, it should be an investment not a loan, and working for lower salary is just a way of life in a start up. Both of these practices are apt to make it much harder to raise capital because investors want their money used for future activities—not to pay for past obligations.

A business owner approached me several years ago trying to raise several hundred thousand dollars for his company. When I pressed him for the details, I learned that much of this money would be used to pay delinquent withholding tax obligations plus penalties. As you might guess, I let that one go by.

Of the three types of investors, venture funds are likely to come up with the lowest valuation; corporate venture funds are likely to have somewhat higher valuation because they will attribute value to other factors, and individual investors and informal venture groups will probably have the highest valuation.

From the above discussion it should be clear that the further down the road your company is before you approach a venture investor the higher the valuation may be. The reason is that the numbers can be based to a greater extent on reality rather than on estimates.

Chapter 20

The Business Plan

An important part of raising start up financing for any business is to have a good business plan. A top quality business plan is absolutely critical if you expect to secure money from almost any source—banks, individual investors, formal venture funds, another company or going public. This will often be condensed into a much shorter summary document called an investment proposal which is intended to be used to introduce your company to potential investors. The basic information, though, will be similar to that contained in the business plan. The investment proposal will be discussed in more detail in Chapter 21.

More has been written on the subject of planning in general, and the preparation of business plans in particular, than almost any other business discipline. An immense amount of material is available telling you how to write a business plan. I urge you to read as much as you can. Some of it will be great,

much contradictory, and some wrong. That does not matter. The more you read, the better understanding you will have of the process. Then follow the suggestions contained here. It is good advice that will put you well on the road to having a good business plan.

How important is the business plan? As I said, it is crucial! I urge everyone even thinking about starting a business or trying to raise capital to write a business plan before they go very far down the road. Modify and change it when necessary, but do not try to run your business without one. It has been said, "If you don't know where you're going, any road will get you there."

Included in my first book, *Start Up, An Entrepreneur's Guide to Launching and Managing a New Business,* are two excellent sample business plans. One is for a company planning to sell smoke alarms intended for use in children's bedrooms. After the alarm wakens the child, the next thing to be heard is the parent's voice telling the child not to panic and instructions on what to do next.

The other is for a travel agency written about six years ago by a former student of mine. The agency is in business with annual sales of about $2 million. However, because of modern technology, including Internet and services such as CompuServe and America Online, the travel industry is experiencing a revolution. Included with the business plan of the travel agency are the owner's comments about what she is doing to continue to have a successful business in the face of these new forces.

If you read my other book, these two plans give you an idea of what several entrepreneurs used to guide them in planning, starting, managing, and/or raising capital for their businesses.

Recently I have thought a lot about this subject and have come to the conclusion that I should differentiate between a "plan for the business" and a "business plan." My definition of a plan for the business implies a strategy, which may or may not be in writing, while a business plan implies a written document.

You can reasonably ask which is most important: the plan for the business or a written business plan. Is not the process of thinking it through and making the fundamental strategic decisions more important than putting it in writing? I believe the thinking process is more important than the document, much more important. But the discipline of putting the plan on paper will make

the thinking process more effective and you will end up with a better plan for the business. Also, a written plan can be shared with others. And obviously a plan intended to be used for raising capital from any source must be in writing.

In general, the main purpose of a business plan is for use as a road map in managing your business. This can be modified for use in raising capital. The information in either of these plans will be generally similar, but the emphasis will be different. For example, a plan intended to be used as a road map probably does not need to include detailed biographies of the key management. In a sales document for raising capital or obtaining a loan, the background and experience of management may be the most important part. I suggest that you first prepare a business plan to be used as a road map, an operating plan for running the business. This can then be modified as needed for use in raising money.

How long should a business plan be? How many pages should it have? Many entrepreneurs rebel at the prospect of writing a business plan, but when they finally decide to do so, they write one about 200 pages long. Most business plans are far too long and far too detailed. As a result, they are less effective than they might be. It is my belief that 30 or 40 pages is long enough, perhaps even too long. Longer plans are much less likely to be read.

Then there is the question of who should write the business plan. Many entrepreneurs are uncomfortable writing such a formal document. Engineers and scientists in particular are often intimidated by the process. They frequently assign the task of writing the business plan to others such as a business plan consultant, their lawyer or their accountant. I do not advise using a lawyer or accountant, but under certain circumstances using the services of a professional business plan writer may be the right thing to do. But please remember that the planning decisions for an enterprise must be the effort of the key person or small key group if they are to make any sense at all. Get help with editing, get someone to correct your spelling and grammar, even get someone to write the plan for you. But be sure that the key strategic decisions about the business are yours. Any knowledgeable reader will know in an instant when a business plan was prepared entirely by a surrogate.

As far as the format of the plan is concerned, again I suggest caution. Today we are in the age of desktop publishing and multimedia. Computer magazines are full of articles about how to include graphics, color, different typefaces, many types of charts, etc., in your written documents. Physical appearance is fast becoming more important than content. I suggest you forget all of this and keep your plan simple. Use only one or two different typefaces. In the text, use a typeface with serifs, such as Times Roman, with proportional spacing to make it easier to read. And use graphics only where they add meaning to the plan—not for the purpose of adding flash.

Another thing to consider in writing a business plan is whether or not to use a personal computer software program which guides you through the process. There are a number available at prices in the $100 range. I have some experience with one of these and it did a pretty decent job. In essence, what these programs usually consist of is a simple word processor, an outline for a plan, and one or more sample plans.

Shown below is an outline of a business plan that I like. There is nothing magical or unique about it—it just covers all of the bases and puts the contents in logical sequence.

Outline of a Business Plan

- Title page
- Table of contents
- Executive summary
- General description of business
- Goals and strategy
- Brief background
- Product/service description
- Market description
- Competition
- Marketing and selling strategy
- Manufacturing and quality control
- Organization and management
- Board of directors/advisors
- Financial plan
- Present stock ownership and investment
- Use of funds
- Capitalization plan
- Return to investors
- Assumptions and risks
- Supporting material

The rest of this section will include brief comments on each part of the plan and a description of their purpose.

Title page

Obviously, the title page should include the name of the company and the words "Business Plan." Not so obvious, it seems, is that it should also include an address, telephone number, fax number and perhaps an e-mail address. On a number of occasions I have had to call the information operator in order to learn the telephone number of the company whose plan I was reading.

Table of contents

This should be a page or so long, and is more important than you might think. Many readers have hot buttons. They like to read about cash flow, or marketing strategy, or some other narrow interest before reading the entire plan. The table of contents directs them to the right place. Obviously, the pages must be numbered.

Executive summary

Here you must capture the entire essence of your business in one, two, or three pages. Some people write this first—others write it last. I think last is better. It is a critical part of the plan and the only part some audiences may read. Many will read no further if the executive summary does not whet their curiosity. You cannot spend too much time working on this section.

General description of business

Here is where you present the "Big Idea." What is your offering (product and/or service) and what market will you address? Why did you choose this offering and market, and why are they attractive? Be sure to comment on your distinctive competence and how it supports your selections.

Goals and strategy

State briefly the goals you have for the business and the general strategy you intend to follow to achieve these goals.

Brief background (optional)

This is to set the stage for the remainder of the plan, if appropriate. It could include a description of other ventures in which individuals on your team have been involved, and anything else you want to highlight by way of introduction.

Product/service description

This and the next section are the heart of the business—and the heart of the business plan. Identify the important attributes of your product/service and the benefits that it provides to your customers. Be certain your proposal differentiates, concentrates and innovates in meaningful ways as we have already emphasized so strongly.

Market description

Include comments about the resources you need and what you consider to be the major success factors. Forecast how you expect your market will grow or change over the next few years. Brief descriptions of market research studies and projections by industry experts might be included to substantiate your projections.

Competition

List your competitors and identify their strengths and weaknesses. Include estimates of their market shares and profit levels, if possible. This section will give the reader an idea of how tough it will be to get your business going. One venture investor I know says that when he sees the words, "We have no competition," in a business plan it is almost a sure predictor of failure.

Marketing and selling strategy

This should be an action plan on how you expect to get customers to buy your product or service. Selling strategy is a serious weakness in many plans. Do a good job here. Make it a strength. Describe available distribution channels external to the firm and how you intend to use them.

Manufacturing and quality control

Include some comments on how you will produce your product or deliver your service and how you will assure continued good quality. While this will, you hope, become an important operating problem in the future, it is not often a key part of the business plan.

Organization and management

This is considered an extremely important section by many investors. Include a description of your organization and how you expect it to develop over the next few years. Your management team is of critical importance. I suggest you include a short description of their background in the heart of the plan and more detailed resumes in an appendix. Be sure you have identified the key skills that are needed, and that you

have first-rate players covering these key skills. I am a strong believer in including references in a resume or biography especially if you can use people who are known to the intended reader. Include addresses and phone numbers because you want it to be easy for the reader to contact your references if they choose to do so.

Do not make individual resumes too long. Academics are the worst offenders. They often equate quality with length. One of my doctors, who is a well known researcher in his field, recently sent me a copy of his resume as part of a fund raising effort and it was more than 200 pages long.

Board of directors/advisors

List the people you have or expect to have on your board of directors or board of advisors. Do not load your board with relatives or employees. Investors like to see a fairly small board, which includes successful business people with strong skills in functional areas key to your business. Tell how often the board meets and whether the directors/advisors have a financial commitment to the company.

Financial plan

Financial projections are a key part of a business plan. They provide the reader an idea of where you think the business is going. Perhaps more importantly, they tell a lot about your intrinsic good sense and understanding of the difficulties the company faces.

Often, financial projections are optimistic to an outlandish extent. And they are always prefaced with the words, "Our conservative forecast is...." Do not use the word "conservative" when describing your forecast. Be careful not to use the "hockey stick" approach to forecasting; that is, little growth in sales and earnings for the first few years followed by a sudden rapid upward surge in sales and totally unrealistic profit margins.

Many are the business plans I've read where after tax margins of 30 percent and higher are projected in an industry where 10 or 15 percent is considered good performance. Excessively optimistic projections ruin your credibility as a responsible business person.

Include monthly cash flow projections (remember, this is different than profit), and quarterly or annual order projections, profit and loss projections, and capital expenditure projections. In making financial projections, it may be a good idea to include "best guess," "high side," and/or "low side" numbers.

Present stock ownership and investment

Include a list of all present shareholders with a comment about what they contributed to get their stock—money or otherwise. If the list of shareholders is too long, use a summary, but be sure to include the names of large shareholders. Investors like to see the founders of a company have a cash investment in the business in addition to "sweat equity." The level of this investment should have a reasonable relationship to their personal resources. But remember, your chances of raising capital from others will be much easier if you have invested some of your own money.

Capitalization plan

This is the financial deal you are trying to sell. Tell the potential investor how much money you're trying to raise, which should be consistent with your cash flow projections, and what percentage of the company they will own in return for their investment. This can be done in terms of number of shares, percentages or both. Be specific in describing the type of security you're trying to sell (common stock, preferred stock, warrants, etc.) and other alternatives you will consider.

Use of funds

Include a description of how you expect to use the money and of any major capital items you need to get the business going. On large items it may be appropriate to reference actual quotations from credible sources.

Return to investors

Sensible investors want to know what returns they can expect and especially how they will achieve liquidity. Tell them, again perhaps with alternatives.

Assumptions and risks

This is another very important part of the plan, even though I suggest it be placed toward the end. It may be a good idea to suggest other strategies you might consider to reduce risk in the event your original assumptions do not materialize.

Supporting material

Brochures, resumes of key managers, short magazine articles, technical papers, summaries of market research studies, references from people acquainted with the company or the founders can be included. Be careful not to go into too much detail.

You can reasonably ask how you can possibly pack all of the above in 30 or 40 pages. The answer is, "With great difficulty." But remember, people who read business plans appreciate brevity and view it as an indication of your ability to identify and describe in an organized manner the important factors that will determine the success of your business. If the plan is so long that it intimidates the reader, you are the one who suffers.

Chapter 21

Converting the Business Plan Into an Investment Proposal

The general partner of a medium-sized venture fund told me recently that he sees about 1,200 investment opportunities a year and invests in four or six. This means that you must have a pretty good business idea and be a pretty good salesman if you are to have a prayer of surviving to the end. I do not know what the ratio of submitted plans to committed loans is for a bank, but my guess is that it is also pretty high.

One of the early decisions an entrepreneur must make is what is the best way to approach a potential venture investor in order to have the best chances of successfully getting through the very complex and involved decision process of obtaining venture capital.

The first thing you must decide is how to make the initial contact. Should you telephone the potential investor and try to describe your deal? Should you try to have a friend or associate who is acquainted with the venture investor make the initial contact as an introduction before you make contact? Should you send a complete business plan and hope against hope it successfully gets through the complex evaluation process?

Making this process a little easier is the fact that there are comprehensive lists of venture funds available that show their areas of interest, address and telephone number, and names of senior people. This means you probably should not have to make several hundred calls in order to find some reasonably good prospects.

If you ask people in the venture capital industry what the best first approach is, you surely will get almost as many answers as the number of people you ask. So the only right answer is, "It depends." On what it depends you will never be sure; all you can do is make your best guess.

My feeling is that it probably can't be wrong to make a few telephone calls to carefully selected funds. If you can get a personal introduction in advance, all the better. This will probably give you an idea whether you are in the right ball park. If the person you talk to has no interest, he or she may be willing to suggest other funds closer to what you are looking for.

Assuming you get at least a hint of possible interest, then you must decide whether to send a complete business plan or what I call an investment proposal. My definition of an investment proposal is a somewhat expanded executive summary. It should include enough information to get their interest but not so much information that you lose their interest.

Consider the problem of presenting a complete detailed business plan to a venture capital firm from which you are seeking an investment. Even a medium-sized venture fund is likely to receive several dozen business plans each week. With this number to review, and investment decisions to be made, the following is apt to be the sequence of events they go through:

- Four out of five plans will be reviewed and discarded in 10 to 15 minutes or less after a very cursory scan.

- Of the remainder, four out of five will be read thoroughly, an hour or more, and then discarded.

- The rest may be of sufficient interest for the venture investor to either visit the company or invite the management to their office for further discussion. Then many of these will be turned down.

- The remainder, about one out of 100 of the business plans originally submitted, may survive to the point of serious discussion and perhaps negotiation of detailed terms. More of these will fall short than will pass.

- In most cases only a small handful of the several hundred plans submitted will result in an investment opportunity.

How should the plan described in the previous chapter be modified for use in the initial contact for the purpose of raising capital? This is a good question and will vary somewhat depending on the characteristics of the person to whom the proposal is to be submitted. Clearly it is desirable for the entrepreneur to try to learn as much as possible about the individual who is expected to read the plan. Doing this with any degree of accuracy will be very difficult, but try. Calling them on the telephone, as mentioned above, before you send the document may give you some guidance.

I commented earlier about the importance of the executive summary at the beginning of the plan. It may be that the executive summary can serve as your investment proposal. However, it will probably have to be modified to include additional financial information. Also, because venture investors base so much of their decision on the quality of the management this should be in more detail than in the executive summary of the complete document.

This means that the first written document you send to potential investors better be a pretty good selling document to get their attention. Once you have accomplished this, potential investors will surely want to see your entire plan as described earlier; however, if you do not get their interest in step one—the investment proposal—nothing else matters.

As I mentioned earlier there is no sure way to approach a venture investor and get them interested in your deal. I suggest you follow your own judgment, doing things you are comfortable with, but do not overlook the importance of a carefully thought out and planned approach.

Chapter 22

Will the Government Really Give Me Money?

To the complete surprise of many entrepreneurs, there are numerous sources of financial and other types of support available to small businesses from the federal government, most state governments and many county and city governments. These include grants that support research and development, loan guarantees, low-interest loans and, in some states, even direct investment similar to a venture capital fund. Many of these programs are new in the past 10 or 15 years and many entrepreneurs know almost nothing about them.

As you are probably already aware, dealing with the government, at any level, is often time consuming and frustrating. A lot of paperwork is almost always required, and when you begin, you have no assurance of a successful conclusion. But it may well be worth the trouble because for many companies these sources of financial aid have

meant the difference between success and failure.

The following will describe several federal programs in some detail. Also, I will mention some of the programs available in New York state because these are the ones I know most about. However, almost every state has programs of some sort, but they may be entirely different. Some effort will be required to learn what is available in your area.

For starters, I suggest you telephone the Government Printing Office at 202-783-3238 and purchase a copy of a Small Business Administration booklet titled, "The States and Small Business: A Directory of Programs and Activities." The document ID number for this publication is 045-000-002-57-8. The latest edition that I am aware of is dated 1989, but there may be later editions by now. Even though some of the individuals named as the proper contact may have changed, the organizations and functions are likely to be the same. This booklet has a vast amount of useful information for anyone starting a business. I recommend it highly if it is still available.

Another excellent source of information is the U.S. National Technical Information Service (NTIS), which is part of the Department of Commerce and has almost three million reports available describing a huge number of research programs. One report that they have of particular interest to entrepreneurs is the "Directory of Federal and State Business Assistance, 1988-1989: A Guide for New and Growing Businesses." Their telephone number is 703-487-4650 and the document ID number is PB88-101977. Again, this report is fairly old, but there may be a later edition available. A description of NTIS services is also available through the Internet at http:/www.fedworld.gov

At the state and local level, almost every state, county and city has an economic development agency of some sort, which can give you guidance as to the types of programs that are available and where to look. Also, your local chamber of commerce will be able to help you in your search.

Federal programs

Small Business Innovation Research program

This program, which came into existence in 1982, makes financial grants—not loans but grants—known as SBIRs, to small businesses to support research and development activities.

In this program, 11 large government departments that sponsor research and development must set aside a small percentage of their external research and development budgets for companies with fewer than 500 employees. To qualify for an SBIR, the company must be U.S.-owned and independently operated.

The agencies that participate in the SBIR program and their Internet home page addresses follow:

- Department of Agriculture
  http://www.reeusda.gov/sbir.htm
- Department of Commerce
  http://www.oar.noaa.gov/orta/sbir
- Department of Defense
  http://www.acq.osd.mil/sadbu/sbir
  Within DOD there are at least seven sub groups with Internet sites, such as the U.S. Army, U.S. Navy, etc.
- Department of Education
  http://www.ed.gov
- Department of Energy
  http://www.sbir.er.doc.gov.sbir.htm
- Department of Health and Human Services
  http://www.nih.gov/grants/funding/sbir.htm
- Department of Transportation
  http://www.volpe.dot.gov/sbir.htm
- Environmental Protection Agency
  http://www.epa.gov/ncerqa
- National Aeronautics and Space Administration
  http://nctn.hq.nasa.gov/nctn/sbir/sbir.htm
- National Science Foundation
  http://www.eng.nsf.gov/dmii/sbir
- Nuclear Regulatory Commission

Because some of the agencies involved, including the Department of Defense, have very large external research and development programs, this very small percentage adds up to a large amount of money.

Topics of interest are determined by the individual agency. These are generally quite broad, and with so many agencies involved, if you look hard enough you should be able to find one that fits your needs.

The Internet addresses of several supporting agencies are:

1. SBA home page address is http://www.sbaonline.sba.gov
   Then go to "Expanding Your Business" which covers Small Business Innovative Research opportunities (SBIRs).

2. The National Technology Transfer Center home page address is http://www.nttc.edu

If you are not familiar with the use of the Internet as a means to obtain information about the above groups, I strongly urge you to get help from someone who is. The amount of information that is available is simply immense.

The SBIR program is intended to support R&D that will later benefit the sponsoring agency, the company and the country.

I know of one company that received a grant for research in the use of laser devices to weld bowel tissue during surgery, another company that had a grant to develop techniques for ruggedized hand-held personal computers, and another that received several grants for the development of three dimensional imaging for use on a personal computer without the need for colored glasses. The list and variety of projects is endless.

SBIR awards are made on a competitive basis. The program has several phases. Phase One can be a six-month grant of up to $100,000 to determine the feasibility of the idea. This may then be followed by a Phase Two grant extending over a period of up to two years with awards of up to $750,000 for further work refining the ideas and developing prototypes.

These numbers vary from agency to agency. However, in most cases the question of when the program being funded will be commercialized is receiving more emphasis than in the past. The SBIR program does not provide funds to bring a product to market.

Another resource is "Writing SBIR Proposals" and is available from Sandra Cohn Associates at 312-648-0082. It was updated at the end of 1996 and should now be available. The price of earlier editions was about $75. I do not know the price of the latest edition.

To give you an idea of the scope of the SBIR program, in 1991 there were about 3,800 Phase One Awards (about 12 percent of those that applied) and more than 1,025 Phase Two Awards (about one third of those that applied).

I believe the money available to fund SBIRs is now approaching $1 billion a year. So, you can see that an SBIR is something worth pursuing.

Small Business Technology Transfer program

This is a more recent program similar to the SBIR program in which the small company is required to work in partnership with a public sector non-profit research institution of some sort. These programs are known as STTRs and are funded at a level of between 5 and 10 percent of the money available in the SBIR programs. The purpose is to encourage small businesses to work jointly with various types of research institutions for the purpose of developing commercially viable products from earlier stage research programs.

The requirements for a small company to participate in the STTR program are about the same as in the SBIR program. For the nonprofit research institution there is no size limit but it must be located in the United States and be either a college or university, a domestic non-profit research organization, or a federally funded research and development (R&D) center.

Four federal agencies reserve a portion of their R&D funds for STTR programs. They are the following:

- Department of Defense.

- Department of Energy.

- National Aeronautics and Space Administration.

- National Science Foundation.

Their Internet home page addresses are the same as noted under SBIRs.

Small Business Administration, 7(a) loan guarantees

In this program, the SBA provides guarantees to banks making loans to small businesses. This is intended for use by companies unable to obtain loans on their own. Funds may be used to establish a new business, enlarge an existing business, to acquire machinery or equipment, to finance inventory or for working capital. In its 40 year existence the SBA loan programs have helped more than one million small business owners. SBA guaranteed loans vary in size from $20,000 to $750,000 with most in the $150,000 range. A formal application to SBA for a 7(a) guarantee can be made by the bank that declined to make your business a conventional loan.

Banks unwilling to lend to a small business because it is unable to cover the entire loan with personal guarantees and liens on personal assets are frequently willing to lend with a partial SBA guarantee. In 1995 the SBA guaranteed a total of more than 55,000 loans with a value of about $7.8 billion. However, the agency is in the process of reducing the percentage of the loan that it will guarantee and raising fees to the borrowers in order to increase the dollar value of loans that will be covered. According to the SBA, women, minorities and veterans especially benefit from this program.

State programs

The financial aid and assistance programs of states are more diverse than the federal programs. These are usually intended to create or maintain jobs within the state, to attract companies to move to the state or to keep companies from relocating out of the state. For New York, where taxes are high, keeping companies from moving elsewhere is an important priority.

I cannot possibly cover all programs available in all states. Instead, I will describe some that are available in New York to give you an idea of the scope of these programs. In 1994, George Pataki defeated Mario Cuomo as governor and the state has a republican governor for the first time in many years. Since this change in administration occurred, some of the New York state programs have been consolidated and the application process simplified, but that the level of spending is about the same as in the past. Listed here are some programs that are available.

Corporation for Innovation Development (CID)

The CID program is administered by the New York State Science and Technology Foundation and provides debt and equity capital to new technology-based businesses with fewer than 100 employees. CID operates in a way similar to a private venture capital fund but is willing to take greater risk. Its telephone number is 518-473-9741.

Empire State Development Corp.

This agency is new in New York state and has combined a number of smaller programs, including the Urban Development Corporation and the Job Development Authority. More details are available from the agency headquarters in New York City at 212-803-3100. The people I spoke to were very helpful and I was told the best way to proceed is to contact one of the 10 regional offices in or near the area in which you are located. The people in the regional offices will help determine whether there are any programs that might meet your needs. If you have trouble locating the local office for your area, check with your chamber of commerce for help or call their headquarters number in New York City shown above.

Some of the programs of the Empire State Development Corp. can assist small businesses in obtaining loans for various purposes at favorable rates, under certain circumstances can provide significant tax benefits, can help train new employees in certain skill areas needed by the company, can advise and assist in gaining access to various Federal Assistance Programs, etc.

New York Business Development Corporation (NYBDC)

The NYBDC is a quasi-public agency that makes term loans to small businesses with varied collateral requirements and the flexibility to collaborate with or complement loans from conventional lenders. Interest rates are usually competitive. Its telephone number is 518-463-2268.

In addition to this list of New York state programs, there are others administered by local governments, both county and city, either alone or in cooperation with the state, for the benefit of new or small businesses.

When you check into the availability of programs such as these in your area, remember that all involve dealing with a government bureaucracy of some sort. They are often slow, cumbersome and involve much red tape. Under no circumstances can you expect action that will help you meet next week's payroll. Get started early and you may be able to get financial assistance that is not available from any other source.

Chapter 23

Finance a Business With Credit Cards! Are You Crazy?

Using credit cards as a way to borrow has become extremely common in the United States in recent years. It is very easy for almost anyone with a half-way decent job to obtain a card with a credit limit of at least $5,000. My personal situation is not typical but I seem to get a letter a week from banks I never heard of telling me that I have a pre-approved credit line in the $5,000 to $10,000 range and all I have to do is sign and mail back the enclosed form in a postage-paid envelope. The major disadvantage of using credit cards as a source of borrowing is that they usually charge interest rates that are quite high.

My wife and I now have three or four cards and we charge almost everything we buy to these cards. But I always pay the card bills within the time limit specified and never incur interest charges. This has several advantages. First, it gives me free credit for 20 days

or so, and more recently, a frequent flier mile for every dollar we spend. I do not think I am the kind of customer the credit card companies are looking for.

But for an entrepreneur, the use of credit cards represents a somewhat different situation. I know several companies that are today very successful that used credit cards extensively in order to meet payroll and other financial obligations during their early, formative years.

One of these entrepreneurs was a woman who founded and built a successful market research business. Her bank would not give her a loan, and as a practical matter, credit cards were the only alternative she had. When I met her she had about 15 or so employees and almost as many credit cards. The availability of cash through credit card borrowing gave her the opportunity to get the business started.

Why would she do such a thing when interest rates were so high? Simple: She was unable to borrow and unable to find equity investors, and it was the only source of cash available. She was smart enough and had enough confidence in her business ability that the availability of extra cash outweighed the burden of high interest rates.

Interestingly, by the time we got to know each other, her business was in the black and she had achieved excellent growth. I asked her why she was still using credit cards and she said the last time she tried to get a loan the bank rejected her application. I suggested to her that it seemed to me she had passed the critical point where credit cards were her only alternative and that she should go back to her bank and re-apply for a loan. She asked me what she should do if they refused and I said try another bank.

Several weeks later I asked how she was doing and she said she had no trouble getting the loan.

This story must sound a little silly, but it is not. This woman was a skilled entrepreneur with enough confidence in her ability to somehow figure a way to get the business going. The use of credit cards may have been close to the most expensive route she could have taken,

but it was the only source of money she could find, and it worked.

He is another example. A company has annual sales of more than $300 million and is a leader in its industry. During its early days the owner used credit cards frequently to cover a wide range of expenses. The company is now publicly owned and the owner now has a personal net worth of several hundred million dollars.

I have noticed recently that several credit card companies are actively trying to attract companies as customers. The lines of credit available are in the $20,000 range and higher, some have no annual fee, and on the one that sent me detailed information, the interest rates were still high but not outlandish. As a last resort these might be worth looking into. In fact, a recent article in *Business Week* magazine estimated that about 40 percent of companies with sales under $500,000 per year used credit cards to finance some of their operations.

In reading this chapter, do not conclude that I suggest you should use credit cards when you have access to other, lower cost sources of capital. But when no other road is available, take the one you can find.

Chapter 24

Maximizing Owner Value

··

There are many reasons why people start businesses. These include a desire to prove they can do it, the desire to be involved in all aspects of an enterprise, the loss of a job in a big company cutback, greater flexibility in determining one's working hours, and many others. This issue is covered in more detail in my earlier book, *Start Up, An Entrepreneur's Guide to Launching and Managing a New Business.*

However, with few exceptions, one very important objective of almost every entrepreneur is to maximize the value of the company for its owners. This includes privately owned firms as well as partnerships and companies with outside equity investors.

How do you maximize the value of the company? In my view, the first step is to try to identify the things over which you have control that will influence value. This is often very hard to do and in situations where there are several things

on your list, it may be hard to decide which is most important.

At RF Communications, we were publicly owned from the very beginning. By the time we merged with Harris Corp., eight years later, the price of our stock had increased from the $1 a share offering price in 1961 to about $45 per share in 1969 (considering splits). Whether this is the best we could possibly have done we will never know, but it sure wasn't bad. For the initial investors it represented an appreciation of 45 to 1. For the four founders, the gain was even greater.

Over the years I have often thought about the various decisions we made during the life of RF Communications as an independent company and which decisions had the most influence on this increase in value. One of the early decisions we faced was the question of how to invest our limited capital. We concluded as a practical matter that the decision was between trying to maximize growth in sales or trying to maximize growth in earnings. These required different strategies.

Maximizing earnings probably also required that the company grow, but whether it grew at a 10 percent rate or a 30 percent rate would have been less important than how fast earnings increased. To maximize growth in sales you should also be profitable as a means for generating cash, but growing at a rapid rate would be more important than an increase in earnings.

We concluded that in our circumstances, in order to maximize the value of the company to the owners, including ourselves, we had to maximize the price at which the publicly owned stock was trading. We decided that the best way to accomplish this was to try to achieve a rate of profit consistent with the industry in which we did business and, within that constraint, do everything we could to maximize growth in sales.

In the electronics industry at that time net (after tax) profit of 5 percent seemed to be common among the companies with which we competed and we set that as our minimum acceptable profit level. Because earnings cannot be controlled that accurately, we usually exceeded the goal and reported profit of 6 or 7 percent. But our growth rate averaged about 60 percent a year over the entire history of RF Communications as an independent firm, which far exceeded industry standards.

For us, growth was usually determined by investment in either marketing or product development. Marketing investment gives you short term growth and new products give you long term growth—you need both. We invested in both. This seemed to work very well in our situation.

Other types of businesses require different strategies. In a company that reaches its ultimate customer through stores, such as pharmacies, fast food chains, retailers or companies like Discovery Zone, the most important decisions would be store locations and how many stores you try to open, over what period of time, and over what geographical area. Discovery Zone, for example, probably went too far in that it recently filed for bankruptcy and the reason mentioned in the business press was that they tried to open too many stores in too many places over too short a period of time.

This means that the strategy you adopt to maximize growth in the value of the company to its owners varies widely depending on many things. What I suggest is that you analyze your situation very carefully to try to identify those things that you can control that most affect value and to adopt a strategy that will provide the maximum increase.

Chapter 25

Accounts Receivable and Payable, Two Ways to Conserve Cash

....

Accounts receivable is the money owed your company by its customers after you have shipped the merchandise that was ordered or performed the services that were required. It is the money owed after an invoice is sent to the customer.

There are several things about accounts receivable that many entrepreneurs are very careless about. First is that your customers will not pay you until you send them an invoice. In case you do not know what an invoice is, it is what accountants call a bill for money due you.

I am always surprised at how many entrepreneurs are extremely conscientious about meeting delivery commitments on orders they receive, yet after the merchandise is shipped or the service provided they are often very sloppy about sending an invoice. Unless you bill your customers, in all likelihood you will never be paid. Some particularly

conscientious companies even send the invoices before the equipment is shipped. I do not recommend this but I do recommend that the day the equipment is loaded in a truck an invoice should also go into the mailbox.

It is also possible, under certain situations to require advance deposits, sometimes as high as 50 percent or more, at the time you accept an order. This is clearly the best way of all to be paid. Whether you can do this depends on a number of things including how many other sources are available for the thing you are selling, whether the product or service must be customized, how badly your customer needs quick delivery, etc.

Another thing I also recommend is that it is usually a good practice to offer a discount for quick payment. Normally, 1 or 2 percent is sufficient. The reason for this is that many organizations, big organizations especially, have rigid policies to always take discounts. One large

....

company I know of always prints checks a day or two after the invoice arrives in the mail. If a discount is offered, they date the check 10 days later or whatever the discount period happens to be. Then the checks are mailed to arrive within the discount period. If a discount is not offered, they date the check 30 or 60 days later depending on their payment policy and mail it at that time.

There are a number of things a small company can do to speed up collections. Every month or so the head of the company should go over the list of delinquent accounts and place a telephone call to those accounts for the purpose of collecting. Many entrepreneurs are not aware that most big companies have a person whose main responsibility is to pay bills slowly. This is an excellent example of where the squeaky wheel gets the grease. Call the accounts payable manager; if that does not get results call the head of the finance department, and if that does not work call the head of the company. You will be surprised at how often this gets your invoices paid more promptly.

Entrepreneurs are often concerned that being aggressive in collecting invoices will have a negative effect on future orders. My experience is that this seldom happens. The person who makes the purchase decision for whatever it is you are selling very seldom is involved in the payment process. And, they may be just as upset as you that their company does not pay its bills in a timely manner.

A few years ago I had several interesting experiences in doing things to speed

up the collection process. When I self-published the first edition of my other book, *Start Up, An Entrepreneur's Guide to Launching and Managing a New Business,* one of my target markets was for use as a text in college courses in entrepreneurship. College bookstores are notoriously slow bill-payers and I often had to wait 60, 90 days and more before I got a check. Finally it occurred to me that once a professor specifies a text for use in a course, the bookstore had no alternative but to buy the specified text and get copies into the store before classes begin. They have no choice.

After about a year of getting angry, I finally figured out a better solution to the problem and did the following. When I got an order from a college bookstore, usually by telephone, I would ask for a purchase order number. Then I would immediately send them an invoice along with a letter saying that as soon as I received payment I would ship the books. "Cash with order" became my policy and without fail, within a week or so I had a check. As best I can tell I never lost an order because no one in the bookstore has anything to do with the purchase decision and my collection period dropped from about 90 days to about nine days.

Another experience I had was when I was commodore of Rochester Yacht Club. There were a half dozen or so members who were always behind in paying their bills. Threatening letters from the treasurer did not seem to work. The practice I followed was to call the delinquent members at home in the evening about two weeks after their bill was due. After one or two minutes of chit chat, I would say, "Why don't you pay your bill?" Within a few days we always had a check. This took a total of about 15 minutes a month and cut our late dues payments almost to zero. Sometimes the member became annoyed with the commodore's dunning them, but that did not bother me. I paid my bills on time and they should have paid theirs.

My belief is that being aggressive in collecting receivables can help a great deal in reducing the cash requirements of a new business, but that very few new business owners are aggressive enough.

Factoring is another way to speed up the collection process. Very simply stated, factoring is the sale of an account receivable at a discount to a third party. The discounts vary but may be as high as 20 percent, so you must realize that it involves significant cost. When you factor an account receivable, you actually sell the receivable to a factor organization which pays you immediately. This is usually done on a nonrecourse basis. The factor then assumes all of the responsibility and risk of collection. An important issue to be aware of is that your suppliers are usually informed that you are using a factor and are asked to send payment directly to the factor organization rather than to you.

I have never used a factor to collect bills but I understand in some industries it is quite common. If you operate your business at high enough profit margins to afford factoring, I strongly advise you to check out a number of organizations that factor and compare their terms and conditions. Some purchase receivables on

a nonrecourse basis and some require guarantees from your company and sometimes even require personal guarantees. I considered including a sample of a factor agreement as an appendix in this book, but they vary so widely that I decided not to do so. I suggest you consult a lawyer and/or accountant familiar with factoring to advise you.

Accounts payable is the other side of the fence. In addition to trying to figure out ways to get your customers to pay the money they owe you faster, you should also try very hard to think of things you can do to pay the money you owe others slower. This is another way to reduce the cash needs of your business.

To start, it is a good practice to tell all of your suppliers that your standard policy is to pay all invoices in 60 or 90 days. Whether or not your suppliers will accept this depends how much they want your business, which is likely to vary widely.

If there is only one supplier of whatever it is you are buying, the chances are they will refuse. On the other hand, if there are several potential sources, you should go out to competitive bid and make one condition of the purchase process negotiation of payment terms. How important a customer you are to the supplier will determine how much latitude you will have in extending payments. Most entrepreneurs are surprised at how often this procedure works.

If you are in the manufacturing business, another approach to delaying the time that you must pay your suppliers is to schedule the delivery of the parts you use so that it matches your manufacturing schedule as closely as possible.

There is no point in having parts in your inventory six months before you will use them. A better way is to schedule the arrival of parts weeks or even days before they will be used, with you being billed at the time of delivery. This is called "just in time manufacturing" and is an approach used in recent years by many companies.

Just-in-time manufacturing is really not a financing problem, it is a manufacturing issue, but it may result in a delay in accounts payable and the need for less capital. Dell Computer, one of the country's leaders in sale of personal computers by mail order, has a reputation of being expert in the use of just-in-time manufacturing in the management of its business. It may be that you have to be an important customer to your suppliers for them to agree to this approach, but it is worth a try.

Financing your business with suppliers' money, by whatever ethical means you can think of, is another good way to reduce the cash needs of your business.

I read several articles recently in the business press that mentioned a problem that a number of companies have run into lately. It relates to the subject of reducing staff assigned to receivable and payable activities and depending on computers to perform the tasks more efficiently while requiring fewer people to do the work. This does not always work as expected and there are cases mentioned where the same bills are paid twice as a result of slight differences in invoices or the collection of bills is overlooked because the computer is not always able to detect slight errors in the collection process that people are likely to notice. These problems suggest that maybe humans are more apt to find errors or inconsistencies than machines, and companies should be very careful when they attempt to entirely automate these crucial activities.

The two things that I discussed in this chapter (doing everything you can to collect your receivables fast and doing everything you can to pay your payables slowly) may seem obvious. But I am always amazed at how naive many new business owners are of the importance of these issues.

Chapter 26

Franchising & Multilevel Marketing

Two other ways for a small company to build its business without the need for large amounts of outside capital are franchising and multilevel or network marketing (sometimes called direct selling). Both of these are fairly complex. They are often under attack by regulatory agencies and require considerable care in setting up in order to avoid problems at a later date. I strongly advise anyone considering either approach to consult an attorney, expert in these areas, at an early stage. A neophyte or amateur proceeding on his or her own is almost certain to encounter some difficulty that could be avoided by seeking advice and counsel from a specialist. Caution is strongly suggested.

Franchising

Selling a franchise in an established business is a way to reduce the capital needs of a growing company. It can greatly expand the sales capability and distribution for the company's product or service and possibly even generate cash flow in the process. This approach has its own pros and cons, some of which will be discussed here.

In 1990, there were more than 500,000 franchised outlets in operation in the United States with annual sales exceeding $700 billion, about one-third of all retail sales. The franchise industry employed more than seven million full-time or part-time people. There are about 3,000 U.S. companies from which franchises can be bought representing about 60 different industries. From this data you can see that franchising is a way many companies use to expand the marketing capability of the business while at the same time doing it with a reduced amount of capital from other sources.

Lists of franchise opportunities are included in franchise guides and handbooks that can be obtained from most libraries and many bookstores. If you are seriously thinking of selling a franchise, be sure to read some of these at the very beginning of your search so you get a feel for the scope and diversity of franchise businesses.

There are two different types of franchises. One is called a product franchise, where the franchisee obtains the rights to purchase and sell the product of the franchiser, perhaps operating the business under his or her own name rather than the franchiser's name. The most common of this type is an automobile dealership.

The other type of franchise is called a business format franchise. Here it is usual to operate the business under the franchiser's name. Typical of these is a McDonald's or Holiday Inn franchise. In these cases, it is often difficult for customers to know whether they are in a franchised unit or a company-owned unit.

For the buyer of a franchise there are a number of benefits compared to starting a business from scratch. One of the most important is that the failure rate among franchised businesses is lower than among independently created businesses. They are usually buying a proven business idea, and get a lot of help running it.

For example, they begin with a known product or service and receive training and expert guidance in the operation of the business. They gain from the advertising and promotional efforts of the parent company, may receive volume buying economies, follow standardized procedures and operating methods that have proven successful for others,

and get the benefit of new products or services developed by the franchiser. All of these can give the entrepreneur a valuable head start compared to developing a business strategy of his or her own. In effect, they are in business for themselves but not in business by themselves. You as the seller of a franchise must provide the above list of services and benefits.

All sellers of franchises are required by the Federal Trade Commission to give the potential buyer a document called a Franchise Offering Circular. This provides detailed information about your business and is intended to protect the buyer. Many states also have laws that regulate the operation of franchises. Learn about these.

If you are serious about selling a franchise you should consider attending one of seven or eight franchise expositions or trade shows held each year. These will have as many as 400 companies exhibiting for the purpose of selling franchises. For information about these, contact International Franchise Expos, Inc. at 407-647-8521.

Multilevel marketing

Multilevel marketing is a selling approach where the company sells its product to others, frequently called independent distributors or independent consultants. Typically, they buy products from the company and resell to the ultimate user. This is often done through house parties, group sessions, door-to-door selling, and selling to friends, relatives, neighbors and acquaintances. The product, when purchased by independent distributors, is discounted from the retail price so they can realize a profit on the transaction. Normally, the distributors operate as independent contractors rather than employees of the company. They take title to and pay for the product in advance of making a sale.

There's even more appeal to this selling approach. The independent distributors are then encouraged by the company to recruit other distributors, and in return receive a percentage commission on the sales of their recruits. They cannot be paid a fee for finding a recruit. Their payment must be in the form of a commission on the sales of the recruit.

Amway, Mary Kay Cosmetics and Tupperware are several of the better-known companies using multilevel marketing as their main distribution method. I have heard that there are about 2,000 companies that use this approach, most of their independent distributors work part time and about 80 percent are women. Information and very good publications about multilevel selling can be obtained from the Direct Selling Association at 202-293-5760.

In summary, from the company's viewpoint there are three key benefits from both franchising and multilevel marketing.

They are:

1. The company can recruit a large sales force without the expense of adding full-time employees.

2. You can view either of these approaches as an inexpensive way of securing capital for your business. Both the franchisee and the multilevel marketing distributors are independent contractors, owners of their own businesses. Little investment is required from the company. In fact, the franchisee usually pays a fee in advance and then must raise the capital to build whatever facility is needed to carry out the business. In the case of a Holiday Inn, for example, the cost of building an Inn may be in excess of $50,000 per room. Holiday Inn has about 1,400 franchises. I have no idea how many rooms there are in the average Holiday Inn, bu you can see the immense capital investment that would have been required to accomplish this through normal financing channels.

3. Franchisees and distributors, who tend to be entrepreneurs or individuals working part-time to augment their income, are likely to work very hard. They will often have more drive, enthusiasm, and spirit than will regular, full-time employees.

Both of these methods of selling have come under recent criticism for various reasons. In the case of franchising, this happens when the franchisor establishes a company-owned operation in the same area after the buyer of the franchise invested a lot of money and years of effort establishing the market or holds back on the training and management assistance that was promised.

This means that if you are selling franchises to others you must take it as serious business, not simply a windfall source of capital. The franchiser has an obligation to do everything possible to help their franchisees succeed. One thing not too many people selling franchises do is to qualify the buyers. This means they should be sure the franchisee has the necessary knowledge, experience and capital and is committed to being successful. One seller of franchises that I read about receives more than 5,000 requests a year for information, after initial discussions invites about 200 to informational meetings and ends up selling franchises to only about 50.

In the case of multilevel marketing, the company must have a valid product or service. However, a frequent criticism here is that some of these situations may resemble a pyramid scheme where the people who get in early can get rich, but the latecomers are taken for suckers.

Another criticism of multilevel marketing is the great emphasis on recruiting new distributors. This implies that, because of the override commissions across several levels, the distribution costs become excessive. In most cases I do not believe this is a valid criticism. For example, it is not unusual in the normal distribution of consumer products to have a company salesperson selling to a commission representative selling to a distributor selling to a retailer selling to a consumer. Add all the markups in this "conventional" distribution process and you may find the costs are similar to or even more than those in the multilevel process. And the multilevel marketer will usually deliver the product to the user's home at no cost, which in some cases may be an important benefit.

In both cases, these objections can be overcome by the franchiser and multilevel marketer by doing business in an open and ethical manner and making sure that the buyer knows and understands the risks involved. Obviously, not every kind of business is suitable for franchising or multilevel marketing. For those where it is suitable, it may provide an opportunity to greatly leverage your marketing and selling capability in a way that would not be possible to do on your own financial resources.

Chapter 27

Help, Help! Where Do I Go for Help?

When I started a company in 1961 there were very few places to which I could go for help. Today, there are countless places and people that offer help, counsel and guidance. It is no longer a question of whether there is help available but more a question of which sources of help to use.

This chapter lists some that I consider to be of potential value. They are almost certain to be able to give you answers to many questions—and give you greater confidence in your program for becoming an entrepreneur. Many also provide a lot of information and suggestions about the process of financing a new business.

Other entrepreneurs

Perhaps the most valuable help you can get in planning, raising capital or managing a new business is from someone who has already started a business.

I am approached constantly by entrepreneurs and potential entrepreneurs to discuss every imaginable problem related to going out on their own. I seldom refuse to see them and rarely charge a fee. In almost every case I can help them in some way.

You may wonder why I do this and I often ask myself the same question. At one time I was actively seeking investment opportunities and did, in fact, invest in about a half dozen of these situations. But today I no longer make venture investments and still see about 100 entrepreneurs every year. It is something that I enjoy and I guess it provides me satisfaction in being able to help others.

What I am suggesting is that you should get to know a few successful entrepreneurs in your area and try to spend time with them. Make it clear that you are seeking advice, not trying to raise money or sell them anything.

You'll be surprised at how often they are willing to see you, and, almost invariably, they will be able to help you in some way and not expect to be paid. If you can generate enough interest you may even attract an investment.

Internet

When I wrote my other book I had just started using the Internet and did not appreciate its value. Since then, I have used the Internet extensively and it has been of immense value in many of my business activities, including the writing of this book. There is virtually no subject or organization you can think of that does not provide information over the Internet. There are so many articles about the Internet and how it came into existence that I will not repeat its history here, but I will discuss some of the ways it can be used by entrepreneurs in running their business.

Access to the Internet can be obtained through an Internet provider. These are organizations, both large and small, through which you can both access the information available on the Internet or which you can use to have a web page for your company or organization as a sales tool.

The Internet can be accessed through computer information services such as America Online and CompuServe as well as AT&T, many local telephone companies and both local and national specialized service providers.

Today the price of most service providers is in the $20 a month range for unlimited access time. What the price will be a year from now is anyone's

guess, but my belief is that there will be a shake out of some sort or we will need another national telephone system to handle Internet traffic alone.

Putting your product or service on the Internet and offering it for sale is not the subject of this book and will not be discussed. However, I would like to list a number of sources of information available over the Internet which might be helpful to an entrepreneur in developing a plan for a business or in trying to obtain financing for a business.

This list does not pretend to be complete and by the time this book reaches the shelves of book stores there will undoubtedly be many additional sources of information and some of the sources presently available will have disappeared.

Several interesting web sites are mentioned in other chapters of this book. The following is a list of others that would be of interest to someone starting a business looking into:

1. http://www.sbaonline.sba.gov
   This web site includes literally hundreds of SBA publications on every subject imaginable.

2. http://www.inc.com
   This is the web site on *Inc.* magazine and includes articles on many subjects.

3. http://www.entrepreneurmag.com
   This is the web site of *Entrepreneur* magazine and includes many articles from past issues.

4. http://www.ideacafe.com
   This is the web site of an organization devoted to entrepreneurship and small business.

5. http://www.amazon.com
   This is an Internet bookstore that lists the availability of well over a million books, including many on the subject of finance.

6. http://www.sec.gov
   This site includes reports filed with the Securities Exchange Commission by almost every company in the United States that has issued stock to the public. This information is usually hard to obtain in printed form.

7. http://www.thebcnnetwork.com
   This web site lists thousands of business cards.

8. http://www.village.com
   It is possible to incorporate over the telephone using this web site.

9. http://www.jm-publ.com
   This web site has information about venture capital.

10. http://www.aboutwork.com
    This web site has many elements, one being entrepreneurship.

11. http://www.businessfinance.com
    This a web site devoted to raising money for a business.

12. http://www.sba.gov.inv
    This is a web site that list all Small Business investment companies.

13. http://www.scor-net.com
    This web site is almost entirely devoted to problems companies face going public.

As you start using the Internet for help in running your business, including the raising of capital, you are sure to learn about other sites that may be useful.

Books, tapes and videos

Books, audio tapes and videos on the subject of entrepreneurship and the financing of a new business have become very popular in recent years. For example, my other book, *Start Up, An Entrepreneur's Guide to Launching and Managing a New Business*, which I first self-published in 1989 and which is now published by Career Press, is in its fourth edition. At last count it was used either in small business programs or as a text in more than 50 colleges and universities.

There is a company named Amazon that sells books at a discount through the Internet. I understand they list more than one million books in their directory, including mine. Also, I have heard that both Barnes & Noble and Borders are planning to establish web sites through which they hope to sell books.

I read, listen to and watch many of these books, audio tapes and videos about starting a business. Some I find to be extremely informative, and some are interesting but a little short on useful advice. In any case, I advise you to go to your bookstore or library and read, listen to or watch as many as you can find. As a minimum, you will end up a little smarter and it may be that you will garner advice and suggestions that will be of great value.

College courses

Fifteen or 20 years ago, few colleges and universities offered formal courses in entrepreneurship and small business management as part of their curriculum.

Today, there are more than 500 in the United States that offer such courses. In some schools, entrepreneurship and small business management are major concentrations and some universities have large entrepreneurial centers devoted to teaching and academic research in the field. A number have endowed chairs in entrepreneurship.

Some of these courses are taught by successful entrepreneurs who teach part time. These entrepreneurs are willing to devote considerable effort for small compensation to help students along the road to starting and financing a business.

In almost all of these courses, the term project is the preparation of a business plan. I taught entrepreneurship in MBA programs for about 10 years. Most of my students were young people with little or no business experience, individuals who did not yet know whether they wanted to go out on their own. However, when a student either had already started his or her own business, seriously planned to do so or was employed by a small company, I strongly encouraged him or her to write a plan about their own business.

You should consider taking one of these courses. In doing so, you will probably be forced through the discipline to write a real life business plan, and in all likelihood, get a formal, detailed critique of the plan either from the faculty or other students.

In many of these courses, entrepreneurs are invited to address the classes. This is a good way to establish contact with a business owner with whom you can later network on your own.

Small Business Administration (SBA)

SBA offices are spread all across the country. They have countless publications available and many programs in which you may have an interest. The SBA has a Small Business Answer Desk (800-827-5722) which can answer many general business questions including the location of the SBA office nearest to you. They can also provide a list of the many publications and videos available to small businesses at very low cost that may be of value to an entrepreneur.

Recently, the SBA began using the Internet to provide a great deal of information about its various programs. The main Internet address is mentioned earlier.

Small Business Development Centers (SBDCs)

This is another program of great value to small business owners that is supported by the Small Business Administration. SBDCs are usually associated with a community college or state university. They each have a small group of business specialists who will counsel and advise you on a one-on-one basis, and who conduct seminars, programs and courses for entrepreneurs. Often the SBDCs have a library of books, pamphlets and other material. In some cases they publish newsletters with articles of interest to entrepreneurs. There are about 800 of these centers around the country. You can contact the Association of Small Business Development Centers in Washington, D.C. at 703-448-6124, or your local chamber of commerce for the location of the SBDC in your area.

Business incubators

A business incubator is an organization that provides low cost space to new companies on a leased basis. This usually includes modest rental charges, small units of space when necessary, short leases and the availability of shared services that most new businesses cannot justify having on their own. Sometimes business incubators are publicly supported and sometimes privately financed. The types of shared services available will vary, but are likely to include a conference room, copier, fax machine and secretarial services. I have seen one where a law firm and public accountant were among the tenants. The sponsors of the incubator may also be able to provide the new companies with general business guidance and counseling.

A list of incubators can be obtained from the National Business Incubation Assoc., 20 East Circle Dr., Suite 190, Athens, OH 45701, 614-593-4331. Also, your local chamber of commerce will probably be able to guide you to the location of business incubators in your area that are not associated with the above association.

Service Corps of Retired Executives (SCORE)

This is a free program sponsored by the Small Business Administration in which retired businesspeople agree to devote time counseling small business owners. In many cases, SCORE chapters are associated with a local chamber of commerce. You cannot always choose your adviser, but in almost every case you will benefit from the opportunity to discuss your problems with a knowledgeable person.

Small business councils

Many chambers of commerce have sub-groups called Councils. In Rochester, the Chamber has an International Business Council, a Sales Executives Council, a Minority Business Owners Council, a Small Business Council (SBC) and others.

The SBC in Rochester has more than 250 members, mostly owners of small and not-so-small businesses. The council runs seminars on entrepreneurship, occasional breakfast meetings devoted to a wide range of specific problems faced by small firms and monthly evening meetings where extensive networking is encouraged. Also, they organize small groups of owners of noncompeting businesses into advisory boards that meet monthly to discuss mutual problems.

These SBCs can be a valuable resource for an entrepreneur. Check your nearest chamber of commerce to see what is available in your area.

Small business seminars

Seminars are available on almost every imaginable subject of interest to a small business owner. Check the events list in the business section of your local newspaper for information about what is happening in your area. Sometimes these cost hundreds of dollars and sometimes they cost little or nothing, depending on who organizes and runs the seminar.

Several years ago, a woman business owner and I organized and conducted a seminar for women entrepreneurs. It drew about 100 attendees. The fee was $75 and a local bank and public accounting firm provided some financial support. We ended up with a $5,000 profit that we used to set up a small scholarship fund for women business owners in an area business school. Seminars of this type can be a valuable source of information and networking for an entrepreneur.

Many of these seminars are devoted to the subject of securing financing for new businesses.

Entrepreneurial magazines

There are a number of specialty magazines devoted to entrepreneurship and small business management. Some have huge circulations, such as *Inc., Entrepreneur* and *Home Office Computing,* while others are smaller and more focused, such as *Midnight Engineering* and *In Business Magazine.* All try to include articles, book reviews, case histories and other material of interest to entrepreneurs. Almost all of these have web sites. Some of the web addresses were given earlier.

General business publications

Publications such as *Business Week, Forbes, Fortune, The Wall Street Journal,* etc. are devoted almost entirely to business subjects of every kind imaginable. I subscribe to most of them and there are articles of interest to small businesses in almost every issue. Many of these relate to financing issues of various sorts. Most of these publications have web sites, the addresses of which are given in the front pages of the publications.

Professional service organizations

Many public accounting firms, law firms and banks have various kinds of written information and publications that they make available to entrepreneurs and small business owners. Those that I have seen are mostly in the form of pamphlets and small booklets on a variety of subjects. Specifically, I have copies of material put out by Ernst & Young, Price Waterhouse, Arthur Young and KMG Peat Marwick, all large national accounting firms. I know they give them to clients free and charge little or nothing to others. Most of this material is very good.

Venture capital clubs

These groups provide a forum to which entrepreneurs can present an outline of their business plans, usually for the purpose of raising outside capital. In Rochester, we have a group that meets 10 times a year. Typically, there are one or two presentations at each meeting. Sometimes the entrepreneur is successful in raising money, other times not. Recently it has become more difficult. At worst, these groups can be the source of contacts, at best, a source of interested investors.

The best way to determine whether there is such a club in your area is through your local chamber of commerce or to simply ask around. A good source would be other entrepreneurs or bankers, lawyers and accountants with small business clients.

Networking

Then there is networking—meeting and speaking with others who have problems similar to yours and who have knowledge that may be helpful. How do you find people with whom you can share problems and gain useful advice and counsel? Take seminars, attend association meetings, take advantage of everything mentioned here and make a habit of asking for one or two more names of other possible sources of help whenever you talk to anyone about a business problem. Doing this may get you a personal introduction that will make it easier to gain an audience with your next contact. The value of networking will be increased if you are well prepared in advance. Be sure to have at least a good outline of a business plan available and a list of questions or problems you would like to discuss.

Professional associations for small businesses

Finally there are a number of national associations whose main purpose is to help various categories of small businesspeople. Several are:

National Association of Self Employed. This group represents about 320,000 entrepreneurs, most of whom have only a handful of employees. It has a number of publications including a Small Business Resource Guide. Their telephone number is 800-232-6273, and their address is 2121 Precinct Line Rd., Hurst, TX 76054. Their web address is www.nase.org

National Federation of Independent Businesses. This organization has about 600,000 members, and in addition to lobbying in Washington on small business issues, they have a monthly publication. Their telephone number is 800-634-2669, and their address is 600 Maryland Ave. SW, Washington, DC 20024. Their web address is www.nfibonline.com

The Council of Growing Companies. This is an organization of the heads of small and medium-sized companies that provides lobbying, seminars, and conferences for its members. Their telephone number is 301-951-1138, and their address is 7910 Woodmont Ave., Suite 1206, Bethesda, MD 20814.

Summary

When I first began writing this chapter, I was surprised at the long list of people and places an entrepreneur can go to for help—including a lot of help on the subject of financing a new or growing business. I suspect your problem will not be finding sources of help, but deciding how many you should take the trouble to use, and sorting out the contradictory advice you are sure to get. Most are available at little or no cost and most can help you identify and solve problems that would have been much more difficult on your own. Gaining access to some of these sources may require you to be pushy and aggressive from time to time, but the benefits are almost sure to justify the effort.

Chapter 28

Why Companies Fail

Throughout this book I say over and over again that money isn't everything. In various chapters I refer to a number of companies who raised huge amounts of capital yet could not make the grade and failed. By now you have probably learned of others. If you were to ask the founders or senior managers of any of these companies the reasons for their failure, the answer you will almost always get is, "We ran out of money." In most cases I disagree with this conclusion.

When I was a young engineer I worked for a man who once told me the following, "My brother and I started a very successful business but we failed because we ran out of money." Sound familiar? I was quite inexperienced at the time but something about what he said bothered me. It was years later that I concluded that his statement was nonsense for at least two reasons.

The first was that being a success includes not running out of money. That seems fairly obvious.

The second reason is a little more complex. If they were reasonably decent managers, if the product or service that they were offering addressed a market that needed that product or service and if they could get enough orders, the likelihood is that they would not have run out of money. There are very few problems that companies have that more orders won't solve.

So my final conclusion was that yes, they did run out of money, and the business failed. But running out of money was not the cause of their problem, it was the result of another problem—failing to sell enough of whatever product or service the business was based on. In other words, what really caused their problem was not running out of money it was running out of orders.

It is my strong belief that the real reason companies fail is that they are either badly managed, that they fail to adjust their strategy to match the amount of capital they have available, or that they fail to get enough orders for whatever it is that their business is offering.

They underestimate the importance of selling. Then they run out of money.

Obviously there are exceptions to this position, but I repeat the statement of Mary Kay Ash that I quoted in an earlier, "Money isn't everything. You also have to know what you are doing."

Chapter 29

Examples—The Most Important Part of This Book

As I mentioned earlier, this chapter may be the most important part of this book. It includes some real life examples of a number of companies and how they did their initial financing. I have tried to include a wide variety of different types of businesses.

Some of the examples I use are ones that I am personally acquainted with. These are mostly from the upstate New York area. However, I have tried to be careful to be sure that they are representative of that type of company and that the messages they contain will be of value to all readers.

There are probably some differences in financing a new business that vary depending on the area of the country in which the company is located. Silicon Valley, Calif., for example, probably has more venture capital firms than any other area of the United States and many very high visibility success stories. The Boston area (Rte. 128) has many new companies, probably a result of the proximity and influence of MIT. Raleigh-Durham is another area that has spawned many new businesses for reasons I am not sure I understand.

However, in my opinion most of the problems an entrepreneur faces in raising early capital are largely unrelated to the area of the country in which they are located and these examples should be helpful wherever you are.

Most of all, you should remember that the starting of the companies I use as examples was in almost every case not easy for the founders. In most, they had to use a great amount of ingenuity, aggressiveness, refusal to give up and other important entrepreneurial qualities in order to finance the businesses they were trying to start.

Some of these examples I wrote personally based upon information from many sources, including the companies themselves. Some were written entirely by the entrepreneur who started the company and some are a combination, where I wrote a few introductory comments and closing observations (shown in italics) and the entrepreneur wrote the remainder.

The following list includes the names of the companies I used as examples and a brief description of their business. However, I urge you to read them all because each has some unique quality that might be helpful to you in your search for financing.

1. RF Communications Inc., long range radio communications.
2. Career Press, publisher.
3. Galen Medical Centers Ltd., medical treatment for impotence.
4. Custom Software, specialized software development.
5. Intuit Software Inc., Quicken checkbook management software.
6. Lillian Vernon Corporation, mail order jewelry and gifts.
7. Paychex Inc., payroll services for small companies.
8. Yeaple Corporation, personal stereo system.
9. Microchip Technology Inc., specialized semi-conductors.
10. Sea Creations, nautical gift and shell shop.
11. Jolt Cola, a unique soft drink.
12. HCR Corporation, specialized health care.

1. RF Communications, Inc.

Because the company I founded many years ago is the one I am most familiar with I have included it as the first example. Even though RF Communications, Inc. was started in 1961 and merged with Harris Corp. in 1969 many of the things we did apply as much today as they did then. Certainly the sources of initial financing for new businesses have changed over this period, however, I think our situation is a good example of how a group of entrepreneurs can use their imagination and ingenuity to overcome some very difficult obstacles in order to raise the money they think they need to get their business underway.

RF Communications was in the long range radio communications business. The markets it served were government, military and commercial users of this type of equipment, wherever they were located. During its eight years as an independent company, RF Communications sold equipment in more than 100 countries.

At the time I started RF Communications, I held a senior position in the marketing department of General Dynamics Electronics Division (GD), which sold electronics equipment to the government. At the time, GD had about 6,000 employees in its Rochester operation. Prior to that I had been assistant chief engineer, but even then my main job was getting new business.

Before going to GD I had worked for six years as a design engineer at RCA

Laboratories during the early days of television and FM broadcasting. My educational background is a Bachelor of Electrical Engineering (BEE) from Polytechnic Institute of Brooklyn in 1945 and a Master of Science (SM) in Industrial Management from MIT, which I received under a Sloan Fellowship at age 36, a year or so before I went out on my own.

When I made the decision to become an entrepreneur I had a great deal of experience in marketing, a lot in general management experience and a fair technical background. But I did not have sufficient knowledge of any product or service that could be used as the basis of a business. This meant I needed associates who could contribute the skills I lacked.

I approached two engineers at GD, the chief engineer and the assistant chief engineer of the Communications Laboratory, who were both nationally known single sideband engineers. We added a young attorney to the team to assist with the legal aspects of starting a business, but mostly to help us with the process of raising capital.

So we had a team, some good ideas for products, but no money and very little knowledge of what to do next. We set up a crude laboratory in the basement of a local apartment house owned by the attorney and proceeded to begin design of a prototype of our first product and plan the business.

The first thing we did was to form a legal partnership in which we were all equal partners and in which we each invested $5,000. That does not sound like much today, but at the time it was about one third of a year's salary. And, none of us had $5,000.

In my case I also had six young children, a mortgage and a car loan which made my situation even more difficult. To raise $5,000, I used several thousand dollars of savings, borrowed some money from my father, managed to get a small bank loan based upon my executive position at GD and sold an insurance policy.

One of my jobs while working in the basement was to do a cash flow projection for the business we hoped to have. The result was that we would need about $150,000 of additional capital which, considering inflation, would be about $500,000 today. We talked to a few banks about the possibilities of a loan in that amount and quickly decided we should stop wasting their time and ours trying that route.

Then we approached several people who we considered fairly wealthy (in our situation we only knew a few) and got no interest whatever. And venture capital funds had not yet come into existence.

It soon became clear that our only alternative was to go public. We approached several brokerage firms who handled public stock issues. The reputable ones would not give us the time of day and those that would give us the time of day wanted very large commissions and refused to give us any assurance of success. So the next decision we made was to go public and try to sell the stock ourselves without the benefit of an underwriter. This meant we had to get approval from the Securities and Exchange Commission (SEC) and find enough people willing to put up

$150,000 in a company that, as yet, did not even exist. And don't forget we were still working in the basement.

Then the four founders had to decide how we would cut the pie—how many shares of this new corporation each of us would own. As the original founder and president, my share was 33 percent, with each of the other three getting a little less depending on their role.

All four of us prepared lists of everyone we could think of who might invest a few dollars in our deal, and after several months we had about 600 names. In addition we had to decide what percentage of the company we were prepared to sell for the $150,000 we needed and the share price of the stock. We decided to sell one-third of the company for the $150,000 at a price of one dollar a share. The one third number was completely arbitrary because none of us had any experience doing this before. The price we set mostly because it would make the arithmetic simple for potential investors.

On the last Friday in January 1961 we mailed the SEC our application for a Regulation A stock issue and the following Monday the other two GD people and I resigned. We gave them four weeks' notice, which seemed fair at the time.

On Mar. 1, 1961, we moved our company from the basement to a vacant beauty parlor, but we were still waiting for approval from the SEC and were fast running out of the original $20,000 we had invested. Fortunately, about three weeks later we received SEC approval (this would probably take longer today)

and were free to try to raise the $150,000 we thought we needed.

Two other things we did that we hoped would make selling the stock a little easier were to use a local bank as the subscription agent (which meant checks from potential investors were mailed to a bank rather than to our attorney's office) and we retained Price Waterhouse as our public accountant (which was a result of their approaching us, not our approaching them).

On the Thursday following SEC approval, we mailed about 600 offering circulars to the previously mentioned list. Our children hand wrote the addresses on all of the envelopes. On the following Monday morning the bank we used had the longest line in its history waiting for the doors to open and their post office box was overloaded with mail.

To make a long story short we had requests for about $450,000 worth of stock—three times the amount we were seeking. That's the good news; the bad news was that we were only permitted to keep the amount we were asking for, the $150,000. So we had the unenviable task of allocating the stock in a way we considered fair and mailing back checks for about $300,000.

Because of the local publicity we received through this process, two small local brokerage firms began making a market in our shares and almost immediately they began trading for about $2 compared to the $1 subscription price.

We often asked ourselves whether what we had done was smart or dumb.

A case could easily be made that we should have charged a higher price for the one-third of the company we were selling or sold a smaller percentage of the company for $150,000.

My feeling is that what we did was pretty smart. For one thing, all four of us were amateurs, completely inexperienced at selling stock with no idea of what to expect. And our main goal was to raise enough money to get our business underway, which we succeeded in doing. Years later, it occurred to me that when a company sells stock through a public issue it will either be oversubscribed a mile or undersubscribed a mile. The least likely scenario was that the last person on line would purchase the last share available. Obviously, being oversubscribed is the better result.

As it turned out, our business did very well. During the first two years business thrived and we had to do bank borrowing, using receivables as security, which suddenly became possible because we were almost immediately profitable. During RF Communications' entire history as an independent company it had only one loss quarter—its first quarter in business.

Two years after the first offering we had a second at a price of $5 per share, which was also oversubscribed; a year or so after that we had a private placement at $9 per share. Several years later we had another public issue at $17 per share, but this time through a New York underwriter. Shortly after that we were listed on the American Stock Exchange and then had our final sale of stock at a price of $27 per share.

In 1969, RF Communications merged with Harris Corp. at a price of approximately $45 a share (taking splits into effect) which was about two and a half times annual sales, five times our net worth and 43 times earnings.

RF Communications as a unit of Harris Corp. now has about 1,600 employees and sales in the $200 million range.

The process was not easy. Keeping our products ahead of competitors, getting orders and hiring competent employees was a continuous challenge and required immense effort for the years we were independent. Fortunately raising capital was not too difficult, but that was mainly the result of doing all of the other things right. Companies can usually raise money without too much difficulty once they have a successful track record, which was fortunately true in our case.

2. Career Press

Career Press is a medium-sized publisher located in Franklin Lakes , N.J. It was founded in March 1985 by Ron Fry, who has a bachelor's degree from Princeton University. Career Press specializes in personal, self-help-type books. These include books like mine, about how to start a business, as well as books about how to write a resume, how to interview for a job, how to study, the best places to live in the United States, etc. His catalog now has about 200 titles and he publishes 45 to 50 new titles each year.

Before starting Career Press, Fry was the sales manager of a magazine for travel agents located in New York City and later publisher of a travel magazine based in Indiana. The position in Indiana was not to his liking and after a few years he and his wife moved back to the New York City area where he started two businesses—a magazine for travel agents, which he considered a sure thing, and a publishing company—Career Press, which he considered very risky. The magazine was soon abandoned and he gave all of his effort to the publishing business.

Publishing is a very interesting type of business with several unique qualities. To a new, amateur author, which I was in 1989, finding a publisher willing to publish my book seemed like an insurmountable problem. I was turned down by 30 publishers before I decided to self publish the first edition of Start Up, An Entrepreneur's Guide to Launching and Managing a New Business. *To my dismay I learned something I should have learned before writing the book and that is that it is almost impossible to find a publisher willing to publish an unsolicited manuscript.*

I sold about 8,500 copies on my own and eventually made a good profit, but I was out of pocket about $24,000 the day I got the first books from my printer. This high cost means that self publishing is not a realistic alternative for most new authors.

Then I learned something else, and that is that once having self published my own book and sold 8,500 copies it was no longer difficult to find a publisher. Suddenly I had a choice of three

or four. I picked Career Press over several much larger firms and have not regretted that decision.

When an author submits a book to a publisher he or she should keep the following in mind. No one thinks a book is more wonderful than does the author, and it is easy to forget that most publishers are deluged with manuscripts and their main objective is to publish only books that people will buy. If they fail to do this they will not last long as publishers. There is a great deal of competition among publishers to find this type of book. So theirs is not an easy selection process even though you, the author, may not agree with the ones they pick.

Another thing that I find very strange about the publishing business is that it is one of the few businesses in any industry where the buyer has the right to return all unsold books for a full refund—no questions asked. This means that for the publisher, even though he may think that the books are sold, they may not stay sold. This situation is so bad that for low priced, paperbacks of the type you buy in a drug store, the publisher often does not even require that the books be returned in order to credit the buyer with a refund. All they ask is that the covers be returned and the rest of the books go into the trash barrel. Quite frankly, as a businessman I don't think I like this system. My point is that publishing is a tough business.

With these introductory comments, the rest of this chapter is in Ron Fry's words.

To begin, I want to talk about how I financed the publishing business and the things I did right and wrong. First and foremost, I broke what many will tell you (or you will tell everyone!) is at least a cardinal rule of a new business: Create a business plan. I certainly had nothing in writing, and while I try to contend "it was all in my head" the reality was that very little in the way of capital needs or projections were in my head. I pretty much took the position I'd figure it all out as I went along, a sure-fire prescription for disaster that, luckily, we averted (Notice I didn't say "never happened." It did, as you'll see.)

The reality is that I had no clue as to how much I was going to spend, or for that matter, where the heck the money would come from. Some would, accurately, say that this puts the ostrich to shame. It's pretty remarkable that I survived to tell the tale.

My original stake of around $40,000 carried me through the first year, paying all the basics—rent, equipment, telephone, etc. Needless to say I was not paid a salary myself. And I did everything myself, from lugging the books to be shipped down to the post office to doing invoicing late at night, and by hand, on my brother's kitchen table. (Yes, we even stayed with relatives for nearly a year to save the rent. The "savings," of course, went right back into the business.)

At the suggestion of a friend I decided to publish industry specific books and developed a series of four such books, which I termed Career Directories, for magazine publishing, book publishing, advertising and public relations. (This series expanded to more than 10

titles before we sold it to another publisher in 1991.)

I recall running out of money just about the time the first of these books was ready to be printed. I needed about $75,000 to print the quantity needed of all four (between October 1985 and February 1986). I ended 1985 with sales of $35,000, though I doubt much of that had been collected. So I was pretty much broke. And since I was a brand new publisher, the printer I found gave me pretty standard terms—one half down, one half due on delivery. I think I talked him out of the one half down by the third book, but I still needed to pay COD to get my books.

Because of my and my wife's previous earnings, we had managed to develop pretty good credit. Luckily, the credit card industry gave me some Christmas presents that year—a whole slew of "invitations" to get new cards. I happily accepted every such invitation. I probably had two credit cards with a total limit of $10,000 before then. Within a couple of months, I had about a dozen with a total limit of $85,000. Voilà. That's how I paid for the printing. (And it took me two years until I was able to pay them off entirely.) Interestingly, I now have double that number of cards, with more than double the credit limit, as does my partner—more than $300,000 in open, unsecured, personal credit lines. And while it is now exceedingly rare for us to have to touch them, it *has* happened that a major market downturn or a rash of slow payments from major accounts has necessitated a quick infusion of cash for 30 or 60 days. So they still come in plenty handy. (Although now we go out of our way to have only those that have no annual fee, so credit is there when we need it, at no cost *until* we use it.)

Career Press didn't make a profit for three years and we didn't become profitable enough to pay me a salary until five. So for *five* years we lived on my wife's salary, which represented about 60 percent of her income. The other 40 percent—bonuses and commissions paid quarterly—went into the business, like clockwork, every three months. By the end of five years, we had invested roughly $200,000 all told (the original $40,000 plus another $30,000+ per year). And the credit card money. And of course, my own time, which netted me a big fat zero for all that period.

And, it wouldn't have been enough if we hadn't gotten lucky in two other ways. Two years after starting, we were still very much behind the eight ball. My then-accountant had a brother who was looking for wacky, high risk investments. I certainly qualified. For 6 percent of the company, he took over as part-time CFO—doing financial projections, regular quarterly statements, and all the other stuff I had certainly never had time for—and supplied and programmed a computer that took over all the accounting, billing, accounts receivable, accounts payable, payroll and other similar functions (all the stuff I had been doing by hand at night). Not long afterwards (within a year), our cash flow position was so bad he agreed to put up a sizable amount of money—enough to get us out of our immediate hole—in return for a slightly bigger (though still minority) share.

Joe Zipper is still my part-time CFO (he only shows up a half-day a week, doing most of the work by modem), responsible for our much larger computer system and its network of dozens of other PCs, modems, faxes, etc., for overseeing all accounting, staying in touch with the bank, continually assessing cash needs and, if necessary, finding ways to fulfill them.

The other way I got lucky was back in 1987 (though, again, it's "luck" that continues to this day). My printer had been working for me for all of a year. We had printed four books in 1985-86 which were fully paid for. We wound up printing 10 or so in 1987 for which he gave us terms (net 30 days). Well, after paying overhead and all that good stuff (and promotion and advertising, and, and, and), I wound up having nothing to pay the printer. And I owed $117,000.

That's happened to publishers before, and what usually happens next is that the printer embargoes all the inventory still around and stops printing anything new, even reprints, until paid in full.

My printer continued to print new books—on 90 day terms, yet—and allowed us to pay off the $117,000 over the next two years. So he effectively financed my business as well. Needless to say, he's still my printer. And, we now do above $1 million a year with him. Loyalty sometimes pays off.

One last point: We are *still* not in the cash flow shape we should be, and the main culprit is that we were undercapitalized from the very start and never managed to become "over-capitalized." We've had to weather the occasional cash flow storms, the unlimited peaks and valleys of business cycles because of my own inability to plan 12 years ago, and a lack of enough cash. Of course, not having any idea how much I really needed made planning pretty difficult.

The good news is that we're off to the best start (30 percent ahead of the best four months in our history), and if we keep it up for about 12 more months, may finally be sufficiently capitalized!

I was not aware of the financial problems that Ron Fry went through getting Career Press off the ground. If I had known I might not have picked him to be my publisher. However, after working with his company for about five years I can honestly say he never failed to pay my cash advance or royalties on time.

My conclusion is that Ron Fry's story is a good example of the struggle and ingenuity that is often needed to get a new business "off and running."

3. Galen Medical Centers, Ltd.

Galen Medical Centers, Ltd. is a company located in Arlington, Virginia. The founder of Galen, George Oprean, is not a medical doctor, yet the business he started was based on a system that can be used to cure impotence in men. The system requires that the individual inject chemicals into his penis. In most cases this causes an erection that lasts for several hours. The system is not patented but has been approved by federal authorities for this use. I asked Oprean to give me a short description of his background and how he raised the capital needed to start the business. The following is his story that I consider fascinating.

Bill Stolze asked me to write this section for the book. Why? Because Bill knew that I broke all the rules and faced what the soothsayers would say was truly a "mission impossible." But I have a belief and a motto that has carried me through some very difficult times: "Winners never quit and quitters never win."

My educational background is in the State University of New York plus Syracuse University from which I have degrees in education and marketing. Early in my career, I had what I thought was the ideal job, but as a result of a corporate merger, I was fired. At the time I had about $100 in the bank, no golden parachute, a new house, a six month old baby, and two weeks' severance pay. It was at this point in my life that I decided to start my own business in order to control my own destiny. Then it was probably called "crazy"; today it is called "Entrepreneurship." In the long run, it proved to be the right decision.

During my career I started a number of different companies and purchased one. Those I started were in the marketing, advertising, and film production businesses. The one I purchased was in the competitive swimwear business. Several of the ones I started were successful and two were complete busts. So

I had some experience in start up financing because all of these companies were started with other peoples money.

I first met Bill in 1990 on the recommendation of a friend, and from the start, the chemistry between us was good. Bill made it clear that he was no longer making venture investments but that he would read my business plan, listen to my ideas, guide me through the Rochester venture capital maze and help me get in front of groups of potential venture investors.

This seemed like a good start. However, I faced some obstacles:

1. I had just gone through bankruptcy in Nashville. It was a company I bought from a friend without doing enough due diligence. The moral here: Do not buy companies from friends without first doing your homework.

2. The company I wanted to start was a company that dealt with and treated impotence. This was a big market, but at that time a taboo subject.

3. I was not and am not a physician.

4. I had no credentials in the medical field.

5. I had no staff, no management infrastructure—all I had was a list of high priced consultants.

6. My background was exclusively in marketing and film production.

7. I had no cash.

However, I believed and knew that I was right and that my concept for a freestanding medical clinic dealing only with impotence would work. What would you say the odds were of my being successful? Little or none, right? But I had no choice.

My only chance of raising capital was from individuals. Venture capital funds, bank loans, and public offerings were options not available to me. So my ultimate strategy, which was cast in concrete at the time, was to find individual investors. This is the approach I embarked on.

Bill arranged for me to speak at a breakfast meeting of a group of sophisticated investors at a hotel in Rochester. There were four presenters and we each had 10 minutes. I was the last to go on

The groups that preceded me were very good; they had it all—the visual aids, the charts, the offering circulars, the attorneys and accountants, their $400 suits with the $200 shoes and $50 ties. I had none of that, except for an introduction from one of the most respected businessmen in the room, Bill Stolze. It came to be my turn and I really did not know until the very last minute how I was going to approach this subject with this ultraconservative group of men who probably all had a problem with impotence, and like most men, would not admit it.

So imagine the scene: Bill introduces me and tells the audience that I have something very interesting to talk about and then turns it over to me for my ten minutes.

There is 30 seconds of silence and I say, "Thank you for inviting me this morning. My presentation has to do with the sale of sex and drugs. (Pause.) And the ability or inability of a man to achieve an erection strong enough and hard enough to penetrate his partner."

There was dead silence and then a few laughs, the ice was broken, and then I got into my presentation. The numbers were outstanding, the potential market was fantastic, but the concept was totally outlandish to them. I could not imagine those men talking to their wives, accountants or attorneys and telling them they wanted to invest in an erection factory. But they did ask good questions and they did get good answers.

What happened after that was classic. I got all kinds of accolades—the best presentation, great idea—all the good things but no money—and no invitation to call and make an appointment.

It took me another nine months of banging on doors and beating on Bill's ear. This included getting thrown out, politely, of course, from physicians' offices and businessmen's offices before I got a breakthrough. Back to, "Winners never quit and quitters never win." It was a small breakthrough, a tiny hole that could possibly be enlarged, and it was greed that was the motivating factor.

Just to digress for a moment. As a potential entrepreneur seeking funding, you have to remember at all times that the money man is there for one reason—"What's in it for me." I don't care how good the idea is or how good the team is, it is the smell of blood and financial gain that opens an investor's pocketbook. Potential entrepreneurs must recognize this and use it to their advantage. Sometimes it works and sometimes it

doesn't—but those are the rules of the game.

When Bill started his own company, the offering was not oversubscribed because the investors knew and loved Bill and his partners. They saw the potential for profit. The market-makers did not make a market because they liked Bill—they saw the potential for profit. And call it what you like, but it is just plain old-fashioned desire for a financial killing.

After all those months trying to find investors, I finally pushed someone's greed button. I needed $250,000 net. An "in between" guy wanted a commission and no options. So what did I do? I raised the ante to cover his cut and offered the single investor 20 percent of the company. Everyone was in agreement and the lawyers, who I could now afford to pay, put the deal together and it was closed.

I chose the Washington, D.C. area for the first clinic. It had the demographics, the population base and the income base. My original projections called for three new patients a day, but when we opened we got 12 a day. From the day my company started, we did not have a month, quarter or year without a profit.

Now there are copy cats—the very same people who said it would never work—but that is an issue for another chapter or entire book.

Bill wanted this story of how Galen Medical Centers raised its initial capital because it is off-the-wall and cannot be found in other books. But if you believe in what you have and believe in yourself, you can do it. It will not be easy and there are more vultures out there than there are real people, but it can be done. In fact what we created was a whole new industry, a whole new concept for medicine. We drove the market in an area which was taboo at the time.

Today, Galen Medical Centers is flourishing and looking forward to an initial public offering and a national roll out. I think that if there is anything to be learned from this, it is that if you really have entrepreneurial blood flowing through your veins, you cannot look back. If you cannot beat the obstacles, go around them, and above all, keep focused.

4. Custom Software

The following describes a company in the custom software business. All of the information included is accurate and describes an existing business, but for professional reasons the owner has requested that he and his company not be identified. We will call the company XYZ Software and the owner Peter Smith.

Peter Smith has a bachelor's degree in economics from Ohio State University. Before starting his own business he worked as a software engineer at a photographic subsidiary of a large U.S. corporation. They were located in a city with a population of about 700,000 in the metropolitan area. The area included several very large companies and many small- and medium-sized firms. The unit he worked for had about 1,200 employees. Smith married shortly after finishing college and his wife taught at a local elementary school.

In 1986, his employer announced that he was closing down the photographic business and Smith was offered the opportunity to transfer to another unit in another city. He decided instead to start a business of his own doing software consulting for other companies in the area.

The type of business he specialized in at the beginning, and still puts major emphasis on today, is writing custom software for a wide number of clients employing graphical user interface on personal computers to solve a variety of business problems.

In the beginning he was his only employee and his place of business was his home. By then he had one child, but between his very small cash flow from the new business and his wife's income as a teacher they were able to live in a decent life style without the need for bank borrowing. And he received no financial assistance from relatives or friends.

Smith's business grew slowly. As he was able to find additional clients he began employing other programmers. They were full time employees, not contract people. However, because they were always working at the customer's plant or office, Smith continued to work from his home and did not need a place of business that provided a work area big enough for all the people he employed.

His billing policy was to send invoices to clients twice monthly with payment due in 30 days. This policy is still strictly enforced and no discounts of any kind are ever offered.

The services he sold were very specialized and were not generally available from other software firms in the region. Because of this, he was able to grow the business at a comfortable rate and never had to raise working capital by borrowing or selling equity. As a practical matter his only expenses were salaries and benefits. His office and overhead expenses were negligible.

About four years ago, when he had three children and his family had moved to a new home, he decided to move the business out of his home. His place of business now has five office workers in addition to himself and occupies a space of about 1,600 square feet.

However, over the past few years his perseverance paid off and he has been able to grow at a much faster rate. Today, XYZ Software employs about 67 people in addition to Smith. Their annual sales currently exceed $4 million and his pretax profit ranges around 20 percent. He estimates that whenever he employs another programmer he only has to invest about $14,000 before that individual's revenue stream covers his or her salary and expenses.

What has all of this meant to Smith and his family? Recently he moved to another beautiful home, which he owns without a mortgage, and he lives a very comfortable life style free of debt. He is building up a financial portfolio that will send his three children to the colleges of their choice and permit him to retire, if he chooses, at a fairly young age.

Most interesting to me, though, is that he was able to create a new business entirely with his own resources without the need for outside financing.

In thinking about how he was able to accomplish this, I draw a number of conclusions:

1. He started a business selling a service in which he was an expert, giving him a competitive advantage over others in the field.

2. Between the income his wife earned as a teacher, his personal savings, and the fact that he ran a very spartan operation for several years as his business grew, he was able to get the business underway entirely on cash flow, without either borrowing or selling equity.

3. Through very astute management, he took work only from customers who had a substantial need for his services and were willing to pay a price that represented a fair profit for Smith over and above the cost of providing the services.

4. He did not hire people in anticipation of new business; he hired them after he had a client for which they could work almost from the first day of their employment. Therefore, they could generate revenue within weeks of coming on board.

5. He runs a tight, efficient operation without the perks and embellishments that many entrepreneurs feel are necessary in order to impress either customers, employees or both. Because his customers rarely visit his place of business, he does not need a very fancy facility.

6. He has tight standards on collection, and if a customer proves to be slow at paying for the services he provides, he takes no further business from them.

7. Finally, he tries very hard to only employ people who excel in designing custom software. Most measure up to his high standards, but if they don't, they soon become former employees. In other words he is a very tough manager.

What about the future? Smith has now started another business in addition to the one described above. This new business will provide complete computer services, including both hardware and software. The software will do electronic data invoicing, electronic purchase orders, etc., for companies with sales in the $30 to $40 million range. It will also solve the date problem many organizations face as we approach the 21st century.

When he started this new business he had the opportunity of getting a substantial financial investment from an institutional venture capital firm but decided not to do so because of the possibility of losing control. Instead, he formed a team with four other people who have complementary computer skills. Together they invested $241,000 of their own money with Smith still maintaining a majority interest.

Depending on the success of this new venture, Smith may consider securing additional capital either from a public offering, an investment from a venture capital fund or merging with a larger organization. My guess is that with his record as an entrepreneur any of these alternatives should be possible.

5. Intuit Software, Inc.

Intuit came into existence in 1983. It was founded by Scott Cook and Tom Proulx, and its first product was a checkbook management computer program named Quicken. Quicken would print checks, keep a directory of all checks written over an extended period of time, put each check into a category that you define and assist greatly in balancing your checking account each month. In addition, the program would print out reports that you define, which are of great assistance in preparation of tax returns or keeping business records.

Cook has a degree in economics and math from the University of Southern California and an MBA from Harvard Business School. Before starting Intuit, he had worked at a number of jobs including a marketing position at Proctor & Gamble. Proulx was in his fourth year at Stanford University, majoring in electrical engineering/computer science.

When Intuit was started, there were about 40 other personal finance software packages on the market. Proulx did most of the design work on early versions of Quicken.

The company's initial capital was about $350,000, which was raised by Cook from personal savings, a home equity loan, a loan from his father, credit cards, and an equity investment from two outside investors. Through the first few years of Intuit's existence, Cook and Proulx approached more than two dozen venture capital funds. They were very polite, but all said, "No, thank you."

One thing that Cook and Proulx did that was probably the most important in influencing the success of Intuit was to spend a great amount of time and effort determining what features the users of a program such as Quicken would most value. This made Quicken a "stand out" product compared to other financial management programs available at the time.

I recall that I used a competitive product to Quicken during the late 1980s that received very high reviews in a computer magazine. Soon I purchased an upgrade from that company, and when I loaded it into my computer it erased my data files. Then I switched to Quicken, purchased a number of upgrades, and never had another problem.

In the early years, Intuit had serious cash flow problems that took a lot of skill on Cook and Proulx's part to overcome. In 1985, after their initial product development was completed, they literally ran out of money. At the time, they had seven employees, which immediately dropped to four because they could not pay anyone's salary. Yet, they persisted.

One of Intuit's first attempts to market Quicken was through banks. Cook and Proulx had exclusive arrangements with banks in 11 states. While the banks were able to sell a fair number of programs, this was clearly not a long term solution to their marketing problem. In 1985, they introduced an Apple II version of Quicken which had a very positive effect on sales. The original version was for use with IBM compatible personal computers which were, at the time, used mostly by companies. The Apple II was widely used in private homes, the primary market Intuit was targeting.

With no salaries to pay, their expenses were very low and they gradually had a reasonable revenue flow. They began advertising in various computer publications directly to ultimate users and found that for each dollar they spent on advertising they developed two dollars' worth of sales. These ads had another important benefit in that many people reading the ads and deciding to purchase Quicken went to their local computer store seeking a copy. Many of the stores had never heard of Quicken, but because of an obvious demand began stocking it.

Sales grew rapidly and the company very soon was profitable. In 1990, Intuit suddenly became an attractive investment to the California venture capital industry and three funds bought several million dollars of Intuit stock. To Scott's surprise they began getting calls from other funds wanting to get in on the deal—what a change from six years earlier. The final result was that three funds became investors and two of them have representation on the Intuit board of directors.

Interestingly, none of the venture funds' investments went to the company. It went to the early investors, even though small in number, who had waited seven years for a return. Obviously, by this time Intuit sales were growing, their expenses were still quite low and they were very profitable, so suddenly they were able to get bank loans when needed to carry them over the slow periods.

In March 1993, Intuit had a public offering and raised about $30 million, and its stock began trading on NASDAQ.

Over the next few years, Intuit embarked on an aggressive program to expand its offering and started an active program to build sales outside of the United States.

In October 1994, Intuit announced its intention to merge with Microsoft. These discussions were terminated in May of the following year as a result of opposition from the U.S. Justice Department. Microsoft still offers a product competitive with Quicken. But Intuit is one of a small number of companies that continues to thrive after a major attempt by Microsoft to enter its market.

Currently, Intuit has versions of most of its products for use with Windows and Macintosh. Many are upgraded on a regular basis, which generates substantial continuing sales from an existing customer base. A significant part of Intuit revenues come from the sale of supplies and services.

In fiscal 1996, Intuit's sales were more than $530 million and it had about 3,100 employees in the United States and 290 overseas. I recently read that there are about 10 million users of Quicken. While they still have competitors, Quicken is clearly the dominant product in its market.

Intuit also offers a highly rated business version called QuickBooks, for use as an accounting program for small companies, as well as a number of other financial management programs and services. Recent activities of Intuit include a series of mergers, acquisitions and divestitures.

As you can probably guess from my comments, I consider Quicken to be an outstanding product and Intuit to be an outstanding example of how a new company struggled for years to establish itself in an extremely competitive market, and succeeded.

6. Lillian Vernon Corporation

In 1996, Lillian Vernon wrote an autobiographical book titled, *An Eye For Winners, How I Built One of America's Greatest Direct Mail Businesses*. In addition to the personal content, Lillian describes in detail how she started and grew her business—operating for many years almost entirely on her own resources, which were very limited. It is one of the best books on entrepreneurship that I have read and I recommend it highly. It is published by Harper Collins Publishers, Inc.

Lillian Vernon started her business in 1951. Her name at the time was Lilli Menasche Hochberg. Lilli had been raised in Leipzig, Germany, during the early 1930s. She was a child of an affluent Jewish family and her father owned a successful women's wear manufacturing business.

After Hitler came into power in 1933 and began persecuting Jews, her family lost its home and business and moved to Amsterdam. This was followed several years later by a move to the United States. They arrived here in 1937 and lived in upper Manhattan, where her father started a series of businesses—some successful, some not. Lilli and her family became citizens in 1942.

Lilli could speak no English when she arrived in the United States but soon learned the language. She began working at part time jobs at age 14, finished high school and attended New York University for two years. After dropping out of New York University, she married and moved to Mount Vernon, N.Y., where her husband managed a dry goods shop, and Lilli continued to work part time from her home. She also Americanized her name to Lillian. This is where her life as one of our country's most successful woman entrepreneurs began.

At the time of Lillian's marriage women rarely worked—they were expected to stay home, take care of the household, have children and raise a family. However, because she was brought up in a family that owned a number of businesses where she worked regularly, she developed many entrepreneurial qualities. Shortly after her marriage she became pregnant with her first child. She stayed at home during the early period of her pregnancy but soon became bored with the household routine. Her husband's income was sufficient for them to live on but they always had a need for a little more money.

Her father had a leather manufacturing business by then and Lillian had an idea for two unique products that she wanted very much to test to see if the idea could be used to generate money to supplement the family income. The products were a handbag and a belt, and the unique feature was that both were personalized to include the initials of the customer. From their wedding gifts she and her husband had accumulated savings of $2,000, which Lillian used to launch a business.

Since the product was aimed mostly at teenagers she decided to run her first ad in *Seventeen Magazine*. The ad, which she prepared herself, was a fraction of a page and cost $495 dollars for one insertion. Toll-free 800 telephone numbers did not exist at the time and credit cards had not been invented.

Lillian's initial goal was to sell a few hundred purses and belts and, to her complete amazement, within three months she received $32,000 worth of orders for the products, each order accompanied by either a check, cash or money order. Her father made the purses and belts and Lillian went to his plant and personally engraved the initials of the buyers.

She continued to advertise in *Seventeen*, gave birth to the first of two children, and her business continued to thrive.

Lillian was a very methodical person and kept lists of all buyers of her products in a small card file, which later became the basis of her catalog mail order business. A short time after the business got underway, she decided she needed an adding machine to keep track of her finances but she could not afford to buy one. Instead, she visited the manager of a local bank. Of course he would not give her a loan, but he did let her come to his office each Friday morning and sit at the corner of his desk using his adding machine.

By 1954, sales hit $41,000 and her husband left his job to join her in the business. At about the same time Lillian began attending product trade shows to find additional items to sell, including jewelry. Her all-time most popular product, incidentally, which she sold for 45 years, is a monogrammed bookmark. In 1957, Lillian began manufacturing her own jewelry, and in 1960, she incorporated as Vernon Products, Inc., which was changed five years later to Lillian Vernon Corporation.

In 1956, Lillian Vernon published its first four page catalog, which was soon expanded to 32 pages. The mail order business expanded rapidly and by 1970 broke the $1 million mark in revenues. By 1982 sales reached $60 million—all financed by cash flow.

In 1983, Lillian Vernon got her first loan of $13 million but she was able to get out of debt fast. In 1987 the company went public, raising about $28 million, and was listed on the American Stock Exchange. This money was used primarily to build a national distribution center in Virginia Beach in 1988. By 1997, sales exceeded $240 million, and the company employed more than 3,500 people during peak seasons.

Today, Lillian Vernon regularly mails 179 million catalogs each year and ships almost five million packages annually with more than 20 million items. Much of Ms. Vernon's book, which I mentioned earlier, is devoted to the problems of running a mail order business, compiling mailing lists, creating catalogs, finding new and unique products, and identifying market opportunities. These things will not be discussed here.

However, the fact that she started her business with total capital of $2,000 and ran it entirely from internally generated cash flow for many years is the important message I want to convey. Lillian Vernon Corporation is one of the most impressive examples of bootstrap entrepreneurship in the history of this country.

7. Paychex, Inc.

Paychex, Inc. is a payroll service company specializing in providing services to companies with between one and 200 employees. It was founded in 1970 by B. Thomas Golisano and has since grown to become a company with more than 4,000 employees. Paychex has 70 processing branches in 34 states and the District of Columbia. Its sales exceed $350 million and it serves over 260,000 clients. As part of its service, Paychex prints paychecks for its clients and now prints more than two million checks a week.

Golisano is a graduate of Alfred Technology with a degree in business. Before starting Paychex he was sales manager for a payroll service provider, mostly to larger clients. The rest of this section is in the words of Tom Golisano, describing the process he went through creating an extremely successful business that required using almost every type of financing available.

I think the most important thing that drove me to start Paychex was the nature of my prior job. At the time, I was sales manager for a payroll processing firm called Electronic Accounting Systems (EAS). Like the traditional payroll processing providers during the mid 60s and early 70s, most of EAS's marketing and sales effort was directed at companies with between 50 and 500 employees. I think their rationale was that the larger the client, the better the revenue and profit potential for the company.

However, it seems to me that if you drive down any street in the United States today and look at the businesses out there you certainly get the impression that most of them have fewer than 50 employees. One day I went to the library and found a publication called "County Business Patterns." It was put out by the federal government based upon payroll tax returns. I learned that about 98 percent of all American businesses have fewer than 100 employees and 93 percent have fewer than 50.

From this I concluded that there was a market niche out there in which no one had an interest. However, I also concluded that in order to be successful addressing this small company market, you had to do three things differently.

First, you have to make it very easy for small companies to transmit their payroll data to the processor each pay period. Up until that time it was customary to have the client fill out a complex computer input sheet. It was an error prone procedure that required skills most small businesses did not have. Instead of having the client fill out the complex computer input sheet, I decided that it would be great if they could just call in the information on the telephone. A payroll specialist would read the name of each employee and the client would tell them how to process that person's payroll. Any changes in wage rates or exemptions, marital status or address could also be made over the telephone.

A typical client with 20 employees can complete this chore in three or four minutes. It is very simple for the client and it can be done from anywhere.

Next, provide the client with payroll tax returns. Only one company in the country provided that service at the time. In the United States employers are unpaid tax collectors. They are required to collect taxes from their employees and remit the funds to federal, state and local governments on a timely basis. The fines and penalties for non-payment are severe. So I concluded that this could be an important adjunct, or addition, to the preparation of paychecks. To give you an idea of what a difficult chore this is, remember that in New York, a company with five employees must file a minimum of 42 payroll tax returns each year. This is a very onerous task for small firms.

Finally, costs had to be controlled. Payroll processors at the time had a very high minimum processing charge. For example, if you had five people on your payroll, the minimum charge was something like $24 a pay period. This was a large burden for a very small company. My belief was that we could substantially reduce the minimum processing charge and sell our service to many more very small companies. In fact, when Paychex started our minimum charge was $5 for the first five employees. Today it is still less than $10.

I put these three ideas together and went to the management of Electronic Accounting Systems with a proposal to go after this low end market. They rejected my idea. I think they were concerned that certified public accountants (CPAs) would look unfavorably upon a payroll processing firm that prepared payroll tax returns.

My intuition was that they were wrong and that CPAs would look favorably on our doing payroll tax returns. This assumption proved to be correct and CPAs have become an important source of new client referrals for Paychex.

Well, when Electronic Accounting Systems told me they were not interested in this concept I left my job there to start Paychex. When I started Paychex I only had a total of $3,000. Starting a business, even in 1971, with only $3,000 was probably impossible. If I had to do it over again I probably would not, but I felt so secure in what I was doing that even though I did not have enough money, I started anyway. The $3,000 lasted about 30 days. Then I found myself in a situation where I was borrowing money using consumer installment loans from several banks. I borrowed money from relatives, I even used my credit card to meet our payroll on a few occasions. I did all the things undercapitalized companies must do to survive. I was not able to get out of debt until 1977 or 1978.

It only took me a couple of weeks to get my first customer. Getting customers was not as big an issue with me as it might be in other cases because I had two years' experience in selling payroll service and I knew the market was there. The credibility issue was a bigger problem because here I was starting out as the new payroll processing company in town with zero clients. That was an issue during the first few months but after we had 30 or 40 clients it became much easier.

I did not put Paychex offices in other cities until 1974. It happened as a result of a comment made by a friend of mine who worked at EAS with me. This friend walked into my office one day and said, "Tom, it looks like this Paychex is going to be successful. How can I get involved?" I came up with the idea that we could each put in some money and start a corporation in which we each had 50 percent ownership. It was to be located in Syracuse, N. Y. and patterned after Paychex. It was a joint venture partnership—a separate company.

A few months later, an employee of one of our clients walked into my office and said to me, "This service is terrific—it can be sold in other cities. I want to go down to Miami, Fla., and start a Paychex office there." I said "That's great. I would like to be partners with you." He said, "No, I don't want to be your partner, but I will be your franchisee." So we put together a very loose franchise agreement and he moved to Miami and started a Paychex operation down there.

After these two offices got going I could see that it could be done and represented an opportunity. I began the process of going out and finding people to start Paychex offices in other parts of the country.

Over the next four years, this approach evolved into 11 joint ventures and six franchise operations. The total cost on the average to get a new Paychex office to the break-even point was somewhere between $35,000 and $50,000. If it were a franchise, the franchisee had to pay all of it. In the case of a joint venture we split whatever amount it turned out to be. The people in Washington, D.C. got it going for $22,000; that was the lowest. I think the highest was more than $100,000. It was a matter of the capability of the person and how fast he or she could build sales volume.

Before long, I decided that it would be very desirable to have a single integrated company and bring the joint ventures and franchises back into the parent. There were a number of factors for this decision. The first thing I began to realize was that even though these people that I got involved with were very entrepreneurial and very aggressive, I started to notice a difference in their ambition level. Some of the people were very aggressive in opening multiple office locations and others only wanted to open one and rest on their laurels. That began to bother me because I started to see some undeveloped territory.

The second thing I realized was that some of the people were very good in the sales side of our business but not very good operationally and vice versa. So we were not doing a very good job of skill matching.

The third reason was that these individual corporations, even though they were working, were very weak. It was very difficult for them to buy computers and to upgrade offices; it was just a weak environment in which to operate.

And fourth, no one had given any thought to how they would cash out when the appropriate time came. I think many entrepreneurs never think about this when they start their venture.

I needed to integrate these independent business units. I wrote a business plan and sent it out to the group in early December 1978. It was an outline for a consolidation of the 18 separate Paychex operations. It included spending three years building the sales organization to open new markets and the next two years concentrating on building profitability. The end goal was to either become a publicly owned corporation or to merge.

Of course, when I presented this plan it created a lot of consternation and generated many telephone calls because the people really did not understand my rationale. Just a year or two earlier I had encouraged them to become entrepreneurs and now I was suddenly telling them we should consolidate. I was suggesting we should combine into one larger company and that we should all be shareholders and employees of that company.

In February 1979, we all met around a big table down in the Bahamas and spent an entire day discussing the virtues and downsides of this kind of consolidation. The next morning we sat around the big table again and I went around the room asking each person whether or not they would agree to this consolidation. They all agreed to it.

One key question they all had was how much stock each one of them would receive for their contribution to the new corporation. That was done by formula by myself and two others. The final point we reached was that once we announced how much stock each one of the individuals was going to get in this new corporation we did not allow any negotiation. I knew as soon as I allowed one person to negotiate and change his or her stock allocation every one of them would be standing outside the door and the task never would have been accomplished. I just decided I was going to stand firm and it was going to be take it or leave it.

One thing I did was to give the people the option of continuing on their own if they chose. If a person decided they did not want to become part of this new venture, we guaranteed them we would not open a Paychex branch in their city. Fortunately, none of the group decided to continue on their own.

While Paychex was growing, there were several people outside the company on whom we leaned for advice and counsel. In 1981, the University of Rochester and the Hambrecht & Quist Venture Capital Fund bought substantial equity stakes in Paychex. This was before we became a public company. Those two organizations had people, namely Phil Horsley at the University of Rochester and Grant Inman at Hambrecht & Quist, who became members of our board of directors.

They are both still on our board, and in addition to their expertise in the area of general management, they had great expertise in the area of finance and going public. Their relationship with Wall Street and stock analysts has been extremely helpful to us.

The money the University of Rochester and Hambrecht & Quist invested to get a stake in Paychex did not go to the corporation. It went to existing shareholders. The real benefit was that it gave some of our shareholders liquidity before we had a public offering. That was very important because many of us had gone for many years without any way to cash in.

We never brought in any additional equity capital before we went public. We borrowed money from banks and at one point our loans were even classified. We used every method available to raise capital. Everything from home equity loans to family borrowing to borrowing from banks to borrowing larger amounts from banks to venture capital to going public. I think we used them all.

In 1983, Paychex became a publicly owned company. We did it for a number of reasons. Obviously, most important was to provide liquidity for our shareholders. By then we had approximately 85 or 90 shareholders with varying stakes in the company. This included the original joint venture people and franchisees who each owned from 2 to 6 percent of the company. The other outside shareholders had been very patient and very supportive, but it was time to do something to give them their rewards.

Another reason we went public was that we were able to raise about $7 million for the company, which we immediately spent in developing a greatly improved online computer system. This gave us a great economic advantage in offering our payroll services. Also, it gave us more visibility and more credibility with our customers.

Finally, being a public corporation made it easier to recruit key employees. A publicly owned company gives the perception that you are more stable and will probably have a longer existence. You also have the additional benefit that you can give employees more visible incentives such as stock options, which are very important.

To this day, I never regretted the decision to go public. Some people say that dealing with the Securities and Exchange Commission (SEC) is a problem. Fortunately, we had a chief financial officer, Tom Clark, who was responsible for maintaining a good relationship with the SEC and making sure we were always in complete compliance.

Also, we always looked at the Wall Street community as providing us with a sense of discipline. You hear a lot of CEOs tell how burdensome it is to run their company on a year-to-year, quarter-to-quarter basis. We have never looked at it that way. We think the outside investor market gives us a structure and discipline and makes us focus better on our responsibilities. Quite frankly, I have never felt that being a public corporation had any negatives.

It is of interest that the market we serve is not becoming saturated, even though we have many new competitors. If you add up all the companies doing payroll processing in the United States, combined they have less than 14 or 15 percent of the total market. The rest of the market is still doing its payroll manually or has some sort of in-house system.

It remains almost a virgin territory. Paychex, with 260,000 clients, has about 3 percent of the market we serve and seven years ago we had 3 percent of the market we served. Remember that many Fortune 500 companies are downsizing. People are starting small companies today who would not have considered it 10 or 15 years ago. Even though Paychex has a great track record of client growth over the last 10 years, we are only growing at about the same rate that the market is growing.

I view Paychex as being a niche based company—we concentrate on our offering and we concentrate on our target market. I think if you analyze all the great companies of the world you will find a similar quality.

We made the decision years ago, as we consolidated the franchisees and joint ventures, that we would focus on geography with current payroll products. Rather than diversifying into other services, we knew we could establish more branch offices selling the same product and make money at it. So the theme was to do it in as many geographic areas as possible and build the distribution network. Then we would have a client base that we could sell additional products and services to. The ability to sell additional products to existing customers is a lot easier than selling new products to new customers but we tried to find the right time to make that move.

In recent years we have expanded the services we offer our clients. The other things we now offer include employee handbooks; Section 125 Cafeteria Plans; and administration of health, workman's compensation and disability insurances. We also offer other employee type products, even as basic as writing job descriptions and the posters that go on the company billboards regarding state labor laws.

Now, of course, Paychex no longer has any trouble borrowing and the banks are seeking us rather than chasing us away. Also, with the rapid growth and good profit that we have had recently, cash flow from operations covers much of our capital needs.

8. Yeaple Corporation

Yeaple Corporation was started by Ron Yeaple in 1975. At the time, Yeaple was on the faculty in the MBA program at the University of Rochester. Before he started teaching he held various management positions at Sybron Corp., Xerox and General Dynamics.

Yeaple's first product was a personal audio output device for use in stereo systems in place of loudspeakers or headphones. It was called the "Yeaple Personal Speaker System." The market he addressed included people who wanted to listen to excellent quality audio without bothering others in the same room using a device that did not attach them to the stereo system and was not as uncomfortable as headphones.

The system consisted of a plastic panel about 10 inches high and 21 inches wide bent to create an arc of about 45 degrees parallel to the floor. There was a 4-inch loudspeaker near each end of the plastic arc. This unit was supported by an adjustable stand which held the speaker unit behind a chair or sofa on which the listener was seated. The listener's head would rest comfortably inside the curved plastic head support and the there would be speaker just a few inches from each ear.

Because of something called the near-field effect, the listener would hear excellent low frequency (bass) sound as well as higher frequency (treble) sound. However, because their ears were so close to the speakers the volume could be set low enough so as not to disturb others in the same room. And because their head was not literally attached to the system by a cable they were free to move around, could hear other sounds in the room and could get up and down without removing a set of headphones.

Ron started the business with $5,000 of his own money. Then he had a private equity placement and raised an additional $50,000 by selling units of $5,000 each to individual investors. I bought two units for $10,000. This money was used to design the device and build some models. These were sent to reviewers in several stereo publications and the reviews were all excellent.

I purchased one of his systems for use in my home. Its performance was excellent and after almost 20 years I still have it in my living room. Unfortunately, the system never caught on in the home stereo market and after selling only a handful of units he terminated the program.

Yeaple's second product was a stereo pillow to use while listening to music in bed without disturbing your spouse. Again, the speakers were close to the listeners ears and the quality of the sound was very good. He sold about 1,200 of these, mostly to bed manufacturers and retailers at very low margins. One of the main uses was to make sales pitches in show rooms. Again this product did not catch on in the mass home stereo market.

His final product was completely unrelated to the stereo business. It was a device that dentists could use to test patients for periodontal diseases. Again, his product was only moderately successful, the main market being dental researchers rather than family dentists. He sold a fair number at good prices, but eventually Yeaple Corporation sold this dental business to another company and ceased operations.

During the life of his company, Yeaple rarely took a salary and worked mainly evenings and weekends while continuing his teaching career as a source of income to support himself and his family. Even though the dental business eventually became profitable, Yeaple finally concluded that the likelihood of the business growing to the point where it would provide a decent return to its investors was very small.

You might ask why I am telling this story about a little company that did not achieve nearly the success we had all hoped for before it ceased operations. The reason is that during these very difficult years one day I received an envelope in the mail from Ron. It was a check for $10,000, the amount of my original investment. Most of this was accumulated as a result of Ron's working for no salary during most of the life of the business.

I told Ron it was not necessary to return my money because I invested understanding the risk. He said he felt a strong, continuing obligation to his shareholders and did not think it was appropriate for him to begin taking a salary while the probability of their getting a decent return was small. He actually apologized for not being able to include interest or some capital gain.

In all of my experience as an entrepreneur and as an investor in new businesses, I have never known of another person who took their responsibility to their shareholders as seriously as Ron Yeaple. This action was an important lesson for me. Ron Yeaple is an honorable person who has my greatest respect.

9. Microchip Technology, Inc.

The following example is very unusual. It was brought to my attention by a friend of mine, Paul Brentlinger, a partner of Morgenthaler Ventures. It is unlikely that readers of this book will be involved in similar situations. However, it so fascinated me that I thought it might be a good example of how innovative a person with imagination can be when trying to get a business going.

The story began a number of years ago when a company named General Instrument (GI) entered the semiconductor business. GI was headquartered in New York City at the time and has since moved to Chicago. Its main business is the design and manufacture of equipment for the cable television industry. It owned a business unit, located in Phoenix, Ariz., that designed and manufactured field programmable 8-bit microprocessors. Initially, their main market was for computer type games and several other similar applications.

I do not know whether GI started this business from scratch or acquired it as a going operation through merger or purchase. However, the business began to have problems and hired as the head of the unit a man who had formerly been in charge of all of the very successful semiconductor operations of a major corporation. Shortly after he arrived, the unit was reorganized as a wholly-owned subsidiary of GI with the name of Microchip Technology, Inc.

He did a good job running the new subsidiary, but in several years GI made the decision that this was a business that it should not be in and put it up for sale. However, no willing buyers were found.

The manager of the unit knew some people in the venture capital industry and approached them with some ideas about spinning off GI's micro-processor subsidiary, Microchip Technology, as an independent company. His goal was to develop new products as well as new applications for existing products.

In 1989, three large venture capital funds bought into his idea and invested $12 million in a new independent company as working capital. But the most unique thing about the deal was that GI agreed to give its microprocessor unit to the new company free of charge. The cost of giving it away was apparently less than the cost of closing it down. The new company retained the Microchip Technology name. It received all of the assets of the business and assumed all of its liabilities. A short time later, three other venture funds invested several million dollars more in the new business for working capital.

Microchip then developed several new lines of semiconductor products in addition to the microprocessors. The markets that Microchip now serves includes automobiles, hand tools, telephones, pagers, answering machines, and many others.

By 1992, the company had sales of more than $70 million and was profitable. In 1993, it had more than 500 original equipment manufacturer (OEM) customers and sold to more than 4,000 other customers worldwide through distributors.

Its customers and end users included Sony, Whirlpool, Samsung, Mercedes Benz, Panasonic, Apple Computer, Northern Telecom, United Technologies and General Electric. They had plants in Chandler, Ariz., and Kaohsiung, Taiwan.

Another interesting aspect of this situation results from the existence of a balance sheet item known as good will. If a company acquires another company for a price higher than the selling company's net-worth, the difference is known as good will and is normally shown as an asset which must be written off over the next several years. This results in a decrease in the profits of the buying company.

In the Microchip deal, the good will was negative because the cost was zero, but the company to which it was given had a significant net worth. Writing off negative good will results in an increase in profits for several years.

In 1993, just four years after Microchip became independent, they went public and raised $19.5 million at a price of $13 a share. (Taking three subsequent 3 for 2 splits into account, this is equivalent to about $3.85 a share.) After underwriting costs, this resulted in the company's realizing proceeds of more than $15.7 million and a number of selling shareholders realizing more than $2.4 million.

Since then, the stock has been trading on NASDAQ. While the price of Microchip stock, as in most high-tech companies, has had its ups and downs, generally it has done very well. Through the past 12 months the stock price has been more than $40 and was quoted at $35 in early May 1997, as this example was being written.

The overall result is that the venture fund investors have done very well as have some executives of the company, who either owned stock or had options. You do not see deals like this every day but I am told that they are not all that unusual in the institutional venture capital fund industry. The opportunity for fast growth in a large market in a company with experienced management is usually considered a very attractive investment situation.

For someone heading up a subsidiary of a large corporation, this Microchip example might be viewed as a way to get a new business started.

10. Sea Creations

Sea Creations is a nautical gift shop located in Port Jefferson, Long Island. It was purchased by a woman named Susan Hoeffner in 1987. Susan was raised on Long Island in a middle-class family and has a degree in advertising from Farmingdale State University. Her husband, Lee, was also raised on Long Island and has an engineering degree from Hofstra University. They have two children.

This story starts in 1973 when Susan and Lee bought a Carvel franchise located in Setauket. Carvel is a national chain of ice cream specialty shops. The Hoeffners paid $70,000 for the franchise. When I asked her where they got that kind of money she said that only $20,000 was in cash and the remainder was paid to Carvel on the installment plan over six years. Then I asked her where they got $20,000 and she said it was a combination of savings and money they made on the stock market, mostly from a very good investment in Coca-Cola.

Running a Carvel ice cream shop is very hard work. They are open seven days a week, usually for 10 or 12 hours a day. But it provided them with a good family income.

After eight years they concluded that they had had enough of the ice cream business and decided to sell their franchise. Guess what? They sold it for $195,000, about half in cash and the remainder payable over several years.

Then, together with Susan's brother and his wife, they purchased a restaurant named Country Kettle, located in Stony Brook, for about $45,000, which they ran for about two years. They then sold the restaurant for $100,000, another very profitable transaction.

At this point, Susan and Lee both took some courses and entered the residential real state business. Since Lee's interest was in buying and selling real estate, not the brokerage business, a short time later he took a position as a building inspector. After that he became administrator of the Village of Lake Grove, also on Long Island, a position he still holds.

Susan shifted from residential real estate to commercial real estate and in 1987 came across a small shell shop in Port Jefferson that was for sale. For those not acquainted with that area of New York, Port Jefferson is on the north shore of Long Island, right on the sound, and is the southern end of a ferry line that runs between there and Bridgeport, Conn. The price was $55,000 and at the time the shell shop was grossing about $110,000 a year.

For some reason I thought shell shops bought their products from people who picked up shells walking on Long Island beaches. This is not the case. The shells are normally purchased from distributors who get them from places like the Philippines, Florida, Japan, India and Africa.

One of Susan's first moves was to drastically change the product mix of the business to include jewelry and other gifts with a nautical motif. Within a year or so the sales volume increased from $110,000 a year to almost $230,000.

Her store was located in a small mini-mall and the owner of the adjacent shop decided to move his business. Susan rented his store, which about tripled her space. Her sales volume is now about $330,000 a year. The shop is open seven days a week, but the hours are somewhat less than those of the ice cream business. She has three or four part-time employees helping her run the shop.

The character of her business is now much different than the business she bought. Only about 15 percent of sales are from shells, about 40 percent from jewelry and the rest from gifts. But the thrust of the business is still all nautical.

The income from this business is very good because there are no other shell shops nearby and Susan is a very shrewd and hard working business person. Recently there have been many articles in the business media and even a book suggesting that "entrepreneurs are made not born." I do not think this is true in Susan's case, she is an excellent example of a born entrepreneur. And I can very proudly say, she is also my niece.

11: Jolt Cola

Jolt Cola was founded in 1985 by C.J. Rapp at age 25. The product on which he based the company was a soft drink named Jolt. What differentiated it from other soft drink beverages at the time is best described in the company's motto, "Twice the caffeine." This strategy was, of course, almost the exact opposite of other soft drink companies, which were emphasizing low sugar and no caffeine.

Rapp has a BA in sociology from the State University in Potsdam, N.Y. He said, however, that his degree was really in night life and ice hockey. After college he worked for a plastics division of Beatrice Foods, and later worked for an ingredients supplier named Sweeteners Plus.

When he started Jolt, Rapp's target market was young people. Today, these same folks are referred to as Generation X. In fact, they are people 16 to 32 years of age. More importantly, they are people who live a very hectic life style and want a product that provides the stimulation they need.

Rapp's initial financing was his personal savings, a six-figure loan from his father and about $100,000 of equity investment from 12 private investors. The loan from his father was paid back exactly two months after the first case of Jolt was sold.

At present, Rapp still owns an estimated 88 percent of the company and the remainder is still owned by the initial investors. His company owns no bottling plants; instead, the finished goods are purchased from contract manufacturers. This process substantially reduces the need for large amounts of operating capital.

I recall vividly when Jolt first announced its high caffeine cola. The product was so unusual that it received a huge amount of national publicity both in the press and on national radio and television talk shows. It was featured on the show *Late Night With David Letterman*. Even Bill Gates mentioned the success of Jolt Cola during an interview on MTV.

More recently Jolt products have been seen being consumed by members of the cast on television shows such as *Murphy Brown, Lois & Clark* and *Suddenly Susan*, as well as in motion pictures such as *Jurassic Park* and *Hackers*. This publicity provides the company an incredible amount of national visibility at virtually no cost.

Establishing a new soft drink in traditional channels of distribution, such as super markets and restaurants, is a large challenge for a small company. Because of the huge amount of publicity it received and the immediate acceptance by its target consumer, Rapp was fortunate to gain retail shelf space and acceptance in eating establishments more from a "pull strategy" than a "push strategy." When it became clear that Jolt was a product having genuine consumer demand, it became much easier to gain distribution.

Over the past 12 years, Rapp has increased sales for his company by following several strategies. First was to add several additional products to its line of soft drinks; some of these products contain ingredients that have boost similar to caffeine, and some are products that are simply described as premium. Examples include XTC Energy Drink, Pirate's Keg gourmet root beer and Blu Botol natural water.

A second strategy was to enter the international market. Initially, Jolt targeted only the United States and Canada. But after achieving considerable success in Japan, they decided to expand throughout Asia and Europe. At present, one or more of their products is sold in 22 countries. With Jolt being in the forefront, the company believes it will do business in more than 30 countries by the turn of the century.

Another source of revenue comes from the fact that Jolt has licensed several companies to use the Jolt name and logo on nonbeverage products. Among others this includes energy bars, candy, snowboards, sporting accessories and apparel. Together this concept provides additional revenue and helps create consumer awareness.

In view of the diversified product line, they changed the name of the company and the consumer imagery. It is now Global Beverage Company—makers of Wet Planet Beverages. Global Beverage Company should sound important to their distributors and suppliers. Wet Planet Beverages should sound fun to their consumers.

Because it is a private and closely held corporation, obtaining financial data is not possible. But analysts estimate company sales exceed $10 million. To date, all of this growth was accomplished with the original $200,000 financing. The company is entirely debt free. The instant popularity of Jolt generated a near-immediate positive cash flow. As a result, the growth of Jolt has been accomplished primarily through internally generated cash flow. For a company that does business in 22 countries, many are surprised to learn that it has only 18 employees.

How about the future? Rapp mentioned that he has been approached by several underwriters who suggest that he take the company public. To date, he has declined all offers. Whether Rapp can continue this strategy in the future depends on a number of factors. For instance, Coca-Cola and Pepsi have recently introduced products that are more competitive with Jolt.

Jolt is an excellent example of a company, started on what can only be considered a financial shoe string, that built itself to be a substantial competitive force in the soft drink market with an extraordinary product targeting a unique market niche. I do not know whether C.J. Rapp conducted any formal market research at the time he started the company, or whether he depended on his personal judgment alone. Rapp's judgment said that it would be a success, and he was right.

12. HCR Corporation

Health Care Resources (HCR) was founded by Louise Woerner in 1978. HCR, headquartered in Rochester, N.Y., *with a branch in Washington, D.C., provides home health care services and health information and consulting services.*

Home care services include nursing care, five types of therapeutic services (like physical therapy or speech therapy), complementary services (like massage therapy and nutrition counseling), and assistance with activities for daily living (like bathing and dressing). HCR consulting services are provided to clients like the U.S. Public Health Service and the National Institute of Health. Several years ago, after very serious heart surgery, I used HCR's services for a number of weeks and I cannot describe how valuable it was.

HCR is the only privately held home care organization in New York state where health care institutions and home care agencies are dominated by, and in some cases limited to, not-for-profit organizations. HCR's leadership position in home care is illustrated not only by its growth (employing about 700 people today), but by such factors as its participation in programs sponsored by the US Public Health Service. Also, HCR was selected by Mosby (the leading health care publisher) to write the practice guidelines for home care in high risk maternal and child health.

Louise Woerner holds an MBA from the University of Chicago Graduate School of Business. She was one of the early women to attain this degree, graduating in 1965. Following her graduation, she worked in various management positions for about 15 years. At the time she started HCR she was the executive vice president for J.A. Reyes Associates, Inc., a management consulting firm in Washington, D.C.

One of the early problems Woerner encountered was the regulation of health care in New York state, which was revised to cover home care after she started the business. Woerner decided to pursue the highest credential in the industry, even though New York had limited that designation to not-for-profits. But they failed to realize that Louise Woerner is a determined woman. After a three year effort she got the state to revise its rules and regulations and HCR became the first for-profit certified home health agency in the state, paving the way for other for-profit organizations.

In recalling how I obtained financing for the start up of my business it is hard not to note how old I am, which I do not intend to do. In 1978, interest rates were on their way to an all time high of about 25 percent, there were not as many women business owners as there are today, and health care was a much smaller piece of the gross domestic product. All of these things made it harder to obtain financing.

Bill Stolze indicates in his first book that texts don't always give an accurate indication of how the world works. This was the case for me. Even though I was an MBA with some accumulated assets, including a home and 15 years of professional experience, I could not get the $10,000 I needed to start my health service business.

I financed my business initially from my salary with the management consulting firm. It was clear that the new business could not afford me. Instead, I hired a person junior enough to manage my company at a salary I could afford until cash flow improved.

My office equipment, supplies and decorating budget was about $1,000.

After buying the necessary used desk and chairs, I was left with $20 for amenities. Among my purchases was a poster, which I still have, that said, "You have to labor in the fields before you can reap the harvest." My office was in a basement, which we referred to as the lower level. I also bought a plant and a grow light. The plant died almost immediately. Lack of capital gave me an excellent lesson on making do, which continues to be a useful one. My company always runs lean.

A second source of financing was my line of credit on my MasterCard: $3,000. This could be quite a different story today, when credit card companies send pre-approved cards for tens of thousands of dollars, and many people have many cards. I had one. Just the same, the $3,000 was much needed, and I don't think I would be here today if it weren't for MasterCard.

People talk about underfinancing and I understand the problems it creates. However, it also creates a discipline that is valuable to an organization. Some of our key staff and I still joke about picking paper clips up off the floor.

Innovation was also often the result of having to solve problems creatively. That is another discipline that is with us today, and I continue to be impressed with how easy it is for us to think of innovative ways to produce a result— almost always better than the solution that comes from throwing money at the problem.

A third source of financing was supplier credit. We became expert at collecting our receivables very quickly and working closely with our suppliers so we could use their money to the maximum extent possible. Keeping commitments and communicating well were as important to many suppliers as was very fast payment. We were also loyal customers to the people who worked with us, never undervaluing the relationship that enabled us to use supplier credit when it was necessary.

When the business grew to the extent that internal financing was totally impossible, I began a steady process of looking for a bank to obtain a loan. By this time, I had an established banking relationship for our new business, knew the branch officer, and had receivables.

Just as recommended by the texts, I prepared financial projections to show the bank along with our business plan. We had monthly projections for three years and quarterly projections for the next two years for a total of the magic five years of projections.

The bank with whom we had our accounts was not interested in making us a loan. Here was a good lesson—I should have thought more carefully about how to select our bank for the accounts we had for ourselves and for our employees.

I then began the painful process of looking for a new bank. The important thing to remember is that it just takes one. I worked through the recommendations of our professionals for contacts. Our attorneys and our accountants had people they thought might be interested in the business, but no one was. After about the fourth presentation, I was quite discouraged, but there was no other way to grow my business; I had to continue.

The fifth presentation was to Chase Manhattan, a money center bank that I thought was not at all a fit. Meeting with the officer was certainly an experience. He said he couldn't lend me less than $40,000 (I had wanted $25,000), and he didn't have time to listen to my presentation. He had checked on me through a couple of telephone calls, was satisfied I had the personal collateral as well as the receivables, asked for my personal guarantee, handed me some papers and walked me to the door, so that he could get to some "real" clients.

We enjoyed an excellent relationship with Chase for many years, and I am grateful to them and to several of their key executives for our success and even our survival through a rough spot. Today I find myself beginning another phase. In setting up a related business, I am working with an equity investor. The lessons of the past should stand me in good stead.

Louise Woerner continues to enjoy her hard-earned entrepreneurial success. She was honored by the Rochester Institute of Technology with the Herbert W. VandenBrul Award for Entrepreneurship for "improvements in the economy of the community and for innovative management skills which have changed an industry." She also received the Presidential Award for Entrepreneurial Excellence, which was bestowed upon her by President Reagan in 1986 at the White House Conference on Small Business.

Named one of Rochester, New York's 15 most influential community leaders by the Rochester Democrat & Chronicle, Ms. Woerner's rapidly growing business has sales in the multimillion dollar range.

Summary

In summary, I would like to review what an entrepreneur should do if he or she wants to improve the chances of the business succeeding and of being able to raise the start up capital that will be needed.

For a new business to succeed, it must do many things right, not just raise capital. The strategy of the business must be sound. It is important that you have created an offering, either product or service, that addresses a market with a need for that offering. It is important that you have assembled a management team with the skills and experience needed to run the business. Finally, it is important to remember that raising money, by whatever route you choose, requires selling as well as entrepreneurial skills.

You must identify the things that will be attractive to potential investors or lenders and present them in a way that convinces them that your chances of succeeding are good. Here are some of the questions you should ask:

1. Should I start the business alone or with a team? Many people starting a business have never run a business before and are unlikely to have all of the necessary skills. Starting a company with a small group of others with skills that complement yours will, in my opinion, greatly improve your chances of success. Bringing together what I call a Mr./Ms. Inside and Mr./Ms. Outside can combine people who have product or service skills with people who have marketing, management and financing skills.

2. What is my distinctive competence? You should try very hard to identify some distinctive competence that you or the members of your team have that can serve as the basis of the business. This is often the idea for the product or service upon which the business will be based, but it can also be other things such as marketing skills, financing skills, etc. You do not have to be good at everything, but you must be very good at something.

3. What advantages do small businesses have? Another good thing to do is to analyze the large companies with which you will undoubtedly be competing and try to identify areas in which they have a natural advantage over small companies. Large company advantages usually are the result of access to large amounts of capital.

Then try to identify the things the small companies can do that give them a natural advantage over large companies. Small company advantages could include a willingness to accommodate the unique requirements of small groups of customers and the flexibility to move fast on almost every problem a business faces. The start up business should obviously emphasize those things where they have a natural advantage and avoid those things where the large companies have the advantage.

4. How can I differentiate, concentrate and innovate? These three things are of great importance to a new business. Try to lead—not follow. If your offering is the same as your larger competitor, your only approach to getting more business is to drop your, price and that is the road to Hell.

Then try to find a niche, either in a product niche or a market niche, at which you can excel. Niche strategy is almost always the best basic strategy for a business, regardless of its size. The niche you select should be large enough to provide a reasonable opportunity to

succeed but not so large as to attract too many large company competitors.

It is also very important to find ways to innovate in all aspects of the business. Innovation in product and service are obvious but it is also possible to innovate in pricing, marketing, customer service and many other aspects of the enterprise. These three words, "Differentiate, Concentrate, and Innovate" are of crucial importance in any new business.

5. How do I offer my customers "better value"?. I consider pricing to be one of the fundamental strategic decisions of a new business. People do not make their purchase decisions based upon price alone—they make them based upon value, which includes both benefits and price. If you surround your offering, whatever it may be, with benefits that your customers value, you will be able to sell at a higher price. This means that the likelihood of your business being profitable will increase dramatically.

6. How do I finance the business? Finally, you reach the point where you can intelligently estimate the financial needs of the business. Then you should try to identify sources of capital that might be appropriate and what steps you should take to raise that amount of money.

Interestingly, there are two things that should be kept very much in mind when thinking about the problems of financing a new or growing business. They are, "What can you do to raise more capital?" and, "What can you do to need less capital?"

Notice that securing financing is only one of a number of things entrepreneurs should do to improve their chances of success. Making the decision process even more complex is that some of these decisions are highly interrelated. Assuming that you are satisfied with your strategy on the above list of issues you must then answer the following questions:

1. How much money do I need? This is done best by making a detailed cash flow projection. A crucial point in the life of every new business is when the direction of cash flow goes from negative to positive. This must happen before the firm runs out of money. In its simplest terms, the furthest negative point on the cash flow projection represents the amount of capital the firm needs.

2. How much money can I put into the business myself? Do you have the resources and/or personal borrowing power to supply the amount of money that will be needed to reach the point where cash flow goes from negative to positive or you must raise money from others.

3. What risks am I prepared to take in return for the money I need? and **How much of the ownership in the business am I prepared to give up?** If you need money from outside sources you must then decide the amount you think you can raise from others, either through borrowing or through the sale of a part of the ownership of your business—equity financing. If you sell equity in the business, you must also decide what percentage of the ownership you are prepared to give up in return for the additional capital you think you need.

Finally, you have to decide the best way to close the gap between what you can invest personally and what you need. Remember that most companies during their early years are likely to need to raise money from more than one source. The level of difficulty in getting financial support depends on many factors, but I think it is safe to say that raising money is never easy.

Where do you look?

This discussion assumes that the entrepreneur has determined how much capital is needed to launch the new business. Possible sources of early capital for the entrepreneur include:

1. Personal savings and borrowing. Most entrepreneurs finance the early start up stage of their business with personal savings. If the company is formed by a team, it is their combined personal contributions. This amount of money can often pay the cost of building prototypes of products, limited market research, filing a patent application, incorporating and the preliminary steps of more formal financing.

Service businesses do not require much capital, and I have seen a number of such ventures use only the personal savings of the founder as well as retained earnings of the business. Whether to use your own money rather than seeking outside investors is a complex decision. On one hand you keep complete control; on the other you reduce the financial risk and increase the potential.

2. Borrowing from relatives, friends and business associates. Another source of funding is loans from family, friends or business associates. Borrowing money from this group probably does not require lengthy negotiation. It does represent a very large personal obligation, and could seriously affect your relationship with whomever it is you borrowed from.

3. Banks and other professional lenders. Banks and other professional lenders may be used alone or in combination with other sources. However, this type of borrowing is often difficult to get for a new business. The bank's reward for making a loan is usually limited to interest and it rarely has the opportunity to increase this reward if the company that borrows is exceptionally successful. Any loans you are able to get will probably have to be secured with a personal guarantee, which puts all of your personal assets at risk.

4. Individual venture investors. Individual investors have become a common source of capital in recent years. They are sometimes called "angels." These are usually people who are interested in investing in new businesses, understand and are willing to take the risk and are willing to wait a number of years for a return.

5. Formal (institutional) venture capital funds and small business investment companies. These are another possible source of capital. They can be either private groups or groups backed by the Small Business Administration. Large amounts of money are usually available for investment in new businesses but are often very difficult for an early start up business to get.

6. Corporate venture investor. Another source of capital that may also be an alternative is another company. Many large firms in recent years have established internal venture investing groups, sometimes formal and sometimes informal, that are willing to invest in new businesses. Their goals are to expand their business in a direction that they are already in or as a form of diversification.

7. Going public. Almost every financial expert you are likely to ask will advise you against even thinking about this alternative. However, I know of many companies that have gone public very early using an underwriter or on their own. Recently, the Securities Exchange Commission has eased some of the restrictions on small businesses going public which may make this route more attractive.

8. Federal, state and local governments. The federal government, most state governments and many local governments have financial programs intended to encourage people to start businesses or to help existing businesses grow.

There is no right answer

Which of these approaches is best? It's hard to say. There is seldom a right or wrong answer, and the best you can hope for is an answer that works.

Epilogue

In writing this book, I have tried to include as much of my personal knowledge and experience as possible, as well as the knowledge and experience of others, to help those readers who have ideas for a business and are faced with the problem of financing. The information here is generally of a very practical nature and includes example after example to illustrate the points I am trying to make.

My goal was to identify and discuss some of the key issues that will help improve the chances of your business being a success, in addition to the raising of money. One thing I try to emphasize over and over again is that money isn't everything. There are many things, in addition to raising money, you must do right if you want your business to succeed. These other things mostly involve having good management, having good products and addressing good markets. And if you do all of these other things right raising money will suddenly become much easier.

Remember that there are very few right or wrong answers to the problems of starting and/or financing a business. The best you can hope for are answers that work, and you will never know whether another approach would have had a better result.

Hard work and persistence are important qualities in almost every successful entrepreneur I know. You will find ways to meet and overcome adversity. No one in his or her right mind will suggest that starting, financing, or growing a business is easy. It is not; it is hard. But it can be the most exciting business experience of a lifetime. And when and if you succeed, it can have professional, emotional and financial rewards beyond belief. Also, being an entrepreneur gives you infinitely more freedom to control your own life and your own destiny.

If you found this book helpful, please tell your entrepreneurial friends to read a copy if you think it will be of value to them.

In closing, I wish all of you who are trying to finance the start up or growth phase of a business the best possible success. I hope this book has helped. Please contact me if you have suggestions to help make future editions more valuable. I can be reached through the publisher. Good luck to all of you.

Medium-Sized Institutional Venture Capital Fund Term Sheet

This is a term sheet used by a medium-sized institutional venture capital fund. The fund has asked not to be identified. Most of their investments are in start up or very early ventures. They realize that to some of their potential investees this agreement may seem unnecessarily restrictive and may not be acceptable in its present form. They greatly prefer to discuss the agreement face-to-face with investees so they can explain the reasons for some of the conditions that may seem unreasonable.

Also, this should be viewed as the starting point of the negotiations and may vary depending on many things, such as how far along the company is in the development of its product, whether it has generated any sales, whether it has raised money from other sources, etc.

Start Up Financing

_____ __, 1996

THE TERMS SET FORTH BELOW ARE SOLELY FOR THE PURPOSE OF OUTLINING THOSE TERMS PURSUANT TO WHICH A DEFINITIVE AGREEMENT MAY BE ENTERED INTO AND DO NOT AT THIS TIME CONSTITUTE A BINDING CONTRACT, EXCEPT THAT BY ACCEPTING THESE TERMS _____ (THE COMPANY) AGREES THAT FOR A PERIOD OF 90 DAYS FOLLOWING THE DATE OF SIGNATURE, PROVIDED THAT THE PARTIES CONTINUE TO NEGOTIATE TO CONCLUDE AN INVESTMENT, THEY WILL NOT NEGOTIATE OR ENTER INTO DISCUSSION WITH ANY OTHER INVESTORS OR GROUP OF INVESTORS. AN INVESTMENT IN THE COMPANY IS CONTINGENT UPON, AMONG OTHER THINGS, COMPLETION OF DUE DILIGENCE AND THE NEGOTIATION AND EXECUTION OF A SATISFACTORY STOCK PURCHASE AGREEMENT.

TERM SHEET

I. Issuer:

_____ Corporation
(a _____ "C" Corporation, hereinafter referred to as the "Company").

II. Purchasers:

Venture Fund II, L.P.

_____

_____

(hereinafter collectively referred to as the "Investors")

III. Security: Series A Preferred Stock ("Series A Preferred")

IV. Total Proceeds: $1,250,000

*V. Disbursement
of Proceeds:*

At closing, Investors would advance investment funds as follows:

Venture Funds	$_____
_____	$_____
_____	$_____,000

Pre-money valuation is $2,250,000

VI. Post-Investment
Ownership:

Investors	____%
	____%*
_____	____%*
_____	___%*
Option Pool	10.0%*

* - Common Stock

*The Option Pool would consist of options for shares of Common Stock which would be awarded to current and future employees of the company as an inducement for employment or a reward for achievement. Stock options and all common shares outstanding at closing would vest on a four (4) year schedule. All future options issued by the company for management employees and directors will vest over a four (4) year period following effective issue date.

VII. Closing Date:

Closing for the investment would be targeted for October 31, 1996, provided that all requirements for the closing have been met or expressly waived in writing by the Investors and that sufficient investment capital is available to complete the financing from investors acceptable to   Venture Fund II, L.P.

VIII. Board Representation:

Initially the Board of Directors would consist of not more than seven (7) persons. Holders of Series A Convertible Preferred Stock would be entitled to two (2) representatives on the Company's Board of Directors one of which will be selected by   Venture Funds, II, L.P.   Board of Directors meetings would be scheduled on a monthly basis until such time as the Board of Directors unanimously votes to schedule them less frequently. Additional directors, to include outside industry representatives, or as a condition of securing additional financing, must be acceptable to the Preferred shareholders and the other existing Directors. Such approval will not be unreasonably withheld.

Investors' representatives would be appointed as members of all Board committees (including the compensation committee), each of which would consist of three members. Each Investor would also have the right to one observer at all Board or committee meetings, which observer would be able to participate in discussions, but would not have a vote. The Company would reimburse each Director's reasonable expenses incurred in attending the board meetings or any other activities (e.g., meetings, trade shows) which are required and/or requested and that involve expenses.

Outside directors who are compensated with stock options will vest over a four (4) year period.

IX. *Addition(s) to Management*:
Only if applicable

DESCRIPTION OF SERIES A PREFERRED

X. *General:*
Unless otherwise specified, the Series A Preferred would have rights, preferences and privileges senior to the Common Stock.

XI. *Dividends:*
A 10% dividend would accrue as of the closing date to holders of the Series A Convertible Preferred. Accrued dividends would be payable (a) if, as and when determined by the Company's Board of Directors, (b) upon the liquidation or winding up of the company, or (c) upon redemption of the Series A Preferred. No dividends may be declared and/or paid on the Common Stock until all dividends have been paid in full on the Convertible Preferred Stock. The Convertible Preferred Stock would also participate parri passu in any dividends declared on Common Stock. Dividends will cease to accrue in the event that the Investors convert their holdings to Common Stock.

XII. *Liquidation Preference:*
In the event of any liquidation, dissolution or winding up of the Corporation, whether voluntary or involuntary, the holders of Series A Preferred Stock would be entitled to receive, prior and in preference to any distribution of the assets or surplus funds of the Corporation to the holders of the Common Stock the amount of $_____ (purchase price) per share of Series A Preferred Stock (as adjusted for any combinations, consolidations, stock distributions or stock dividends with respect to such shares) plus all unpaid dividends on such shares for each share of Series A Preferred Stock then held by them. If upon the occurrence of such event, the assets and funds distributed among the holders of Series A Preferred Stock would be insufficient to permit the payment of the full preferential amount, then the distribution would be distributed among the holders of the Series A Preferred Stock, ratably based upon their relative liquidation preferences per share. After the payment of such liquidation preference, the holders of the Series A Preferred Stock would share on a prorata basis with the holder of all other Capital Stock of the Corporation in any available distributions.

A consolidation or merger of the Company or sale of all or substantially all of its assets would be deemed to be a liquidation or winding up for purposes of the liquidation preference unless the net proceeds of such sale, consolidation or merger of the Company were in excess of $20,000,000 and the per share consideration following such transaction is greater than the current liquidation preference of the Series A Preferred, in which event automatic conversion would take place.

XIII. Conversion:

Right to convert: Each share of Series A Preferred Stock would be convertible, at the option of the holder, at any time after the issuance of such share, into such number of fully paid and non-assessable shares of Common Stock as is determined by dividing an amount equal to the Series A per share purchase price plus all declared but unpaid dividends on each share of Series A Preferred Stock by the then applicable Series A Conversion price in effect on the date the certificate is surrendered.

XIV. Automatic Conversion:

The Series A Preferred would be automatically converted into Common Stock, at the then applicable conversion price, upon the sale of the Company's Common Stock in an initial public offering ("Public Offering") at a price equal to or exceeding five (5) times the Series A Preferred original purchase price of $____ per share in an offering which after deduction for underwriter commissions and expenses related to the issuance is not less than twenty million dollars ($20,000,000).

XV. Antidilution Provisions:

In the event of stock splits, stock dividends, reorganizations, mergers, consolidations or sale of assets, there would be a proportional adjustment in the conversion price and in the number of shares of Common Stock to be received upon conversion.

In the event that the Company issues or sells any Common Stock (at any time after the original issue date for the Series A Preferred Stock) or warrants, options, convertible securities or other rights to purchase Common Stock ("Common Stock equivalents") at a price per share less than the then-effective conversion price of the Series A Preferred, the Preferred shares would be provided anti-dilution protection in accordance with the following formula:

$$\text{Conversion Price} = \frac{(P1)(Q1)+(P2)(Q2)}{Q1+Q2}$$

where:

P1 = conversion price in effect immediately prior to such issue;
Q1 = number of shares of Common Stock deemed outstanding before the new issue;
P2 = price per share received by the Company for such issue;
Q2 = number of shares of Common Stock issued or deemed issued in such transaction

The above would not apply to future shares of Common Stock issued for acquisition or future shares of Common Stock issued for management options; both of these events would, however, require joint approval of the Series A Investors.

XVI. Voting Rights:

The holders of each share of Series A Preferred Stock would be entitled to the number of votes equal to the number of shares of Common Stock into which such share of Series A Preferred Stock could be converted and would have voting rights and powers equal to the voting rights and powers of the Common Stock.

XVII. Restrictions and Limitations:

Consent of at least 66 ⅔% of the Series A Preferred, voting as a separate class would be required for any actions which:

i) alter or change the rights, preferences or privileges of the Series A Preferred;

ii) increase the authorized number of shares of Series A Preferred;

iii) increase the authorized number of shares of any other class of Preferred Stock;

iv) create any new class or series of stock which has preference over or is on parity with the Series A Preferred;

v) involve a merger, consolidation or reorganization or sale of all or substantially all of the assets or sale of more than 50% of the Company's stock, or;

vi) involve a repurchase or other acquisition of shares of the Company's stock other than pursuant to redemption provisions described below under "Redemption".

vii) amend the Company's charter or bylaws.

XVIII. Redemption:

After five (5) years and at the request of the holders of at least 66 ⅔% of the Series A Preferred, all or part of the Series A Preferred shares may be redeemed at the higher of a) 110% of the purchase price plus all accrued but unpaid dividends, b) book value or c) fifteen (15) times the previous two fiscal years' average after-tax earnings.

XIX. Conditions precedent to Investors' obligation to invest:

(i) Legal documentation satisfactory to Investors and Investors counsel.

(ii) Satisfactory completion of due diligence.

(iii) Approval by   Venture Fund II, L.P. and the Boards of Directors of the other investors participating in the contemplated financing.

(iv) Before closing, the Company would obtain employment agreements with key employees which would include satisfactory (to Investors) non-compete, non-disclosure and vesting language.

(v) The Company would obtain and maintain life insurance on _____ in an amount equal to the total amount of the investment, with proceeds payable for the benefit of the Company, with rights of the Series A Preferred Investors to put shares to the Company.

(vii) Any debt including interest accrued thereon owed by the Company to any members of management would be converted to equity prior to the first closing. Any other debt to principals, key employees and/or founders would also be converted unless such cases are discussed and approved in advance of the completion of the legal documentation and included therein.

XX. Founder's Shares:

The unvested portion of these shares may be repurchased by the Company at the sole discretion of the Board of Directors upon employee's death, disability or dismissal for cause, or if employee voluntarily resigns. Under any of the foregoing circumstances, the price paid for the unvested shares will be determined as follows: (1) Shares repurchased upon death or disability will be at a price equal to the fair market value as determined by an independent appraiser, (2) Shares repurchased following dismissal for cause or voluntary resignation will be at employee's average cost per share.

Cause shall be defined as:

a) conviction in a court of law of any crime;

b) willful violation of specific and lawful directions from the Board of Directors of _____ or excessive absenteeism which persists for a period of thirty days after a written notice is given of such absenteeism or violation;

c) fraud as determined in a court of law;

d) a material failure of the founder to perform or observe the provisions of his employment agreement which persists for a period of thirty days after a written notice is given of such failure to perform or observe;

e) breach of any of the covenants or obligations contained in the final agreements negotiated as part of this agreement which persists for a period of thirty days after a written notice is given of such breach;

In the event that a sale, merger or IPO of the company is completed with the approval of the majority of the Preferred shareholders, then those shares that are unvested shall be considered as having been fully vested at the time of such sale or merger.

For purposes of this agreement, management's cost for their shares (____% of the common stock equivalents) at closing shall be deemed to be valued at $_____ per share.

XXI. Registration Rights:

The Investor would have the following registration rights with respect to their shares:

(i) Two long-form demand registrations at the Company's expense.

(ii) Unlimited piggyback rights, except that the underwriter would have the right to limit what is sold, so market price is not adversely affected.

In addition the founders will also get unlimited piggyback rights subordinate only to those of the Investors.

(iii) Semi-annual S-2 or S-3 demand registrations (or short-form registrations), if the company qualifies for the use of such short-form registration statements, at the Company's expense.(iv) The Company would not grant new piggyback rights or other registration rights unless they are subordinated to those granted to the Investors.

(v) The Company would comply with all necessary requirements to enable the Investor and any transferees to sell shares under Rule 144 after an initial public offering or if the Company otherwise becomes an SEC reporting company.

XXII. Right of First Refusal:

Holders of Series A Preferred and management would be offered, on a prorata basis and on the same terms as offered to or negotiated by third parties, the right to purchase all or any portion of equity securities (or rights to acquire equity securities, such as warrants, options, convertible debt, etc.) as the company may propose to offer. Such first refusal rights would not apply to shares of Common Stock reserved for employees via stock options or shares of Common Stock issuable upon conversion of the Series A or Series A Preferred or for shares issued for an acquisition which have been approved by the Series A Preferred shareholders.

In the event that any of the holders of Common or Preferred Stock proposes to sell or otherwise transfer any shares of stock of the company, or any interest in such shares, the Series A Preferred Investors and management would have a prorata right of first refusal on such shares, on the same terms as offered to the selling shareholders by any third party.

XXIII. Right of Co-Sale:

In the event that certain employee-shareholders desire to sell some or all of their Common shares to another party, Investor would have the right to sell its prorata shares on the same terms.

XXIV. Covenants:

The following would not be authorized without majority approval of the Board of Directors:

(i) Capital expenditures (including expenditures under capitalized leases) in excess of $100,000 in any fiscal year or any single capital expenditure exceeding $25,000.

(ii) Dividends paid on Common Shares.

(iii) Issuance of capital stock or securities convertible into capital stock.

(iv) Any debt which would increase the company's total indebtedness by more than $50,000 in any fiscal year.

(vi) Establishment of or investment in any subsidiary.

XXV. Monitoring Covenants:

The Company would furnish to the Investor the following:

(i) Monthly reports. Within 20 days following the end of each month, an income statement, cash flow and balance sheet for the prior monthly period. Statements would include year-to-date figures compared to budgets, with variances delineated.

(ii) Annual Financial Statements. Within 90 days following the end of the fiscal year, an unqualified audit, together with a copy of the auditor's letter to management, from a Big Six accounting firm or equivalent, which firm would be approved by the Investor.

(iii) In the event the Company fails to provide monthly reports and/or financial statements in accordance with the foregoing, Investor would have the authority, at the Company's expense, to request an audit by an accounting firm of its choice, such that statements are produced to the satisfaction of the Investor.

(iv) Annual Budget. At least 60 days before the end of each fiscal year, a budget, including projected income statement, cash flow and balance sheet, on a monthly basis for the ensuing fiscal year, together with underlying assumptions and a brief qualitative description of the company's plan by the Chief Executive Officer in support of that budget.

(v) Non-compliance. Within 10 days after the discovery of any default in the terms of the stock purchase agreement, or of any other material adverse event, a statement outlining such default or event, and management's proposed response.

XXVI. Purchase Agreement

The purchase of the Company's Series A Preferred Stock would be made pursuant to a Series A Convertible Preferred Stock Purchase Agreement drafted by counsel to the Investors which would be mutually agreeable to the Company and the Investors. This agreement would contain, among other things, appropriate representations and warranties of the Company, covenants of the Company reflecting the provisions set forth herein and other typical covenants, and appropriate conditions of closing, including among other things, qualification of the shares under applicable Blue Sky laws, the filing of a certificate of amendment to the Company's charter to authorize the Series A Preferred, and an opinion of counsel. Until the Purchase Agreement is signed, there would not exist any binding obligation on the part of either party to consummate the transaction. This Summary of Terms does not constitute a contractual commitment of the Company or the Investors or an obligation of either party to negotiate with the other.

XXVII. Other:

(i) Legal expenses incurred by the Investors would be paid at closing by the Company from the proceeds of the investment. The Investor would make all reasonable efforts to see that this expense does not exceed $17,500. Once this term sheet is signed _____ would accept responsibility for legal fees incurred by the Investors if the transaction does not close. _____ will also secure a quote from legal counsel which will reflect a cap for services of $_____.

(ii) It is understood that the Investors, in the course of their ordinary business would, from time to time, provide the financial results of their portfolio companies to outside investors and to others whom they deem appropriate. In all such cases, the Investors would exercise their best judgment to protect the confidentiality of the information submitted.

(iii) Initial base salary for _____ would be $_____. Initial base salary for _____ would be $_____. Annual increases would not exceed 10% unless approved unanimously by the compensation committee.

XXVII. Exclusivity:

(i) Upon the acceptance hereof, _____, its officers and shareholders agree not to discuss the sale of any equity or equity type securities, provide any information to or close any such transaction with any other investor or prospective investor, unless Purchaser is unable to close this transaction under similar terms to those contained herein on or before _____ __, 1996, or Purchaser waives its rights under this provision in writing.

(ii) The undersigned agree to proceed in good faith to execute and deliver definitive agreements incorporating the terms outlined above and such additional terms as are customary for transactions of the type described herein. This letter expresses the intent of the parties and is not legally binding on any of them unless and until such mutually satisfactory definitive agreements are executed and delivered by the undersigned. This letter of intent may be signed by the parties in counterparts.

Date _____   By: _____

                          _____
                          President & Chief Executive Officer
                          _____ Corporation

Date _____   By: _____

                          For the Venture Fund

Date _____   By: _____
                                              (Purchaser)

Large Institutional Venture Capital Fund Term Sheet

....

This is a term sheet used by a large institutional venture capital fund—Morgenthaler Ventures, headquartered in Cleveland, Ohio. This agreement seems less objectionable than the term sheet in Appendix I, probably because Morgenthaler usually invests in companies that are further along and somewhat less risky than an early start up.

_____SYSTEMS, Inc.
Sale of Series B Preferred Stock
Summary of Terms

Offering:

666,666 shares of Series B Preferred Stock ("Series B Preferred") of _____Systems, Inc., a Delaware corporation (the "Company"), at a price of $1.50 per share.

Rights,
Preferences,
Restrictions:

(1)   Dividend Provisions: The holders of the Series B Preferred shall be entitled to receive dividends in preference to any dividends on Common Stock and on a pari passu basis with the Series A Preferred Stock at the rate of $0.12 per share per annum when, as and if declared by the Board of Directors out of funds legally available therefor. Dividends shall be non cumulative.

shall

(2)   Liquidation Preference: In the event of any liquidation or winding up of the company, the holders of the Series B Preferred be entitled to receive in preference to the holders of Common and on a pari passu basis with the holders of Series A Preferred, an amount equal to the sum of (a) $1.50 per share of Series B Preferred plus (b) all declared but unpaid dividends on such shares (the "Preferential Amount"). Payment of the Preferential Amount shall be made on a pro rata basis. A merger, consolidation or reorganization in which the company is not the surviving entity shall be treated as a liquidation.

(3)   Conversion: Each holder of Series B Preferred shall have the right to convert its shares at any time into shares of Common at the initial conversion rate of 1:1. The conversion rate shall be subject to proportional adjustments for stock dividends, stock splits and similar recapitalizations.

(4)   Automatic Conversion: Series B Preferred shall be automatically converted into common, at the then applicable conversion rate, upon (a) the closing of a firmly underwritten public offering of shares of Common of the Company; or (b) at the election of holders of the majority of Series A and Series B Preferred, voting together as a class.

(5)   Voting Rights: The holders of each share of Series B Preferred shall have the right to that number of votes equal to the number of shares of Common issuable upon conversion of Series B Preferred. The Series B Preferred shall vote with Common on all matters except as specifically provided herein or as otherwise required by law.

Information Rights:	So long as an investor continues to hold 5% or more of the outstanding shares of the company (on an as-converted basis), the Company shall deliver to the Investor annual and quarterly financial statements. The annual financial statements will be audited by an accounting firm of nationally recognized standing.
Registration: Rights:	(1) Company Registration: The investor shall be entitled to "piggy-back" registration rights on up to 3 registrations of the Company (other than the first such offering, which may be solely for the account of the company); provided, however, that the Company and its underwriters shall have the right to reduce the number of shares proposed to be registered in view of market conditions. In any such cutback, the shares of selling shareholders will be cutback before any shares being sold by the Company.

(2) S-3 Rights: Investors shall be entitled to an unlimited number of demand registrations on Form S-3 (if available to the Company) so long as such registered offerings are in excess of $1,000,000; provided, however, that the Company shall not be required to file more than one Form S-3 Registration in any twelve (12) month period.

(3) Expenses: The Company shall bear the additional registration expenses (exclusive of underwriting discounts and commissions and special counsel to the selling shareholders) of all piggy-backs and three S-3 registrations.

(4) Transfer of Rights: The registration rights may be transferred to any transferee acquiring more than 5% of the outstanding shares of the company (on an as-converted basis), provided the Company is given written notice thereof.

(5) Termination: Registration rights will terminate on the tenth anniversary of the Company's initial public offering. In addition, registration rights will terminate as to any individual Investor once that Investor owns less than 1% of the outstanding stock of the Company and is free to sell all of said stock to the public pursuant to Rule 144 (including Rule 144(K)).

(6) Other Provisions: Other Provisions shall be contained in the Agreement with respect to registration, including cross-indemnification, the period of time in which the Registration Statement shall be kept effective, a 180 day lock-up provision and the ability of the Company to delay S-3 registration for up to 150 days.

Board of Directors:	The Board of Directors shall consist of between three and seven members, with the exact number specified by the Board. John Smith (fictitious) will be elected to the Board upon the closing of the offering, bringing the Board to five members.
Purchase Aggrement:	The investment shall be made pursuant to a Stock Purchase Agreement reasonably acceptable to the Company and the Investors, which agreement shall contain, among other things, appropriate representations and warranties of the Company, covenants of the Company reflecting the provisions set forth herein, and appropriate conditions of closing, including an opinion of counsel for the Company.

Appendix III

Short Term Bank Loan Agreement

....

This is a short term loan agreement (demand promissory note) used by a large New York bank. The bank has asked not to be identified. My guess is that for a small borrower, the bank may not be willing to modify this agreement except under very special circumstances.

Start Up Financing

GRID DEMAND PROMISSORY NOTE

_____, _____

_____, 199__

For value received, the undersigned unconditionally (and if more than one, jointly and severally) promises to pay ON DEMAND, regardless of any other provision of this Note (including the determination of any Interest Periods), to the order of _____ ("Bank"), at its office located at _____, or to such other address as the Bank may notify the undersigned, the sum of _____ _____ **Dollars ($**_____) or such lesser unpaid principal amount of the loans made to the undersigned by the Bank and outstanding under this Note.

This Note includes any Schedule or Rider attached hereto.

Interest. The undersigned promise(s) to pay interest on the unpaid balance of the principal amount of each such loan from and including the date of each such loan to but excluding the date such loan shall be paid in full at the following applicable rates (check Other Rate box if applicable):

Variable Rate: A rate of interest per year which shall automatically increase or decrease from time to time so that at all times such rate shall remain equal to that rate of interest from time to time announced by the Bank at its head office as its prime commercial lending rate (the "Prime Rate") **plus** ____%. Changes in the rate of interest hereunder shall be effective as of and for the entire day on which such change in the Prime Rate becomes effective.

and

☐ Other Rate: see Rider(s) attached hereto.

Interest shall be payable, as to a Variable Rate loan, on **the** ____ **day** of each month and as to an Other Rate loan, on the last day of each Interest Period, or if such Interest Period is more than 90 days, then on the 90th day after the date of such loan and on the last day of such Interest Period, unless otherwise specified on a Rider attached hereto, in respect of the corresponding principal. Interest shall be calculated on the basis of a year of 360 days and payable for the actual number of days elapsed.

After any demand for payment under this Note and any failure by the undersigned to make such payment, the interest rate on this Note shall increase by an additional four percent (4%) per year effective on the date of such notice.

Payments. All payments under this Note shall be made in lawful money of the United States of America and in immediately available funds at the Bank's office specified above. The Bank may demand payment of this Note at any time in whole or in part. The Bank may (but shall not be obligated to) debit the amount of any payment (principal or interest) under this Note when due to any deposit account of (any of) the undersigned with the Bank. If the undersigned are more than one, all obligations of each of the undersigned under this Note shall be joint and several. This Note may be prepaid without premium unless otherwise specified on a Rider attached hereto. The Bank may apply any money received or collected for payment of this Note to the principal of, interest on or any other amount payable under, this Note in any order that the Bank may elect.

Whenever any payment to be made hereunder (including principal and interest) shall be stated to be due on a day on which the Bank's head office is not open for business, that payment will be due on the next following banking day, and any extension of time shall in each case be included in the computation of interest payable on this Note.

If any payment (principal or interest) shall not be paid when due other than a payment of the entire principal balance of the Note upon demand, the undersigned shall pay a late payment charge equal to five percent (5%) of the amount of such delinquent payment, provided that the amount of such late payment charge shall be not less than $25 nor more than $500.

Authorizations. The undersigned hereby authorizes the Bank to make loans and disburse the proceeds thereof to the account listed below and to make repayments of such loans by debiting such account upon oral, telephonic or telecopied instructions made by any person purporting to be an officer or agent of the undersigned who is empowered to make such requests and give such instructions. The undersigned may amend these instructions, from time to time, effective upon actual receipt of the amendment by the Bank. The Bank shall not be responsible for the authority, or lack of authority, of any person giving such telephonic instructions to the Bank pursuant to these provisions. By executing this Note, the undersigned agrees to be bound to repay any loan obtained hereunder as reflected on the Bank's books and records and made in accordance with these authorizations, regardless of the actual receipt of the proceeds thereof.

Records. The date, amount and interest period (if applicable) of each loan under this Note and each payment of principal, loan(s) to which such principal is applied (which shall be at the discretion of the Bank) and the outstanding principal balance of loans, shall be recorded by the Bank on its books and prior to any transfer of this Note (or, at the discretion of the Bank at any other time) endorsed by the Bank on the schedule attached or any continuation of the schedule. Any such endorsement shall be conclusive absent manifest error.

Representations and Warranties. If the undersigned is other than an individual, the undersigned represents and warrants upon the execution and delivery of this Note and upon each loan request hereunder, that: (a) it is duly organized and validly existing under the laws of the jurisdiction of its organization or incorporation and, if relevant under such laws, in good standing; (b) it has the power to execute and deliver this Note and to perform its obligations hereunder and has taken all necessary action to authorize such execution, delivery and performance; (c) such execution, delivery and performance do not violate or conflict with any law applicable to it, any provision of its organizational documents, any order or judgment of any court or other agency of government applicable to it or any of its assets or any material contractual restriction binding on or materially affecting it or any of its assets; (d) to the best of undersigned's knowledge, all governmental and other consents that are required to have been obtained by it with respect to this Note have been obtained and are in full force and effect and all conditions of any such consents have been complied with; (e) its obligations under this Note constitute its legal, valid and binding obligations, enforceable in accordance with its terms except to the extent that such enforcement may be limited by applicable bankruptcy, insolvency or other similar laws affecting creditors' rights generally; (f) all financial statements and related information furnished and to be furnished to the Bank from time to time by the undersigned are true and complete and fairly present the financial or other information stated therein as at such dates or for the periods covered thereby; (g) there are no actions, suits, proceedings or investigations pending or, to the knowledge of the undersigned, threatened against or affecting the undersigned before any court, governmental agency or arbitrator, which involve forfeiture of any assets of the undersigned or which may materially adversely affect the financial condition, operations, properties or business of the undersigned or the ability of the undersigned to perform its obligation under this Note; and (h) there has been no material adverse change in the financial condition of the undersigned since the last such financial statements or information. If the undersigned is an individual, the undersigned represents and warrants at the times set forth at the beginning of this section, the correctness of clauses (c), (d), (e), (f), (g) and (h) above to the extent applicable to an individual.

No Commitment. This Note does not create and shall not be deemed or construed to create any contractual commitment to lend by the Bank. Any such commitment in respect of this Note can only be made by and shall only be effective to the extent set forth in a separate writing expressly designated for that purpose and subscribed by a duly authorized officer of the Bank.

Security. As collateral security for the payment of this Note and of any and all other obligations and liabilities of the undersigned to the Bank, now existing or hereafter arising, the undersigned grants to the Bank a security interest in and a lien upon and right of offset against all moneys, deposit balances, securities or other property or interest therein of the undersigned now or at any time hereafter held or received by or for or left in the possession or control of the Bank or any of its affiliates, including subsidiaries, whether for safekeeping, custody, transmission, collection, pledge or for any other or different purpose.

Certain Waivers. The undersigned waive(s) presentment, notice of dishonor, protest and any other notice or formality with respect to this Note.

Costs. The undersigned agree(s) to reimburse the Bank on demand for all costs, expenses and charges (including, without limitation, fees and charges of external legal counsel for the Bank and costs allocated by its internal legal department) in connection with the preparation, interpretation, performance or enforcement of this Note and the Facility Documents.

Notices. All notices, requests, demands or other communications to or upon the undersigned or the Bank shall be in writing and shall be deemed to be delivered upon receipt if delivered by hand or overnight courier or five days after mailing to the address (a) of the undersigned as set forth next to the undersigned's execution of this Note, (b) of the Bank as first set forth above, or (c) of the undersigned or the Bank at such other address as the undersigned or the Bank shall specify to the other in writing.

Assignment. This Note shall be binding upon the undersigned and its or their successors and shall inure to the benefit of the Bank and its successors and assigns.

Amendment and Waiver. This Note may be amended only by a writing signed on behalf of each party and shall be effective only to the extent set forth in that writing. No delay by the Bank in exercising any power or right hereunder shall operate as a waiver thereof or of any other power or right; nor shall any single or partial exercise of any power or right preclude other or future exercise thereof, or the exercise of any other power or right hereunder.

Governing Law; Jurisdiction. This Note shall be governed by and construed in accordance with the laws of the State of New York, Connecticut or New Jersey, depending on the location of the the Bank office set forth in this Note. The undersigned consent(s) to the nonexclusive jurisdiction and venue of the state or federal courts located in such state. In the event of a dispute hereunder, suit may be brought against the undersigned in such courts or in any jurisdiction where the undersigned or any of its assets may be located. Service of process by the Bank in connection with any dispute shall be binding on the undersigned if sent to the undersigned by registered mail at the address(es) specified below or to such further address(es) as the undersigned may specify to the Bank in writing.

Maximum Interest. Notwithstanding any other provision of this Note, the undersigned shall not be required to pay any amount pursuant to this Note which is in excess of the maximum amount permitted to be charged by national banks under applicable law and any such excess interest paid shall be refunded to the undersigned or applied to the principal owing hereunder.

Commercial Transaction. IF THE UNDERSIGNED IS A CONNECTICUT DOMICILED ENTITY OR RESIDENT, EACH OF THE UNDERSIGNED HEREBY ACKNOWLEDGES THAT THIS NOTE AND THE TRANSACTIONS CONTEMPLATED HEREBY CONSTITUTE COMMERCIAL TRANSACTIONS WITHIN THE MEANING OF SECTION 52-278a OF THE CONNECTICUT GENERAL STATUTES. EACH OF THE UNDERSIGNED EXPRESSLY WAIVES ANY AND ALL RIGHTS, CONSTITUTIONAL OR OTHERWISE, WITH RESPECT TO NOTICE AND HEARING AND ANY RIGHTS UNDER CHAPTER 903a OF THE CONNECTICUT GENERAL STATUTES IN CONNECTION WITH ANY PREJUDGMENT REMEDY AVAILABLE TO THE BANK.

Borrower Waivers. THE UNDERSIGNED HEREBY KNOWINGLY, VOLUNTARILY AND INTENTIONALLY WAIVE(S) (TO THE FULLEST EXTENT PERMITTED BY APPLICABLE LAW) ANY RIGHT TO A TRIAL BY JURY OF ANY DISPUTE ARISING UNDER OR RELATING TO THIS NOTE, AND AGREES THAT ANY SUCH DISPUTE SHALL, AT THE BANK'S OPTION, BE TRIED BEFORE A JUDGE SITTING WITHOUT A JURY.

IN ADDITION, THE UNDERSIGNED WAIVES THE RIGHT TO INTERPOSE ANY DEFENSE BASED UPON ANY STATUTE OF LIMITATIONS OR ANY CLAIM OF DELAY BY THE BANK AND ANY SET-OFF OR COUNTERCLAIM OF ANY NATURE OR DESCRIPTION.

Reg Bnk Note 1   26286   May 10, 1995
Legal 330

Short Term Bank Loan Agreement

Bank Account No. to be charged for Disbursements and _____ Payments:

_____

Address for notices:

_____

_____
By:_____

_____   Print   Name
_____

_____   Title:
_____

_____
By:_____
Telecopier No. (_____) _____ - _____
                                          Print   Name

_____   Title:

_____

                                          By:_____

                                          Print Name _____

                                          Title: _____

Start Up Financing

SCHEDULE TO GRID PROMISSORY NOTE
of _____ dated _____, 199_.

Date of Loan	Interest Period	Amount of Loan	Interest Rate	Amount of Payment	Aggregate Principal Balance Remaining Unpaid	Notation Made By

Reg Bnk Note 1   26286   May 10, 1995
Legal 330

Appendix IV

Long Term Bank Loan Agreement

This is a long term loan agreement (term promissory note) used by the same bank as in Appendix III. Again, for a small borrower my guess is that they may not be willing to modify this agreement except under very special circumstances.

Start Up Financing

TERM PROMISSORY NOTE

$ _____   _____, _____

                                                          _____, 199__

     For value received, the undersigned unconditionally (and if more than one, jointly and severally) promises to pay to the order of _____ ("Bank"), at its office located at _____ _____, or to such other address as the Bank may notify the undersigned, the principal amount of _____ _____Dollars ($ _____) (the "loan").

     This Note includes any Schedule or Rider attached hereto.

     Terms of Repayment. The entire amount of principal, and remaining accrued interest on, this Note shall be due on _____ (the "Maturity Date"). Installments shall be payable as follows **[check one]**:

       ☐   In _____ consecutive principal installments of $_____ each due on the _ _____ day of each _____ commencing on _____, 199__.

       ☐   As set forth on a Schedule of Principal Payments attached hereto as a payment Rider.

       ☐   In _____ payments of principal and interest of $_____ each, beginning on _____, 199__, and continuing on the same day of each successive month.

     Interest. The undersigned promise(s) to pay interest on the unpaid balance of the principal amount of the loan from and including the date of the loan to but excluding the date the loan shall be paid in full at the following rate **[check one]**:

       ☐ Variable Rate: A rate of interest per year which shall automatically increase or decrease from time to time so that at all times such rate shall remain equal to that rate of interest from time to time announced by the Bank at its head office as its prime commercial lending rate (the "Prime Rate") **plus** ____%. Changes in the rate of interest hereunder shall be effective as of and for the entire day on which such change in the Prime Rate becomes effective.

      OR

       ☐ Fixed Rate: A rate of interest equal **to** ____ % per year.

     Interest shall be payable on **the** _____ **day** of each month (commencing on the first such date occurring after the date of the loan), unless otherwise specified on a Rider attached hereto, on the Maturity Date, and on any prepayment of principal. Interest shall be calculated on the basis of a year of 360 days and payable for the actual number of days elapsed.

     After the occurrence of an Event of Default set forth below, the Bank, at its option, by written notice to the undersigned may increase the interest rate on this Note by an additional four percent (4%) per year effective on the date of such notice.

     Payments. All payments under this Note shall be made in lawful money of the United States of America and in immediately available funds at the Bank's office specified above. The Bank may (but shall not be obligated to) debit the amount of any payment (principal or interest) under this Note when due to any deposit account of (any of) the undersigned with the Bank. If the undersigned are more than one, all obligations of each of the undersigned under this Note shall be joint and several. The Bank may apply any money received or collected for payment of this Note to the principal of, interest on or any other amount payable under, this Note in any order that the Bank may elect.

Reg Bnk Note 3   26285   May 10, 1995
Legal 334

Whenever any payment to be made hereunder (including principal and interest) shall be stated to be due on a day on which the Bank's head office is not open for business, that payment will be due on the next following banking day, and any extension of time shall in each case be included in the computation of interest payable on this Note.

If any payment (principal or interest) shall not be paid when due other than a payment of the entire principal balance of the Note due upon demand, the undersigned shall pay a late payment charge equal to five percent (5%) of the amount of such delinquent payment, provided that the amount of such late payment charge shall be not less than $25 nor more than $500.

Prepayments. **(Applies only to a Fixed Rate loan)**   Any prepayment of principal of the loan evidenced by this Note (whether by voluntary payment, acceleration upon default or otherwise) must be accompanied by a payment equal to the sum of (a) accrued interest on the principal amount prepaid to the prepayment date and (b) a prepayment charge equal to the sum of (i) the amount, if any, by which (A) the present value of all future scheduled principal and interest payments discounted to the date of prepayment at a rate equal to the average yield of U.S. Treasury securities having maturities matching the average life of the loan remaining **on the prepayment date**, exceeds (B) the present value of all future scheduled principal and interest payments discounted to the date of prepayment at a rate equal to the average yield of U.S. Treasury securities having maturities matching the average life of the loan **on the original closing date** and (ii) ____% of the principal amount prepaid. In the event of a partial prepayment, the amount referred to in (i) above shall be prorated by multiplying said amount by a fraction, the numerator of which is the principal amount prepaid and the denominator of which is the unpaid principal amount of the loan on the prepayment date immediately prior to prepayment.

As used herein, the "average life of the loan" means a period of days equal to the quotient of (x) the sum of the products obtained by multiplying each portion (as determined below) of the amount prepaid by the number of days from the date of prepayment to the installment date for such portion, divided by (y) the amount prepaid. The portion of the amount prepaid applicable to each installment date for purposes of this calculation shall be the portion of the principal amount prepaid that would be applied on such installment date if the amount prepaid were applied to the installments in the inverse order of maturities.

A determination by the Bank of the amounts payable pursuant to this provision shall be conclusive absent manifest error.

All partial prepayments shall be applied to the reduction and payment of principal in the inverse order of maturity.

Authorizations. The undersigned hereby authorizes the Bank to make the loan and disburse the proceeds thereof to the account listed below and to make repayments of the loan by debiting such account upon oral, telephonic instructions made by any person purporting to be an officer or agent of the undersigned who is empowered to make such requests and give such instructions. The undersigned may amend these instructions, from time to time, effective upon actual receipt of the amendment by the Bank. The Bank shall not be responsible for the authority, or lack of authority, of any person giving such telephonic instructions to the Bank pursuant to these provisions. By executing this Note, the undersigned agrees to be bound to repay the loan obtained hereunder as reflected on the Bank's books and records.

Records. The date and amount of the loan and each payment of principal, and the outstanding principal balance of the loan, shall be recorded by the Bank on its books and any such record shall be conclusive absent manifest error.

Representations and Warranties. If the undersigned is other than an individual, the undersigned represents and warrants upon the execution and delivery of this Note, that: (a) it is duly organized and validly existing under the laws of the jurisdiction of its organization or incorporation and, if relevant under such laws, in good standing; (b) it has the power to execute and deliver this Note and to perform its obligations hereunder and has taken all necessary action to authorize such execution, delivery and performance; (c) such execution, delivery and performance do not violate or conflict with any law applicable to it, any provision of its organizational documents, any order or judgment of any court or other agency of government applicable to it or any of its assets or any material contractual restriction binding on or materially affecting it or any of its assets; (d) to the best of undersigned's knowledge, all governmental and other consents that are required to have been obtained by it with respect to this Note have been obtained and are in full force and effect and all conditions of any such consents have been complied with; (e) its obligations under this Note constitute its legal, valid and binding obligations, enforceable in accordance with its terms except to the extent that such enforcement may be limited by applicable bankruptcy, insolvency or other similar laws affecting creditors' rights generally; (f) all financial statements and related information furnished and to be furnished to the Bank from time to time by the undersigned are true and complete and fairly present the financial or other information stated therein as at such dates or for the periods covered thereby; (g) there are no actions, suits, proceedings or investigations pending or, to the knowledge of the undersigned, threatened against or affecting the undersigned before any court, governmental agency or arbitrator, which involve forfeiture of any assets of the undersigned or which may materially adversely affect the financial condition, operations, properties or business of the undersigned or the ability of the undersigned to perform its obligation under this Note; and (h) there has been no material adverse change in the financial condition of the undersigned since the last such financial statements or information. If the undersigned is an individual, the undersigned represents and warrants at the times set forth at the beginning of this section, the correctness of clauses (c), (d), (e), (f), (g) and (h) above to the extent applicable to an individual.

Security. As collateral security for the payment of this Note and of any and all other obligations and liabilities of the undersigned to the Bank, now existing or hereafter arising, the undersigned grants to the Bank a security interest in and a lien upon and right of offset against all moneys, deposit balances, securities or other property or interest therein of the undersigned now or at any time hereafter held or received by or for or left in the possession or control of the Bank or any of its affiliates, including subsidiaries, whether for safekeeping, custody, transmission, collection, pledge or for any other or different purpose.

Default. IF any of the following events of default shall occur with respect to any of the undersigned (each an "Event of Default"):

(a)   the undersigned shall fail to pay the principal of, or interest on, this Note, or any other amount payable under this Note, as and when due and payable;

(b)   any representation or warranty made or deemed made by the undersigned in this Note or in any document granting security or support for (or otherwise executed in connection with) this Note or by any third party supporting or liable with respect to this Note (whether by guaranty, subordination, grant of security or any other credit support, a "Third Party") in any document evidencing the obligations of a Third Party (this Note and all of the foregoing documents and all agreements, instruments or other documents executed by the undersigned or a Third Party being the "Facility Documents") or which is contained in any certificate, document, opinion, financial or other statement furnished at any time under or in connection with any Facility Document, shall prove to have been incorrect in any material respect on or as of the date made or deemed made;

(c)   the undersigned or any Third Party shall fail to perform or observe any term, covenant or agreement contained in any Facility Document on its part to be performed or observed, and such failure shall continue for 30 consecutive days;

(d)   the undersigned or any Third Party shall fail to pay when due any indebtedness (including but not limited to indebtedness for borrowed money) or if any such indebtedness shall become due and payable, or shall be capable of becoming due and payable at the option of any holder thereof, by acceleration of its maturity, or if there shall be any default by the undersigned or any Third Party under any agreement relating to such indebtedness;

(e)   the undersigned or any Third Party: (i) shall generally not, or be unable to, or shall admit in writing its inability to, pay its debts as such debts become due; (ii) shall make an assignment for the benefit of creditors; (iii) shall file a petition in bankruptcy or for any relief under any law of any jurisdiction relating to reorganization, arrangement, readjustment of debt, dissolution or liquidation; (iv) shall have any such petition filed against it and the same shall remain undismissed for a period of 30 days or shall consent or acquiesce thereto; or (v) shall have had a receiver, custodian or trustee appointed for all or a substantial part of its property;

(f)   if the undersigned or any Third Party is an individual, such individual shall die or be declared incompetent;

(g)   any Third Party Facility Document shall at any time and for any reason cease to be in full force and effect or shall be declared null and void, or its validity or enforceability shall be contested by the relevant Third Party or such Third Party shall deny it has any further liability or obligation under any Facility Document or shall fail to perform its obligations under any Facility Document;

(h)   any security agreement or other agreement (whether by the undersigned or any Third Party) granting a security interest, lien, mortgage or other encumbrance securing obligations under any Facility Document shall at any time and for any reason cease to create a valid and perfected first priority security interest, lien, mortgage or other encumbrance in or on the property purported to be subject to such agreement or shall cease to be in full force and effect or shall be declared null and void, or the validity or enforceability of any such agreement shall be contested by any party to such agreement, or such party shall deny it has any further liability or obligation under such agreement or any such party shall fail to perform any of its obligations under such agreement;

(i)   the undersigned shall make or permit to be made any material change in the character, management or direction of the undersigned's business or operations (including, but not limited to, a change in its executive management or in the ownership of its capital stock which effects a change in the control of any such business or operations), which is not satisfactory to the Bank;

(j)   the undersigned or any Third Party shall suffer a material adverse change in its business, financial condition, properties or prospects;

(k)   any action, suit, proceeding or investigation against or affecting the undersigned or a Third Party before any court or governmental agency which involves forfeiture of any assets of the undersigned or a Third Party shall have been commenced; or

(l)   one or more judgments, decrees or orders for the payment of money in excess of $50,000 in the aggregate shall be rendered against the undersigned and shall continue unsatisfied and in effect for a period of 30 consecutive days without being vacated, discharged, satisfied or stayed or bonded pending appeal.

THEN, in any such case, if the Bank shall elect by notice to the undersigned, the unpaid principal amount of this Note, together with accrued interest, shall become forthwith due and payable; provided that in the case of an event of default under (e) above, the unpaid principal amount of this Note, together with accrued interest, shall immediately become due and payable without any notice or other action by the Bank.

Certain Waivers. The undersigned waive(s) presentment, notice of dishonor, protest and any other notice or formality with respect to this Note.

Costs. The undersigned agree(s) to reimburse the Bank on demand for all costs, expenses and charges (including, without limitation, fees and charges of external legal counsel for the Bank and costs allocated by its internal legal department) in connection with the preparation, interpretation, performance or enforcement of this Note and the Facility Documents.

Notices. All notices, requests, demands or other communications to or upon the undersigned or the Bank shall be in writing and shall be deemed to be delivered upon receipt if delivered by hand or overnight courier or five days after mailing to the address (a) of the undersigned as set forth next to the undersigned's execution of this Note, (b) of the Bank as first set forth above, or (c) of the undersigned or the Bank at such other address as the undersigned or the Bank shall specify to the other in writing.

Assignment. This Note shall be binding upon the undersigned and its or their successors and shall inure to the benefit of the Bank and its successors and assigns.

Entire Agreement, Amendment and Waiver. This Note and the Facility Documents constitute the entire agreement between the undersigned and the Bank and may be amended only by a writing signed on behalf of each party and shall be effective only to the extent set forth in that writing. In the event of any inconsistency between this Note (and any Rider(s) attached hereto) and the Facility Documents, this Note and such Riders shall prevail. No delay by the Bank in exercising any power or right hereunder shall operate as a waiver thereof or of any other power or right; nor shall any single or partial exercise of any power or right preclude other or future exercise thereof, or the exercise of any other power or right hereunder.

   Governing Law; Jurisdiction. This Note shall be governed by and construed in accordance with the laws of the State of New York, Connecticut or New Jersey, depending on the location of the Bank office set forth in this Note. The undersigned consent(s) to the nonexclusive jurisdiction and venue of the state or federal courts located in such state. In the event of a dispute hereunder, suit may be brought against the undersigned in such courts or in any jurisdiction where the undersigned or any of its assets may be located. Service of process by Bank in connection with any dispute shall be binding on the undersigned if sent to the undersigned by registered mail at the address(es) specified below or to such further address(es) as the undersigned may specify to the Bank in writing.

   Maximum Interest. Notwithstanding any other provision of this Note, the undersigned shall not be required to pay any amount pursuant to this Note which is in excess of the maximum amount permitted to be charged by national banks under applicable law and any such excess interest paid shall be refunded to the undersigned or applied to principal owing hereunder.

   Commercial Transaction. IF THE UNDERSIGNED IS A CONNECTICUT DOMICILED ENTITY OR RESIDENT, EACH OF THE UNDERSIGNED HEREBY ACKNOWLEDGES THAT THIS NOTE AND THE TRANSACTIONS CONTEMPLATED HEREBY CONSTITUTE COMMERCIAL TRANSACTIONS WITHIN THE MEANING OF SECTION 52-278A OF THE CONNECTICUT GENERAL STATUTES. EACH OF THE UNDERSIGNED EXPRESSLY WAIVES ANY AND ALL RIGHTS, CONSTITUTIONAL OR OTHERWISE, WITH RESPECT TO NOTICE AND HEARING AND ANY RIGHTS UNDER CHAPTER 903a OF THE CONNECTICUT GENERAL STATUTES IN CONNECTION WITH ANY PREJUDGMENT REMEDY AVAILABLE TO THE BANK.

   Business Covenants. The undersigned agrees that until payment in full of the loan, all interest thereon and all other amounts payable under this Note, the undersigned shall perform and comply with the covenants set forth on the Business Covenants Rider annexed hereto.

   Borrower Waivers. THE UNDERSIGNED HEREBY KNOWINGLY, VOLUNTARILY AND INTENTIONALLY WAIVE(S) (TO THE FULLEST EXTENT PERMITTED BY APPLICABLE LAW) ANY RIGHT TO A TRIAL BY JURY OF ANY DISPUTE ARISING UNDER OR RELATING TO THIS NOTE OR ANY FACILITY DOCUMENT, AND AGREES THAT ANY SUCH DISPUTE SHALL, AT THE BANK'S OPTION, BE TRIED BEFORE A JUDGE SITTING WITHOUT A JURY.

Reg Bnk Note 3   26285   May 10, 1995
Legal 334

IN ADDITION, THE UNDERSIGNED WAIVES THE RIGHT TO INTERPOSE ANY DEFENSE BASED UPON ANY STATUTE OF LIMITATIONS OR ANY CLAIM OF DELAY BY THE BANK AND ANY SET-OFF OR COUNTERCLAIM OF ANY NATURE OR DESCRIPTION.

Bank Account No. to be charged for Disbursements and _____ Payments:

_____

Address for notices:

_____

_____

_____

By: _____

_____

Print Name _____

_____

Title: _____

_____

Telecopier No. (_____) _____ - _____

By: _____

Print Name _____

Title: _____

By: _____

Print Name _____

Title: _____

Reg Bnk Note 3   26285   May 10, 1995
Legal 334

Start Up Financing

Business Covenants Rider

SCHEDULE OF BUSINESS COVENANTS

All provisions which do not apply must be crossed out and initialled and dated by the undersigned.

This Rider is referred to in and is attached to the NOTE made by _____ (the "undersigned") to the order of _____ ("Bank") dated _____, 199__ (the "Note").

1.   Affirmative Covenants. The undersigned agrees that it shall:

1.1 Furnish to the Bank:

(a) Within _____ days after and as at the close of each Fiscal Year, a consolidated (and consolidating) balance sheet(s) of undersigned and its consolidated Subsidiaries, and consolidated (and consolidating) statements of income, cash flows and changes in shareholders' equity of undersigned and its consolidated Subsidiaries prepared in accordance with GAAP consistently applied, on a **[check one]** ☐ **audit,**   ☐   **review,**   ☐   **compilation**   basis,   prepared   by _____ or other independent public accounting firm satisfactory to the Bank, and as to audited statements, accompanied by a satisfactory report of such accountants which shall not contain any qualification of opinion or disclaimer.

(b) Within _____ days after the end of each **[check one]** ☐ Fiscal Quarter ☐ month, a consolidated (and consolidating) balance sheet(s) of undersigned and its consolidated Subsidiaries as at the end of each such quarter and related consolidated (and consolidating) statements of income, cash flow and changes in shareholders' equity of the undersigned and its consolidated Subsidiaries for the Fiscal Quarter and from the beginning of such Fiscal Year to the end of such Fiscal Quarter, together with comparisons to the previous year, if appropriate, and to budget projections, prepared in conformity with GAAP consistently applied, and certified by an appropriate financial officer of undersigned.

[additional specific reports that may be required:]

(c) _____
_____
_____

(d) Such other books, records and reports as the Bank may from time to time reasonably request, including an equipment listing; inventory listing, aging and locations; and accounts receivable aging; which information, together with the above financial reports, shall all be prepared in form and detail satisfactory to the Bank.

1.2   Cause to be done all things necessary to preserve and keep in full force and effect undersigned's and its Subsidiaries' existence, rights, licenses and franchises necessary and material to undersigned's operations taken as a whole; and comply with all laws applicable to undersigned.

1.3   Permit representatives of the Bank to visit and inspect any of the properties of undersigned and its Subsidiaries, examine its corporate books and records, and to make extracts or copies of such books and records, and discuss its affairs, finances and accounts with its officers, provided that the foregoing shall only be done at reasonable times and with not more than reasonable frequency, and provided further that the reasonable cost of such inspections and examinations shall be paid by undersigned.

1.4   Cause to be paid and discharged all obligations when due and all lawful taxes, assessments and governmental charges or levies imposed upon undersigned or any Subsidiary, or upon any property, real, personal or mixed, belonging to undersigned or its Subsidiaries, or upon any part thereof, before the same shall become in default, as well as lawful claims for labor, materials and supplies which, if unpaid, might become a lien or charge upon such property or any part thereof; provided, however, that neither the undersigned nor any Subsidiary shall be required to cause to be paid and discharged any such obligation, tax, assessment, charge, levy or claim so long as the validity thereof shall be contested in the normal course of business and in good faith.

    1.5   Maintain with financially sound, reputable and duly licensed insurers, insurance of the kinds, covering the risks and in the relative proportionate amounts usually carried by similar companies in similar localities or as may otherwise be expressly required by the Bank from time to time.

    1.6   Promptly notify the Bank in writing with full details if any event occurs or any condition exists which constitutes, or which but for a requirement of lapse of time or giving of notice or both would constitute an Event of Default under the Note or which might materially and adversely affect the financial condition or operations of undersigned or any Subsidiary.

    1.7   _____

_____

_____

2.   <u>Negative Covenants</u>. Undersigned agrees that it shall not, and shall not permit any Subsidiary to:

    2.1   Incur, create, permit to exist or assume, directly or indirectly, any indebtedness other than:

    (a)   indebtedness to the Bank,

    (b)   trade indebtedness (which shall not include any borrowing, trade acceptances or notes given in settlement of trade indebtedness) incurred in the ordinary course of business and not more than 30 days overdue,

    (c)   Subordinated Debt , and

    (d)   _____

_____

_____

    2.2   Pledge or encumber any of its assets, except:

    (a)   mortgages, liens, security interests or encumbrances granted to the Bank,

    (b)   in the case of real properties, easements, restrictions, exceptions, reservations or defects which, in the aggregate, do not interfere materially with the continued use of such properties for the purposes for which they are used and do not affect materially the value thereof;

    (c)   pledges or deposits to secure obligations under workers' compensation laws or similar legislation or to secure performance in connection with bids, tenders and contracts (other than contracts for the payment of borrowed money) to which the undersigned or any Subsidiary is a party;

    (d)   deposits to secure public or statutory obligations of the undersigned and any Subsidiaries;

    (e)   materialmen's, mechanics', carriers', workers' or other like liens arising in the ordinary course of business, or deposits of cash or United States obligations to obtain the release of such liens; and

(f)   purchase money liens created by undersigned or any Subsidiary in the course of purchasing property, or existing on property at the time of such purchase (whether or not assumed), provided that such lien shall be restricted to the property being purchased, that the indebtedness secured thereby shall not exceed 80% of the lesser of cost or fair market value at the time of purchase, and that the indebtedness secured by such lien is permitted by Section 2.1 hereof and the related expenditure is permitted by Section 2.10 hereof.

2.3   Make or permit to be made any material change in the character, management or direction of undersigned's business or operations (including, but not limited to, a change in its executive management or in the ownership of its capital stock which effects a change in the control of any such business or operations), which is not satisfactory to the Bank.

2.4   Be in violation of any law or regulation, order, writ, injunction or decree of any court or governmental instrumentality or in breach of any agreement or instrument to which undersigned or any Subsidiary is subject or in default thereunder.

2.5   Enter into or be a party to any merger, consolidation, reorganization, exchange of stock or assets, unless undersigned is the surviving corporation and as such satisfies all of the covenants contained in this Schedule; provided further, however, the undersigned will not permit any corporation to merge into undersigned or acquire any assets in exchange for securities of its own issue if immediately after such merger or asset acquisition, assuming full conversion of any convertible securities issued in connection therewith, the shareholders of the corporation merged into undersigned or any Subsidiary would hold 50% or more of the voting power of undersigned or any Subsidiary.

2.6   Organize or cause to exist any new Subsidiaries, without the Bank's prior written consent, which consent may be conditioned, without limitation, upon the execution by such Subsidiary of a guarantee of payment of the Note and all other indebtedness of undersigned to the Bank and of a security agreement covering such Subsidiary's assets and securing such debt.

2.7   Sell, lease, assign, transfer or otherwise dispose of any of the assets of undersigned or of any Subsidiary (including stock of a Subsidiary), except: (a) for inventory disposed of in the ordinary course of business; (b) the sale or other disposition of assets no longer used or useful in the conduct of its business; and (c) that any such Subsidiary may sell, lease, assign, or otherwise transfer its assets to undersigned.

2.8   Make or hold any investment in any securities of any kind other than ownership of stock of Subsidiaries, be or become a party to any joint venture or partnership, or make or keep outstanding any advance or loan except as permitted pursuant to and under Part 2.9. The foregoing provision shall not apply to any investment in direct obligations of the United States of America, certificates of deposit issued by a member bank of the Federal Reserve System, or any investment in commercial paper which at the time of such investment is assigned the highest quality rating in accordance with the rating systems employed by either Moody's Investors Service, Inc. or Standard & Poor's Corporation.

2.9   Loan or make advances to, or guarantee, indorse or otherwise be or become liable or contingently liable in connection with the obligations or indebtedness of any other person, firm or corporation, directly or indirectly except:

(a)   as an indorser of negotiable instruments for the payment of money in the ordinary course of business;

(b)   trade credit extended in the ordinary course of business;

      (c)   advances made in the usual course of business to officers and employees for travel and other out-of-pocket expenses incurred by them in connection with such business;

      (d)   loans to wholly-owned Subsidiaries which have guaranteed all indebtedness of undersigned to the Bank;

      (e)   guarantees by Subsidiaries of undersigned's indebtedness to the Bank.

      2.10   Make expenditures for fixed or capital assets exceeding an aggregate amount of $_____ in any single Fiscal Year.

      2.11   Declare or pay any dividends, purchase, redeem, retire or otherwise acquire for value any of its capital stock, or make any distribution of its assets to its stockholders or permit any of its Subsidiaries to purchase or otherwise acquire for value any stock of the undersigned or another such Subsidiary, except that: (a) the undersigned may declare and deliver dividends and make distributions payable solely in common stock of the undersigned; and (b) the undersigned may declare dividends in its current Fiscal Year which do not exceed the amount of tax liability of the shareholders of the undersigned attributable to the undersigned's undistributed taxable income during any applicable Fiscal Year.

      2.12   _____
_____
_____

3.   Financial Covenants. The undersigned shall maintain the following financial covenants and ratios, to be measured at the end of each Fiscal Quarter unless otherwise stated:

      3.1   A ratio of Consolidated Current Assets to Consolidated Current Liabilities at not less than _____ to 1.

      3.2   Its Consolidated Working Capital of not less than $_____.

      3.3   A ratio of Consolidated Liabilities to Consolidated Tangible Net Worth of not more than _____ to 1.

      3.4   Minimum Consolidated Tangible Net Worth at all times of not less than $_____.

      3.5   Cash Flow Coverage Ratio of not less than _____ to 1.

      3.6   _____
_____
_____

      3.7   _____
_____
_____

4.   Definitions and Rules of Construction.

      4.1   In addition to the terms defined elsewhere in the Note, the following terms shall have the following meanings for purposes of this Schedule:

    "Cash Flow Coverage Ratio" means, in respect of the period for which the computation is being made, and which period shall in each case consist of a twelve month period ending on the last day of a Fiscal Quarter, the ratio of (i) Measured Cash Flow (as defined below) to (ii) the sum of all payments of principal, capital lease obligations, including sinking fund payments and redemptions, which the undersigned is contractually required to pay during such fiscal period.

"Consolidated Current Assets" means, in respect of a Person, all assets of such Person and its Subsidiaries (if any) on a consolidated basis which should in accordance with GAAP be classified as current assets after eliminating inter-company items and prepaid expenses, but in any event excluding any assets which are pledged or deposited as security for, or for the purpose of paying, any Indebtedness.

"Consolidated Current Liabilities" means, in respect of a Person, all Indebtedness of such Person and its Subsidiaries (if any) on a consolidated basis which should, in accordance with GAAP, be classified as current liabilities after eliminating inter-company items (including loans payable to officers and employees of the undersigned) and excluding Subordinated Debt.

"Consolidated Liabilities" means, in respect of a Person, all Indebtedness of such Person and its Subsidiaries (if any) on a consolidated basis which should, in accordance with GAAP, be classified as liabilities after eliminating inter-company items and excluding Subordinated Debt.

"Consolidated Tangible Net Worth" means, in respect of a Person, the consolidated stockholders' equity in such Person and its Subsidiaries determined in accordance with GAAP, except that there shall be deducted therefrom all intangible assets (other than leasehold improvements) of such Person and its Subsidiaries, such as organization costs, unamortized debt discount and expense, goodwill, patents, trademarks, copyrights, contractual franchises, and research and development expenses.

"Consolidated Working Capital" means the difference of Consolidated Current Assets minus Consolidated Current Liabilities in respect of a Person.

"Fiscal Year" means the undersigned's fiscal year consisting of a twelve month period ending on each _____ (if left blank, then presumed ending on each December 31).

"GAAP" means generally accepted accounting principles in the United States of America as in effect on the date hereof and from time to time hereafter, consistently applied.

"Indebtedness" means, in respect of any Person, all items (other than capital stock, additional paid-in capital, retained earnings and deferred credits) which in accordance with GAAP would be included in determining total liabilities as shown on the liability side of a balance sheet as at the date on which Indebtedness is to be determined. "Indebtedness" shall also include, whether or not so reflected, (i) indebtedness, obligations, and liabilities secured by any mortgage, pledge or lien existing on property owned subject to such mortgage, pledge or lien whether or not the indebtedness, obligations or liabilities secured thereby shall have been assumed, (ii) all guaranties made by such Person, and (iii) the amount of any reimbursement obligation in respect of any letter of credit.

"Measured Cash Flow" means the sum of the following items measured on a consolidated basis for the undersigned and its Subsidiaries, if any, for any twelve month period ending on the last day of each of undersigned's Fiscal Quarters:

	(i)	net income,
plus	(ii)	depreciation and all other non-cash charges to income not affecting working capital,
minus	(iii)	all cash or asset dividends on capital stock,
minus	(iv)	all capital expenditures,
plus	(v)	increases in long term debt which shall have been applied to capital expenditures and approved in advance by the Bank.

"Person" means an individual, a corporation, a company, a voluntary association, a partnership, a trust, an unincorporated organization or a government or any agency, instrumentality or political subdivision thereof.

"Subordinated Debt" means indebtedness of the undersigned which shall be subordinated to the loan in a form satisfactory to the Bank in its sole discretion reasonably exercised and to which the Bank shall have given its express written consent.

"Subsidiary" means any corporation or other entity of which at least a majority of the securities or other ownership interests having ordinary voting power (absolutely or contingently) for the election of directors or other persons performing similar functions are at the time owned directly or indirectly by the undersigned.

4.2   All accounting terms not specifically defined herein shall be construed in accordance with GAAP, and all financial data required to be delivered hereunder shall be prepared in accordance with GAAP.

4.3   All references to Subsidiaries or Consolidated Subsidiaries shall be deemed to mean if any shall exist. For so long as undersigned has no Subsidiary, all definitions and covenants referring to undersigned and its Subsidiaries or Consolidated Subsidiaries on a consolidated basis and all references to consolidated and consolidating financial statements shall be deemed to refer to undersigned alone and to undersigned's financial statements alone, respectively, but shall remain applicable in all other respects.

Dated _____, 199___

_____

By:_____

Print Name _____

Title: _____

By:_____

Print Name _____

Title: _____

By:_____

Print Name _____

Title: _____

Start Up Financing

Optional Payment Rider to Note

SCHEDULE OF PRINCIPAL PAYMENTS ON TERM NOTE

The   TERM   PROMISSORY   NOTE   made   by

_____

(the "undersigned") to the order of _____ dated

_____, 1995 is hereby supplemented by the following Schedule of Principal Payments

referred to therein:

Principal Payment	Due Date	Principal Payment	Due Date

_____   _____

By:_____   By:_____

Print Name _____   Print Name _____

Title: _____   Title: _____

Reg Bnk Note 3   26285   May 10, 1995

Legal 334

About the Author

Bill Stolze is a graduate of Polytechnic University of New York, MIT and Rochester Institute of Technology (RIT), with degrees in electrical engineering, industrial management and professional photography. He began his career as a design engineer at RCA Laboratories. Then he was an engineering manager and marketing manager with the Electronics Division of General Dynamics.

In 1961, with three associates, he founded RF Communications. In eight years as an independent company, RF Communications became a world leader in long range radio communications. When it merged with Harris Corp. in 1969, RF Communications had about 800 employees, had sold equipment in more than 100 countries and was listed on the American Stock Exchange. As an independent company RF Communications had only one loss quarter—its first quarter in business

After 10 years with Harris as Vice President and Group Executive he launched a private consulting practice. He is an investor, advisor and consultant to numerous new ventures and is the founder of the Rochester Venture Capital Group.

For about 10 years, he taught entrepreneurship and new venture management in the MBA Programs at the University of Rochester and RIT.

Bill is the author of *Start Up, An Entrepreneur's Guide to Launching and Managing a New Business*, now in its fourth edition. It is used either in small business programs or as a text in more than 50 colleges and universities.

Awards include: RCA Laboratories Research Award for the development and presentation of television receiver circuitry widely used by the industry; Small Business Council's Small Business Person of the Year; Rochester Engineering Society's Engineer of the Year;

Rochester Chamber of Commerce's Civic Award for High Technology; 1995 Entrepreneur of the Year Award in upstate New York, in the category of Supporter of Entrepreneurs in a program sponsored by Ernst & Young, Merrill Lynch and *Inc.* magazine; and Distinguished Alumni and Fellow of the Institute, Polytechnic University of New York.

Mr. Stolze is married, has six children and seven grandchildren. His hobbies include sailing, reading, photography and playing with his grandchildren.

Index